D0482016

The Warsaw Pact

The United Nations University's Programme on Peace and Global Transformation was a major world-wide project whose purpose was to develop new insights about the interlinkages between questions of peace, conflict resolution, and the process of transformation. The research in this project, under six major themes, was co-ordinated by a 12-member core group in different regions of the world: East Asia, South-East Asia (including the Pacific), South Asia, the Arab region, Africa, Western Europe, Eastern Europe, North America, and Latin America. The themes covered were: Conflicts over Natural Resources; Security, Vulnerability, and Violence; Human Rights and Cultural Survival in a Changing Pluralistic World; The Role of Science and Technology in Peace and Transformation; The Role of the State in Peace and Global Transformation; and Global Economic Crisis. The project also included a special project on Peace and Regional Security.

The Warsaw Pact

Soviet Security and Bloc Politics

Gerard Holden

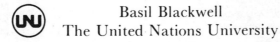

Basil Blackwell
The United Nations University

Copyright © The United Nations University 1989

First published 1989

Basil Blackwell Ltd
108 Cowley Road, Oxford, OX4 1JF, UK

Basil Blackwell Inc.
432 Park Avenue South, Suite 1503
New York, NY 10016, USA

The United Nations University
Toho Seimei Building, 15–1, Shibuya 2-chome, Shibuya-ku
Tokyo 150, Japan

British Library Cataloguing in Publication Data
A CIP catalogue record for this book is
available from the British Library

Library of Congress Cataloging in Publication Data
Holden, Gerard.
  The Warsaw Pact: the WTO and Soviet security policy/Gerard Holden.
    p.   cm.
  Bibliography: p.
  ISBN 0–631–16775–7
  1. Warsaw Treaty Organization.   2. Soviet Union—National
security.   3. Europe, Eastern—National security.   4. Soviet Union-
-Military policy.   5. Europe, Eastern—Military policy.   I. Title.
UA646.8.H65 1989   88–32640
355'.031'0947—dc19   CIP

Typeset 10 on 12pt Baskerville
by Vera Reyes

Printed in Great Britain by
Billing & Sons, Worcester

Contents

Acknowledgements

This study started life as a research report for the United Nations University's Sub-Programme on Peace and Global Transformation, entitled *The Warsaw Treaty Organization: Soviet Security Policy and the Alliance Division of Labour*. I would like to thank the UNU for the opportunity to participate in the project that produced this report, and am especially grateful to my supervisor on the project, Mary Kaldor, for giving me the opportunity and encouragement to undertake the work and to turn it into a book. I am also grateful to the Transnational Institute, Amsterdam, for financial assistance during the later stages of the work and, still more importantly, for intellectual stimulation throughout.

In addition, I have been greatly helped by many people who have, either in person or by correspondence, assisted me in finding material, commented on various earlier versions, and generally made it possible to see the project through. I would particularly like to thank the past and present members of the Military Technology and Arms Limitation Group at the Science Policy Research Unit, University of Sussex; and also, individually, Priya Deshingkar, Christopher Donnelly, Pál Dunay, Alison Flood, Neil Fodor, Mac Graham, Bernard Harbor, Zdenek Kavan, Maureen Kelly, Pat Litherland, Dr Sverre Lodgaard, Rodney McElroy, Michael MccGwire, Peter Morris, Robert Neild, Sheena Phillips, Michael Randle, Tony Randle, Julian Perry Robinson, Stephen Shenfield, Chris Smith, Malcolm Spaven, Claire Trevelyan, Professor Lázló Valki. The librarians of a number of institutions have also helped me over a number of years, particularly those of the Science Policy Research Unit, the University of Sussex library, the School of Slavonic and East European Studies, the International Institute for Strategic Studies, and the British Library of Political and Economic Science. I am also grateful to Tim Goodfellow, Sean Magee, Kate Chapman and Ann Bone of Basil Blackwell, and to Amadio A. Arboleda and Dr. Janusz Golebiowski of the United Nations University, for their editorial and administrative work and assistance; and to Blackwell's three anonymous reviewers for their comments and suggestions.

Gerard Holden, Brighton

Abbreviations

ADC	Alternative Defence Commission
ALB	Airland Battle
CDM	Committee of Defence Ministers (of WTO)
CFM	Committee of Foreign Ministers (of WTO)
C-in-C	Commander-in-Chief
Comecon	Council for Mutual Economic Assistance (sometimes CMEA or CEMA)
CPSU	Communist Party of the Soviet Union
CSCE	Conference on Security and Cooperation in Europe
FOFA	Follow-on Forces Attack
FRG	Federal Republic of Germany
GDR	German Democratic Republic
GSFG	Group of Soviet Forces, Germany
IISS	International Institute for Strategic Studies (London)
INF	Intermediate Nuclear Forces
JHC	Joint High Command (of WTO)
MBFR	Mutual and Balanced Force Reductions
MC	Military Council (of WTO)
Nato	North Atlantic Treaty Organization
NVA	Nationale Volksarmee (GDR army)
OMG	Operational Manoeuvre Group
PCC	Political Consultative Committee (of WTO)
SDI	Strategic Defense Initiative
SIPRI	Stockholm International Peace Research Institute
TC	Technological Committee (of WTO)
TVD	Teatr Voennykh Deistvii (Russian – Theatre of Military Operations)
WTO	Warsaw Treaty Organization.

Introduction

The objective of this study is to contribute to an understanding of European security politics by examining the military and political history and organization of the Warsaw Treaty Organization (WTO). It also aims, more ambitiously, to contribute to the search for alternatives to the present security system in Eastern and Western Europe.

This combination of analysis and a search for alternatives was originally developed within a framework provided by the United Nations University's Sub-Programme on Peace and Global Transformation. Within this framework, a number of Western European and North American scholars have been looking afresh at the political and military relationship between the USA and Western Europe, and have begun to ask what kind of political and security arrangements might be worked out to replace the system which has been in place since 1945. Although the present system of two military blocs with a number of European neutral states interspersed between them retains great reserves of strength, it has been called into question during the 1980s both by popular challenges to the legitimacy of NATO defence policy, and by new searches within transatlantic political elites for ways of reconciling US and European interests. This latter concern has at times been particularly difficult in the areas of East–West security relations and arms control, and also over questions of East–West trade, although the strong commmitment to Atlanticism of the principal West European political elites has so far served to suppress conflicts of interest beneath traditional expressions of concern about the 'decoupling' or 'unravelling' of the Atlantic alliance. These questions acquired a particular immediacy in December 1987 when Ronald Reagan and Mikhail Gorbachev met in Washington to sign the INF Treaty. The deluge of speculation on the future of European security politics unleashed by this event (though hardly caused by it) made early 1988 a particularly stimulating time to be completing this study.

The accumulating uncertainties of the 1980s have produced not only academic reassessments of the US–European relationship, but also a variety of military and political proposals for weakening that linkage, an aspiration which has acquired the label of 'dealignment', and aspirations for a concept of 'Europe' which includes more than its present western half (or perhaps two-thirds).[1] They have also served to draw attention to the need for a comparable reassessment of 'East–East' relations, not so much because it must be assumed that analogous analyses or prescriptions can be made in the field of Soviet–East European relations, but because the widespread questioning of the bloc system of recent years requires that equally serious consideration should be given to the workings of the Eastern bloc. The ingredients of the problem on the Eastern side are all too easy to enumerate: the region's relative economic weakness compared with Western Europe; its importance to Soviet perceptions of the USSR's security; the various national aspirations to greater political autonomy which have been dealt with by military action. It is already an area about which a great deal is written, and obviously it would be a brave analyst who proposed any new plan for solving the problems of Soviet–East European security relations.

A number of the standard themes of Western analyses of the WTO are not examined in any sustained manner in this study. No attempt has been made to assess or reassess the 'European military balance', or to study the WTO's 'reliability' or 'cohesion' as a way of calculating the likely outcome of any war which might occur in Europe. Appendix II provides a limited amount of quantitative data on the contributions made to WTO military strength by the smaller Eastern European countries, but comparisons with Nato are not a major purpose of the study, even though some are made where they seem helpful.

In chapters 1, 2 and 3 the main focus is on the military and political institutions of the WTO, on the organization's origins in a specific era of East–West and East–East relations, and on its evolution since then. Chapters 4, 5 and 6 shift the focus towards the Soviet Union itself and examine in turn the basis of Soviet security policy in Europe, Soviet policies on arms control and disarmament in the region, and the alternative defence debates of the 1980s. It is perhaps inevitable that the study of any alliance should pay particular attention to the policies of its largest member. In the present context, this factor is particularly important in view of the likely impact on European security politics of the generational change in the Soviet leadership symbolized by Mikhail Gorbachev's election as General Secretary of the Communist Party of the Soviet Union in March 1985.

Throughout this study, the WTO is examined in the light of questions which might be asked about any alliance – how much of the alliance's structure and activity is determined by the need for military efficiency in confronting a potential external opponent, and to what extent is the alliance concerned with preserving its own internal political cohesion?

This particular study is unable to deal with the important questions of the economic integration of the Soviet bloc in the Council for Mutual Economic Assistance (Comecon or CMEA) and pays more attention to the WTO's military organization and to its foreign policy activity, even though it might be argued that Comecon is at least as important as an instrument of political cohesion. It is hoped that the examination of a set of predominantly military and foreign policy questions will shed some light on the workings of the present European security system, and will illustrate how the interplay between intra-alliance and inter-alliance issues has shaped that system.

The Russian word *bezopasnost'*, usually translated as 'security', connotes 'absence of danger'. Western commentators have sometimes complained that the Russian concept is difficult to pin down and is an unsatisfactory tool of analysis. There may be some truth in this, but I would suggest that *'bezopasnost''* is no more elusive or problematic than 'security' or 'deterrence'. The Soviet Union and/or the WTO can hardly be accused of a unique failure to provide a sharp and succinct concept to encapsulate the variety of military, foreign-political, domestic-political and economic concerns identified in East and West under the heading 'security'. My own use of the term 'security policy' and concentration on the military and foreign policy dimensions is not intended to understate the problems attached to the concept itself.[2]

The material of this study's early chapters can, I hope, be seen as preparing the ground for the discussion of chapter 6. This chapter asks which of the WTO's internal and external security concerns are consistent with, and which might be challenged by, the varieties of alternative security thinking which emerged in Western Europe during the late 1970s and 1980s. Some of these concepts began to be taken up on the Eastern side in the course of the new fluidity and adventurousness introduced into Soviet arms control diplomacy during Gorbachev's first three years in office, and I have tried to explore their role in the military and foreign policy contexts of Gorbachev's initiatives. Some of the most difficult questions of European security politics in the 1990s will, I suggest, relate directly to the WTO's role in Soviet policy. Will any new phase of East–West detente which may follow the INF Treaty come to challenge the fundamental bloc division of Europe, or will it still fall within the framework of past periods of detente, with their contradictory mixture of competition and co-operation? Any satisfactory answer to these questions, or even an adequate framework for following events, will require an understanding of the dynamics of the WTO, and of the relative importance of internal and external factors.[3]

The question of the relative significance of an alliance's internal and external functions is one whose importance can be appreciated when one examines the existing body of English-language literature on the WTO. A number of different schools can be identified. A substantial body of work written primarily for military audiences, and sometimes by military writers, is in essence oriented towards 'military balance' questions, often with the unstated assumption that Soviet and WTO military policy is a given to which the West must find a response. In this kind of writing, the internal/external question tends to be overlooked or downplayed.[4] A contrasting school of analysis, most closely identified with Christopher Jones, places the focus almost entirely on 'internal' questions, and the possibility of the WTO performing traditional external security functions is excluded almost by definition.[5]

In between these fairly easily identifiable extremes lies a large category of analysis of the WTO which has a more even approach to the alliance, but which tends to deal with questions of WTO cohesion and reliability as issues to be addressed by US foreign policy without much consideration of the possibility that Western European actors may view these issues differently. In practice, these analyses often resolve themselves into simplistic recommendations for the exertion of pressure on identified weak points in the WTO.[6] European analysts seem to be less inclined to oversimplify in this way, but are not immune.

Much of this Western work on the WTO is well-researched and valuable, and this study makes use of a considerable amount of it. However, I would suggest that much of the available material would have benefited from a more rigorous examination of the relative weight of the internal and external alliance functions, since there is a tendency to make unexplained assumptions about their relative importance in a way which colours the subsequent analysis. It is probably no accident that the most impressive books on the WTO, which do not fall into the trap of making these unsubstantiated assumptions, are also the ones which are most cautious in urging policy options on their readers; I am thinking here of Robin Remington's 1971 study. *The Warsaw Pact: Case Studies in Communist Conflict Resolution*, and David Holloway and Jane Sharp's 1984 collection, *The Warsaw Pact: Alliance in Transition?*[7] It will nevertheless become apparent that my own approach has been influenced by a specific background which implies a substantial commitment to policy prescription, namely the 1980s political and theoretical activity of Western European peace movements and peace researchers. At the theoretical level, the writing of this study has helped me to think through the debates between different schools of Left analysis on the nature of the Cold War, in particular between those stressing inter-systemic competition and conflict (Isaac Deutscher, Fred Halliday), and a spectrum of others placing more emphasis on intra-systemic factors (Noam Chomsky, Mary Kaldor, Edward Thompson).[8]

A note on sources and terminology

The sources used in compiling this study are a combination of Western (English-language) and Soviet (English and Russian-language). There are some areas in which information from Soviet sources is relatively easy to find – basic documents and statements of the WTO, a number of institutional questions, and some questions of military strategy. In other areas, more reliance on Western sources has been necessary, and the standard source of *The Military Balance*, from the International Institute for Strategic Studies (IISS), has been used in compiling appendix II.

Many of the Western analyses use more Soviet and Eastern European sources than I have been able personally to use, but inevitably, there are some areas in which the sources themselves stem ultimately from Western intelligence reports. Overall, there is a need for some care in assessing any findings about the WTO. As one recent commentator has put it: 'with an alliance such as the Warsaw Pact, whose workings proceed behind a veil of secrecy, the greatest caution, even humility, is necessary'.[9]

The term 'Eastern Europe' is often controversial in itself, but it is used here in its most conventional sense, to refer to the USSR's six WTO allies – Bulgaria, Czechoslovakia, German Democratic Republic(GDR), Hungary, Poland, and Romania. This usage is not intended to imply any judgement on whether the USSR should or should not be considered part of 'Europe'.

In English usage, the terms 'Warsaw Treaty' and 'Warsaw Pact', are sometimes used to distinguish the treaty document from the organization established by it. Strictly speaking, the full title of the document should be rendered as 'The Warsaw Treaty of Friendship, Co-operation and Mutual Assistance', and that of the organization as 'Organization of the Warsaw Treaty' or 'Warsaw Treaty Organization'. However, 'Warsaw Pact' is also used at times to refer to the entire spectrum of the Soviet–East European alliance system, in its political and economic, as well as military, aspects. In this study, 'Warsaw Treaty Organization or WTO' is preferred for the security alliance, although this does not entail an assumption that political and economic factors can be ignored. 'Warsaw Pact' is used only in direct quotations. The cut-off date for the treatment of events in any depth is 15 August 1988.

1
Origins of the WTO

The Warsaw Treaty was signed in Warsaw on 14 May 1955, by representatives of Albania, Bulgaria, Hungary, the German Democratic Republic,
Poland, Romania, the USSR and Czechoslovakia.[1] A combination of
internal and external factors was at work even at this early stage. The
most immediate cause of the signature of the treaty at this particular time
was the accession of the Federal Republic of Germany to Nato. The FRG
joined the Western European Union in October 1954, and Nato on 5
May, 1955, when the Paris Agreements of the previous October were
ratified.

Within Europe, 1955 did not, of course, mark the beginning of the
Soviet alliance system. It is impossible here to give an account of
Europe's division into two blocs between 1945 and 1955, let alone to
develop any argument about the responsibility borne by the two sides. At
any rate, by 1955 Eastern Europe was already firmly tied to the USSR by
a network of political, economic and military ties. Comecon had been
formed in 1949, though it was hardly a functioning economic mechanism
by 1955. In June 1953 the GDR had suffered the first of a series of crises
within Eastern Europe which seemed to threaten the region's political
stability as part of an alliance of socialist states closely allied to the
USSR.[2]

The FRG's accession to Nato is the event most frequently cited by
Soviet commentators on the origins of the WTO, and since the USSR and
its allies had seen no need to form a multilateral alliance in 1949 at the
time of Nato's own formation, there is no reason to doubt that this was
viewed as an event of great importance. Since the formation of Nato, the
USSR had made a number of diplomatic moves aimed at preventing the
reintegration of the FRG into the Western alliance, including a March
1952 proposal for a reunified and neutralized Germany, and a 1954
proposal (put forward with the USSR's allies) to draw up a collective
European security treaty. Even after the FRG's formal entry into Nato, an
opportunity arose within the UN Disarmament Subcommittee for major
global nuclear and conventional force cuts. This has often been considered
to have been a sadly lost opportunity or 'moment of hope' for disarmament, though it might not have affected the WTO as such even if more
had come of it.[3]

There has been much debate as to whether Stalin or his successors would actually have 'abandoned' the GDR in a German reunification process if terms acceptable to both the USSR and the FRG could have been reached. It does seem quite possible that Stalin's 1952 initiative was serious, and the GDR leadership may well have feared abandonment. Ann L. Phillips has argued that the USSR remained ambivalent in its commitment to the GDR as a separate state right up to 1955, and that the eventual decision was prompted by the need seen after 1953 to increase political and economic support for the weak GDR leadership under Walter Ulbricht. In any event, the 1952 proposal was unacceptable to the FRG leadership of Konrad Adenauer, and by mid-1955 both German states were tied by security treaties to their respective camps.

The threat perceived in the FRG's reintegration into the Western bloc, however, was as much political and economic as it was military. It was feared that a revived West German state would aspire to Germany's former dominant economic, and thus political, role in East-Central Europe. The FRG's accession to Nato, furthermore, was not the only factor at work. Soviet commentators often refer to the development of Western-backed alliances outside Europe as a relevant consideration. The alliances particularly mentioned are Anzus, formed in 1951 (Australia, New Zealand and the USA), Seato (South-East Asia Treaty Organization, including Australia, France, New Zealand, Pakistan, the Philippines, Thailand, the UK and USA), formed in 1954, and the Baghdad Pact, later Cento, formed in 1955 (Central Treaty Organization, including Britain, Iran, Pakistan, Turkey, with the USA as an associate member).[4] This suggests that the WTO was seen as serving a global political/diplomatic purpose of demonstrating the USSR's ability to form its own alliance, but that this amounted to an indirect admission of weakness since the USSR was unable to call on an alliance system as geographically widespread as the USA's.

A number of Western commentators have placed more emphasis on circumstances other than those directly relating to the FRG.[5] It has been argued that military efficiency was important at this early stage, since the practices of the Stalin era, involving stress on sheer numbers of armed forces and close Soviet control of Eastern European military and security establishments, were militarily wasteful and needed revision. Others have considered that immediate military considerations carried relatively little weight at this time, and it was only in the early 1960s that the WTO began to be used seriously as a vehicle for co-ordinating defence policy beyond the measures which had been taken before 1955. According to this view, diplomatic considerations were more important in 1955, partly because by 1955 tentative steps were being taken by the post-Stalin Soviet leadership towards detente with the West, and partly because in those circumstances more subtle methods of managing Soviet–East European relations were needed. A treaty embodying the equal status of the states concerned was seen as making a useful contribution to these objectives.

One point often made is that the signature of the Warsaw Treaty legitimized the presence of Soviet troops in Hungary and Romania, since they would otherwise have had to withdraw once Soviet forces withdrew from Austria with the signature of the Austrian State Treaty. Presumably it would have been possible to regularize the presence of these troops by means of some bilateral arrangements, but the Warsaw Treaty did provide a broad legal basis for Soviet troop-stationing in Eastern Europe. Before 1955 a network of bilateral mutual aid and cultural treaties existed between the USSR and its allies, some of these treaties dating back to 1943 and 1945 (though the USSR had no treaties with the GDR, which only existed as a state from 1949). There also seem to have been some more specific bilateral agreements on military co-operation, although little is known about them. After 1955 new, more public arrangements were made for the stationing of Soviet troops (see chapter 3).[6]

Robin Remington argues that two differing Soviet motivations existed in 1955. On the one hand Molotov, then Foreign Minister, saw the WTO primarily in terms of safeguarding the military security of the socialist camp. For Khrushchev (then First Secretary) and to a lesser extent Bulganin (who replaced Malenkov as Prime Minister in February 1955), the WTO was part of the beginnings of a detente policy towards the West, and it was Khrushchev's conception which took precedence in the treaty text. Perhaps Remington poses the opposing conceptions too starkly, for 'detente' was not then, any more than it was later, considered incompatible with consolidating the unity of the Soviet bloc, but there is certainly evidence of differences within the Soviet leadership and of shifts away from the strictest Stalinist positions (which of course were also taking place in domestic politics). Molotov had central responsibility for the Austrian State Treaty (signed the day after the Warsaw Treaty), but had severe reservations about Khrushchev and Bulganin's policy of rapprochement with Yugoslavia (Khrushchev visited Belgrade later that month). Khrushchev was also preparing for the Geneva East–West summit conference later in the year, at which he met Eisenhower, Dulles, Eden and Faure. This was also the time of the Soviet withdrawal from the Porkkala base in Finland, and of the Soviet leadership's admission of the injustice of aspects of the USSR's past economic relations with Eastern Europe.

In his memoirs, Khrushchev provides some evidence to support Remington's interpretation. He comments (albeit in an interrupted passage which had to be partially interpreted by his American editor) that Molotov expressed doubts about the inclusion of Albania (and possibly other countries) in the alliance, on the grounds, it seems, that the USSR was not really strong enough to guarantee Albania's security. Since the 1948 Soviet–Yugoslav rift had left Albania geographically isolated from the rest of the USSR's allies, this objection would have made some sense. However, it would clearly have been less important for the kind of diplomatic purposes attributed by Remington to Khrushchev, and which he himself alludes to, or for the consideration of 'strengthening the internal situation' in each of the countries involved.[7] Even so, one should retain some caution in speculating on the precise roles and motivation of particular individuals at a time of continued rivalry within the Soviet leadership. (Khrushchev had originally opposed the moderation of foreign policy by Malenkov immediately after Stalin's death, but later adopted positions close to Malenkov's on consumer goods and peaceful coexistence.)

Whatever the precise individual roles may have been, there were clearly some contradictory factors at work at the time of the WTO's formation. The USSR had clearly decided to seek improved relations with Nato and the West, notwithstanding the immediate problems caused by the FRG's action in joining Nato. At the same time, the USSR was trying to consolidate its own bloc, not through the previous Stalinist tactics, but via an alliance which tried to make the equal status of its members more apparent. This is a theme which reappears in the later history of the WTO – the need to pay particular attention to the unity of one's own bloc at a time when relations with the opposing system are improving. Khrushchev's own account of the Geneva summit captures both elements, and also his own nervousness at approaching talks with the Western leaders from a position of relative weakness.[8] Whether or not the USSR would have considered bargaining the WTO away in negotiations with the West, the formation of the alliance did give Khrushchev a bargaining chip of sorts, as well as a visible symbol of the socialist bloc's supposed unity.

The treaty text

The preamble to the Warsaw Treaty identifies the reintegration of West Germany into the Western bloc as giving rise to the need for a counterbalancing alliance.[9] The treaty itself then goes on to commit its signatories to:

- settle international disputes by peaceful means (Article 1)
- work towards the prohibition of weapons of mass destruction (Article 2)
- consult in the event of a threat to the signatories' security, and render assistance as considered necessary in the event of an armed attack in Europe on any one of them (Articles 3 and 4)

- establish a joint command for their armed forces, and a political consultative committee with the power to create auxiliary organs (Articles 5 and 6)
- not join any alliance with conflicting aims (Article 7)
- co-operate in economic and cultural relations, while not interfering in one another's internal affairs (Article 8)
- allow other states to accede irrespective of their social and state systems (Article 9)
- seek a general European treaty of collective security, in which event the present treaty will become ineffective (Article 11).

In some points of phrasing the Warsaw Treaty is modelled on the North Atlantic Treaty of 1949, which established Nato. The North Atlantic Treaty does not actually specify a joint military command, though it does provide for a defence committee which will implement measures for a collective capacity to resist armed attack. However, it is also interesting to compare the two treaties in respect of their coverage of spheres other than defence co-operation. The North Atlantic Treaty, in its preamble and Article 2, makes it clear that Nato is seen as an alliance of states with common political and economic systems and institutions: 'to safeguard the freedom, common heritage and civilization of their peoples, founded on the principles of democracy, individual liberty and the rule of law' . . . 'contribute towards the further development of peaceful and friendly international relations by strengthening their free institutions, by bringing about a better understanding of the principles upon which these institutions are founded, and by promoting conditions of stability and well-being.'[10] The Warsaw Treaty, with its Article specifying openness of accession to all states irrespective of social systems, has no directly analogous clauses. Its Article on economic and cultural relations is politically neutral, though Article 5's commitment to safeguarding peaceful labour could be glossed without too much difficulty as entailing a commitment to a social system.

The North Atlantic Treaty says nothing about the reduction of armaments or the conclusion of a European collective security treaty. Consequently, the WTO has at least a documentary basis for its claim to be particularly concerned about negotiations on security. These clauses lend weight to Remington's argument about the considerations which were most important for the Soviet leadership in 1955, and it was indeed the WTO which pressed originally for the Helsinki process to be set in motion. On the other hand, the WTO has emerged with little credit from its textual claim to political neutrality. Nato can at least argue that it is fairly explicit about being an alliance committed to Atlantic capitalism and bourgeois-liberal parliamentary democracy (to put something of a gloss on the above quotations from the treaty), even if some of its member states, notably Portugal and Greece in the past, and most recently Turkey in the 1980s, have had little to do with the latter. The North Atlantic Treaty also specifies (Article 4) consultation whenever 'territorial integrity, political independence or security' are threatened, which was fairly clearly put in at the time as a pre-emptive legitimation of any intervention which might be deemed necessary in the event of a communist or socialist election victory in, say, Italy.[11] The text of the Warsaw Treaty does not specify any ideological basis for the alliance, still less any right of military intervention in support of such a basis. Indeed, Article 8 specifies non-intervention in internal affairs. Consequently, the treaty could provide no foundation for the armed interventions carried out in Hungary in 1956, and in Czechoslovakia in 1968 (see chapters 2 and 3).

On the same day as the Warsaw Treaty was signed, an announcement was made on the formation of the Joint Armed Forces of the WTO signatories. Marshal I.S. Konev of the USSR was named Commander-in-Chief; the allied ministers of defence or other military leaders were appointed as his deputies and as commanders of allied units assigned to the Joint Armed Forces; a staff was formed with representatives from the member states, to be located in Moscow; and the stationing of the signatories' armed forces was to be arranged by mutual agreement.[12]

The treaty itself was to remain in force for twenty years, to be extended automatically for a further ten years for those who did not renounce it (Article 11).

Developments since 1955

The developments which have taken place in the WTO's forces, institutions and diplomatic activities since 1955 will be examined in detail in the following chapters of this study. In the eyes of most Western observers, the WTO's history has been a matter of successive crisis at strikingly regular intervals. Little more than a year after the treaty's signature, the Hungarian crisis of October–November 1956 erupted. During the course of these events, the Hungarian premier Imre Nagy announced Hungary's withdrawal from the alliance, although his leadership was almost immediately overthrown by Soviet intervention forces and replaced by that of Janos Kadar.[13] At the same time, unrest in Poland was resolved by the appointment of Stanislaw Gomulka as First Secretary of the Polish United Workers' Party, and without the use of force, though confrontation between Polish and Soviet forces was only narrowly avoided.

The Hungarian events were almost repeated in 1968 in Czechoslovakia, though with less bloodshed and with the help of an intervention force which included small detachments from all the other Eastern European states except Romania, as well as a large Soviet force. Subsequently, the reformist Czechoslovakian party leadership of Alexander Dubcek was replaced by that of Gustav Husak.[14]

In Poland in 1980–1, a rapidly-evolving political crisis following the emergence of the independent Solidarity trade union movement ended not in Soviet intervention, but the declaration of martial law in December 1981 and an extensive militarization of Polish politics under General Jaruzelski. Martial law was technically lifted in July 1983, but debate continues over the strategic significance of the Polish events for the WTO and their long-term political significance for Poland.[15]

While these have been the most dramatic events in Soviet–East European relations since 1955, there have been other developments which are worth mentioning before these questions are taken up later in more detail. Apart from the brief period of Hungarian withdrawal in 1956, only Albania has withdrawn from the WTO. No other state has joined, although there were some reports in 1986 that Libya had approached the USSR with a view to joining in the aftermath of the US air attacks on Tripoli and Benghazi. The WTO thus remains a European body, by contrast with Comecon, which has been joined by several non-European states (Cuba, Mongolia, Vietnam).

Soviet publications date Albanian non-participation in WTO bodies from 1962,[16] although in fact the USSR broke off diplomatic relations with Albania in late 1961 after a period of increasing estrangement centring largely on Chinese hostility over Soviet destalinization and policies towards the West, and Albanian support for Chinese positions. Albania finally withdrew in 1968 after the intervention in Czechoslovakia. China had originally sent an observer to the Warsaw Treaty signature ceremony, but China's relations with the USSR worsened during the early 1960s, and the other Eastern European states were not always unreserved in their support for the USSR.[17] Relations with China remained a potentially divisive issue throughout the 1970s.

Soviet relations with Romania also worsened in the 1960s, and in the late 1960s the USSR tried to deal simultaneously with Romania, the Czechoslovakian reform development, and the GDR's fears that detente with the West threatened its interests. After the 1968 Czechoslovakian crisis these pressures seemed to have been contained and, while US–Soviet relations improved with the SALT talks, both the USSR and the individual Eastern European states improved their relations with the FRG and signed treaties 'normalizing' relations and state borders in Central Europe. A further stage in this process was the all-European Conference on Security and Co-operation in Europe, beginning in 1972, and culminating in the August 1975 signature of the Helsinki Final Act.

Although the Helsinki Act became such a bone of contention in the collapse of detente, its signature was seen by the Soviet and Eastern European leaderships alike as a fruit of their longstanding pressure for a European security conference, as specified in the Warsaw Treaty, and an important indication of Western recognition of the political and territorial status quo in Europe. The Mutual and Balanced Force Reduction talks, starting in 1973, were a kind of *quid pro quo* which the West persuaded the USSR to agree to in return for the Helsinki process. It is, of course, hotly debated whether the Helsinki process did amount to an acceptance of the political status quo, and whether US foreign policy, in particular, saw it in those terms. Nevertheless, this was certainly an important Soviet objective and interpretation of the results.[18]

The Polish crisis of 1981 merged with the more general breakdown of detente and continued to sour East–West relations for the first few years of the decade. There were indications of tensions between the USSR and its allies in the 1983–5 period, as negotiations with USA over Intermediate Nuclear Forces were breaking down and the question of Soviet' 'counterdeployments' arose (see chapter 2). Nevertheless, by the time the Warsaw Treaty fell due for renewal in early 1985, disarmament talks between the USA and USSR had been resumed, and a new Soviet leadership under Mikhail Gorbachev was beginning to take the diplomatic initiative, perhaps with some prompting from the Eastern European leaderships. The treaty was duly renewed for a further period of twenty years, with an option of a further ten, and with only one minor change to the original text, on 26 April 1985.[19]

This minor change to the treaty provides a curious footnote. The original version was said to be valid only in the Russian, Polish, Czech and German languages. The 1985 Protocol of Renewal adds Bulgarian, Hungarian and Romanian to the list. This is clearly an understandable way of emphasizing national equality, but it is odd that it was not done originally. (Elsewhere, Russian is specified as the working language of all WTO bodies.) It does suggest that even in 1955 the three northern states of Eastern Europe were seen as being more important, and in a way this might amount to evidence in support of Molotov's conception of the alliance gaining a minor victory over Khrushchev's. Poland, Czechoslovakia and the GDR have always been the USSR's most important political and military partners, even if the GDR was still very weak in 1955. Some analysts have suggested that the USSR originally considered a more limited regional alliance restricted to what is now termed the 'northern tier', and perhaps Molotov's conception had something to do with this. At any rate, this minor but possibly symbolic point about the 1955 text does lend some support to that theory.[20]

2
WTO Political Structures and History

In chapters 2 and 3 of this study, the WTO's institutions are divided rather arbitrarily into 'political' and 'military'. There is obviously a danger of begging questions here, and some of the discussion does not fall naturally into one chapter rather than the other. However, the objective is to establish a framework without presupposing that given bodies have either a military or a political essence. Inevitably, there is some overlap between the two chapters. In both, an outline characterization of WTO institutions is taken from Soviet sources. This outline is then explored in some detail, taking note of historical developments and differing analyses of institutional functions, and related to evidence already presented in earlier chapters. Figure 1 presents basic data from both chapters in diagrammatic form.

The political institutions

The WTO's chief body is the Political Consultative Committee (PCC), which was specified in the text of the Warsaw Treaty along with a joint command for the signatories' armed forces. Article 6 of the treaty empowered the PCC to create additional organs as the need arose, and stipulated that it should be composed of members of government or any other representatives of the signatory states.[1] According to the treaty, the PCC was established 'for the purpose of holding the consultations provided for in the present treaty among the states that are party to the treaty, and for the purpose of considering problems arising in connection with the implementation of this treaty'.[2] The PCC is identified in Soviet sources as the WTO's supreme political body, though there are also times when it appears identified as a military body. Its functions are described as follows in the *Soviet Military Encyclopaedia*: 'At sessions of the PCC the most important foreign policy questions are discussed, decisions are worked out collectively on international questions which affect the interests of all participants in the [Warsaw] Treaty, and the most important problems connected with the strengthening of defence capability and carrying out of the obligation of the states party to the Warsaw Treaty to collective defence are examined.'[3] This gives the PCC a combination of political and military duties, indicating that subordinate bodies of both types report to

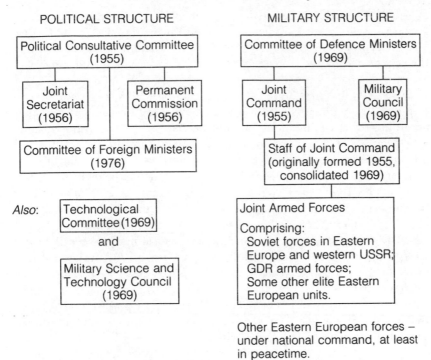

POLITICAL STRUCTURE

Political Consultative Committee (1955)	
Joint Secretariat (1956)	Permanent Commission (1956)

Committee of Foreign Ministers (1976)

Also:

Technological Committee (1969)

and

Military Science and Technology Council (1969)

MILITARY STRUCTURE

Committee of Defence Ministers (1969)	
Joint Command (1955)	Military Council (1969)

Staff of Joint Command (originally formed 1955, consolidated 1969)

Joint Armed Forces
 	
Comprising:
  Soviet forces in Eastern Europe and western USSR;
  GDR armed forces;
  Some other elite Eastern European units.

Other Eastern European forces – under national command, at least in peacetime.

Figure 1   Principal WTO institutions (with dates of establishment)

it. It is often stated that the PCC has no supranational functions and does not impinge on the WTO states' sovereignty.

Although the Warsaw Treaty itself was signed by the prime ministers of the states concerned, from 1960 onwards it was general and first secretaries of the respective parties who signed the PCC's communiqués. The membership of the PCC has been identified as general or first secretaries plus the heads of state or their deputies, ministers of defence and foreign ministers, and central committee secretaries of the respective parties, plus the commander-in-chief of the WTO armed forces and the general secretary of the PCC.[4] Some accounts (for instance, the IISS) suggest that the chief of staff is also a member. The general secretary's post has in the past been mentioned only infrequently, and seemed to involve a much less public profile than the work of Nato's secretary general. In the more adventurous diplomacy of the Gorbachev era, however, the general secretary has become rather more visible, as suggestions have been made of direct talks between the Nato and WTO incumbents. The WTO post now appears to be held by a deputy foreign minister of the country responsible for hosting the next PCC meeting. In Berlin in May 1987, the GDR's Herbert Krolikowski handed over to Poland's Henryk Jaroszek, who was then succeeded by the Romanian Constantin Oancea after the July 1988 Warsaw meeting.[5]

The PCC's first meeting, in Prague in January 1956, saw the power to create additional organs used to set up a *Permanent Commission* (PC) and, according to its communiqué, a Joint Secretariat (JS). Curiously, however, a later communiqué also claims to have set up the JS in 1976, and the later date is sometimes given for the secretariat.[6] Perhaps the original secretariat had not functioned very well, and needed to be revived in 1976. The January 1956 communiqué also specified that the PCC should meet 'when necessary, but no less than twice a year'; the twice-a-year specification has seldom been met, and has been omitted from other accounts of the PCC's obligations.[7] In fact, there were ten meetings between 1955 and 1969, with only four between spring 1955 and spring 1961, and no meeting at all in the period between January 1956 and May 1958. During the Brezhnev period, 1964–82, there were a total of twelve PCC meetings, though a further expansion of WTO bodies after 1969 must have relieved the pressure on the PCC.[8] PCC meetings are now annual, and are rotated around the various WTO capital cities.

The Permanent Commission is described as providing recommendations on foreign policy,[9] while the secretariat is credited by Western sources with preparation of the PCC's agendas and also responsibility for armaments and logistics.[10] Presumably the commission and secretariat have multinational staffs; as a permanent body, the secretariat presumably also implements decisions taken by the PCC (and, since 1976, the Committee of Foreign Ministers). The PCC retains the functions of appointing the WTO's commander-in-chief, chief of staff and general secretary.[11]

The PCC has remained the WTO's senior body, and the presence of the C-in-C on this committee indicates that this is where he reports on the work of the military bodies. A further body was formed in 1976, when the Committee of Foreign Ministers (CFM) was set up by the Bucharest PCC meeting, and the CFM held its first formal meeting six months later in Moscow.[12] This committee was set up shortly after the signature of the Helsinki Final Act in August 1975, although the foreign ministers had been meeting without being identified as a committee since 1959.[13] In addition, summer holiday meetings between the leaders were arranged in the Crimea from 1971 onwards. Presumably a more formal structure was seen as necessary in the new situation created by the signature of the Helsinki Accords, though the founding communiqué does not elaborate on the CFM's functions beyond giving the aim as 'further perfection of the mechanism of political co-operation within the framework of the Treaty'.[14] The CFM now meets twice annually. No major new political institutions have been created since 1976, though there are also working meetings of deputy foreign ministers and foreign ministry officials. The May 1987 PCC meeting in Berlin also set up a working group for information exchanges and a commission to deal with disarmament questions. This disarmament commission consists of representatives of the foreign and defence ministries, and it seems possible that in time it may come to acquire a higher public profile.[15]

In analysis of the objectives of the WTO and of the functions of the constituent bodies described here, there tends to be a sharp dividing line between Eastern commentators who treat the alliance as concerned primarily with European peace and security, and Western treatments which focus more on its domestically repressive or potentially militarily expansionist functions. Both approaches have their drawbacks. The Eastern approach is inadequate in that it seeks to deny the all-too-apparent evidence of the repressive functioning of the alliance system, while a number of Western writers exclude almost by definition the possibility of the WTO performing orthodox security functions in Soviet or Eastern European eyes. Some Western writers have written in a more nuanced way on the WTO's foreign policy functions, and have achieved more discriminating insights into the sometimes common, sometimes divergent interests of the USSR and its allies. The argument of this, and the following chapters, tries to give due weight to both elements.

Intervention and bloc management, before and after 1968

In the earlier discussion of the text of the Warsaw Treaty (chapter 1), mention was made of the text's attempt to suggest ideological neutrality, thereby providing a contrast with the North Atlantic Treaty. Since Article 9 stipulates that the Warsaw Treaty is open to states of any social system, social and political issues should in theory be irrelevant. In practice, this fiction has not been seriously maintained, and WTO mechanisms have played a significant part in sustaining the political cohesion of the Eastern bloc as a whole.

In a basic definitional document, the WTO was described in 1976 as having been formed 'with the aim of defending the gains of socialism'.[16] This is a formulation which, though absent from the treaty, is commonplace in later descriptions of the WTO's purpose. A glance at a selection of material published around 1985, at the time of the WTO's thirtieth anniversary and renewal, gives some indication of the Soviet conception of the alliance.

In one of the Soviet texts already cited, we read: 'The military co-operation of the fraternal socialist countries in the framework of the WTO is a qualitatively new social-historical phenomenon, characterized by the mutual relations between the peoples and armies of the socialist states. This co-operation is based on the objective necessity of the joint defence by the workers of the gains of socialism.'[17] The then WTO C-in-C, Marshal Kulikov, writing in 1985 in the CPSU's theoretical journal *Kommunist*, said: 'On May 14th 1955, they [the socialist countries of Europe] signed the Treaty of Friendship, Co-operation and Mutual Assistance, which has entered history as the Warsaw Treaty, in which were expressed the wish and aspirations of the fraternal peoples for unity, for their collective responsibility to provide for the defence of the gains of socialism, for the preservation of peace and international security.'[18] The existence of the socialist system had pre-dated the formation of the WTO, wrote its Chief of Staff around the same time: after the Second World War 'Socialism moved beyond the frame of one country and formed a world system',[19] and in 1985 the WTO's function was seen to be as important as ever in a period of a US 'crusade' against communism: 'In this situation one can see even more clearly the enormous role which the Warsaw Pact plays in the defence of peace, of revolutionary gains, in securing the progress of socialism.'[20]

To cite these references to the WTO as sustaining a social system is in many ways to repeat the obvious: there exist in Europe (and beyond) two social systems and military blocs in competition with each other, and the political cohesion of these blocs needs to be regularly reaffirmed. However, these axioms need to be recorded to assist in understanding Soviet–East European relations and the role of WTO institutions therein. In addition to the WTO institutions already mentioned, the network of bilateral treaties which existed before 1955 has been updated, so that it continues to provide a distinct mechanism for affirming the obligations between the bloc's states. Many of the bilateral treaties make the commitment to a shared social system explicit in a way which the Warsaw Treaty itself does not.

These bilateral treaties are perhaps best described as 'military-political' in nature and function, and they can be distinguished from the more specific troop-stationing agreements. The most recent round of treaties dates from the 1970s, and they share with a number of other documents, such as domestic Eastern European party programmes and state constitutions, commitments to the alliance with the USSR, the joint defence of socialism and peace, and the 'combat confederation' (*boevoe sodruzhestvo*) of the armed forces of the 'socialist confederation' (*sotsialisticheskoe sodruzhestvo*).[21] The GDR's constitution, for example, states that 'The German Democratic Republic is for ever and irrevocably allied with the

Union of Soviet Socialist Republics.'[22]

A comment frequently made by Western commentators on the WTO is that Soviet proposals to dissolve the WTO are meaningless, since the network of bilateral treaties between the USSR and its allies would not be altered by such a dissolution. Ironically, Soviet commentators have themselves sometimes conceded almost as much; in the words of Valentin Alexandrov: 'Of course the world socialist system will not perish if the Warsaw Treaty Organization ceases to exist simultaneously with Nato under an agreement reached by the two sides. It will not perish because there will remain other components of the strong structure of socialist international relations.'[23] However, this does not necessarily mean that all the functions of the WTO could equally easily be carried out by the bilateral treaty system.

An exception to this pattern is Romania. The 1970 Soviet–Romanian treaty is emphatic about Soviet–Romanian friendship, but is careful not to commit Romania to joint defence of the gains of socialism, and limits Romanian obligations to consultation and the defence of state borders as specified in the Warsaw Treaty itself.[24] These are the distinctions which have been cited in picking Romania out as a non-adherent to the 'Brezhnev doctrine' as spelled out in 1968; a survey of the early history of the WTO will help to clarify how they came to acquire such weight.

The WTO was little more than a year old when the Hungarian crisis erupted in 1956, and the organization as such played little part in its resolution. The crisis can perhaps be seen as reflecting a Soviet failure to realize that destalinization could threaten the very existence of Eastern European regimes in a way in which it did not threaten the Soviet leadership itself. The events of 1956 in Hungary grew out of a combination of worker and peasant discontent and intellectual anti-Stalinism, with Imre Nagy becoming head of government just before the transition to violent conflict. At the height of the crisis, Nagy abolished the one-party system and announced Hungary's withdrawal from the WTO and neutrality. Although the latter step has sometimes been interpreted as a tactical step made to gain Western support, Nagy's own writings before 1956 had displayed an interest in neutrality and the possibility of an independent Hungarian foreign policy. The USSR used its own forces to restore its authority, though it presumably had Romanian and Polish co-operation since some of the troops involved were stationed in those countries. Although the USSR subsequently cited the Warsaw Treaty as a justification for the intervention, there seems to have been no co-ordination through WTO channels, as opposed to Soviet consultation with other Eastern European leaderships, which did take place (including consultation with Tito). Whatever the USSR may have claimed, the

Warsaw Treaty itself certainly did not specify a general right of Soviet intervention. In fact, the intervention was a clear breach of Article 1 (on the non-use of force) and Article 8 (on non-interference in internal affairs), and no PCC meeting seems even to have discussed the Hungarian crisis.

Perhaps because of Soviet concern that there should be no repetition of the Hungarian crisis, the 1960s saw the development under Marshal Grechko of the programme of multinational exercises between Soviet and Eastern European forces. Although significant for military reasons (see chapters 3–4), these exercises were not without political importance. They took place within the conception of 'coalition warfare', which not only laid stress on co-operation on the battlefield between WTO armies, but also stressed ideological ties between states and armies. The multilateral exercises were part of a pattern of multilateral and bilateral WTO institutions which have been documented by Christopher Jones.

Less visible than the well-publicized meetings of ministers and party leaders, these institutions are a careful blend of the military and the political. They include: a committee for sporting links between WTO states and other Soviet allies; a possible directorate for WTO military doctrine which trains the armies according to the shared set of military-political axioms already mentioned; close ties and exchange arrangements between political administrations in the respective armies (though the political administrations themselves existed before the formation of the WTO); co-ordination of military education policy and the training of the most promising Eastern European officers at institutes like the prestigious Voroshilov Academy in Moscow.[25] A key part of Jones's argument is that, in practice, many of these institutions are more bilateral than genuinely multilateral, which enables the USSR to maintain close surveillance of each Eastern European army individually.

One purpose of these institutions is to create a homogeneous military elite, a 'greater socialist officer corps', at the highest level, and to inculcate a specific set of military-political virtues and attitudes in the armies as fighting units. The central political conclusion drawn by Jones from these phenomena is that they are designed to pre-empt movement towards political autonomy in Eastern Europe. No army which is integrated into this system is trained to defend its own national territory, and so would be unable to defend an Eastern European government against Soviet military intervention. Essentially, this aspect of the WTO is a device to limit political development by preventing any military capacity to support an anti-communist, or nationalist and anti-Soviet though still communist, government in the region. By extension, the existing regimes in the region must also rely on the threat of Soviet military intervention to protect themselves from potential domestic threats.

Jones rests his case heavily on Romania's achievement of relative political autonomy and non-participation in these structures. Romania abandoned the multilateral exercise arrangement at an early stage, in 1962–3, and from that time on has steered a course close to non-alignment within the alliance, calling independently for bloc dissolution and distancing itself from Soviet foreign policy in other ways. During the 1960s Czechoslovakia also began to voice some unhappiness with the WTO's political organization. In May 1968, the Czechoslovakian Gottwald Academy floated publicly a number of possibilities for an alternative Czech defence policy, including a Central European security system without the Soviet Union and outright neutrality.[26] The implied criticisms were of Soviet political hegemony within the WTO, and also of Soviet military strategy itself (see chapter 4 for a more military perspective). Jones and others, including Condoleezza Rice, have argued that these developments were a major factor in prompting the Soviet decision to intervene.

Jones's work is particularly relevant to the debate over the politics of WTO intervention, but it also contains a broader argument about the nature of the organization. He argues that although the WTO armies do train for offensive operations against Western Europe, this is not the main purpose of the alliance. The prevention of autonomous territorial defence in Eastern Europe is the main aim, and the offensive posture directed against Western Europe is just a way of discouraging Nato from intervening in Eastern European conflicts.

Jones's central insight is an important point about the interconnections between military, political and ideological 'security' in Eastern Europe. 'Preservation of the gains of socialism' is not just, or even primarily, a question of defence against Nato, but of sustaining a specific social system which might not survive without the constraints of a military alliance. However, my own view of Jones's arguments is that he provides insufficient evidence for ranking the internal political purpose so clearly above the external military role, or even for the claim that it is principally through military mechanisms that internal cohesion is sustained (as opposed to, say, economic incentives or even a genuinely shared perception of a security threat). He sometimes writes with such a disregard for Nato that there appears to be no reason *why* the Soviet Union should regard Eastern Europe as a strategically significant area. But common sense would suggest, and following chapters of this study will argue, that the area *is* militarily important for the USSR as well as being politically vulnerable. Moreover, Jones tends to overestimate the importance of Romania. Even though Romania's territorial defence policy is undoubtedly genuine, Romania remains, in strategic terms, the *least* important of the WTO allies to the USSR. A territorial defence posture in Romania which excludes the USSR is a very different matter from the possibility of one in Czechoslovakia. One really needs to assess the extent, nature and desirability of the political autonomy achieved by Romania before arguing that it is the key to understanding the WTO. Nor is Romania of major importance to the USSR politically, though one has to be careful not to be too dogmatic about the Romanian situation in view of the uncertainties which will surely arise after the end of the Ceausescu era. Jones also tends to write as though the fostering of ideological cohesion were an activity unique to the WTO, and as though the mechanisms he describes provided a highly efficient way of realizing Soviet political objectives, which is questionable.

It is also important to remember that the principles later identified as the 'Brezhnev doctrine' were close to formulations which had been widely used after 1956 and then around 1960–1 in the elaboration of 'socialist internationalism', as a principle governing the supposedly voluntary joint efforts of socialist states. Their elaboration at that time was linked to attempts to assert Soviet primacy in relations with Yugoslavia and China, and so was not new in 1968 and had not originated in concerns related solely to the WTO states.[27]

These reservations do not mean that Jones's work does not provide some useful insights into the political functioning of the WTO. These issues came to the fore in 1968, when the progress of the Czechoslovakian reform movement provoked Soviet concern, then political pressure, and finally multinational WTO intervention.

The critique of national security policy which emerged during 1968 from within the Czech armed forces was only one strand in the political developments which took place in Czechoslovakia. Within the Soviet leadership, there were a variety of other reasons why these developments were seen as threatening, ranging from fear of 'spillover' into domestic dissent and implications for Soviet economic reforms, to fears of the delegitimization of Soviet leadership of the bloc.[28] As far as the WTO itself was concerned, the USSR's difficulty was essentially the same as in 1956 – the Warsaw Treaty did not sanction military intervention by one signatory against another, but intervention might be the only solution if political measures failed. During the summer of 1968, pressure was put on Czechoslovakia in a variety of ways. Military exercises were co-ordinated both inside and outside Czechoslovakia; political meetings took place on a bilateral basis between the Soviet and Czech leaderships, and on a multilateral basis involving other WTO leaders. However, no meeting took place which identified itself as a WTO meeting. Two of the key pre-intervention meetings, in Warsaw in July (excluding the Czechs) and Bratislava in August (at which the Czechs were present) were *ad hoc* meetings of WTO leaders, but not meetings of the PCC or any other WTO institution. Romania attended neither meeting, and the significance of this is plain – Romania would not have endorsed any measures which might serve as groundwork for an eventual intervention. When the decision to intervene was finally taken, after hesitation and probably divisions in the Soviet leadership, the Soviet armed forces themselves took command of the actual operation. (The convening of *ad hoc* meetings was not, however, resorted to only in internal crises; a similar emergency meeting took place in June 1967 during the Middle East War.)

Two particular documents emerged from these meetings which amounted to a revision of the Warsaw Treaty and an extension of its terms to cover internal political developments in a signatory state. The 'Warsaw letter' emphasized collective security and membership of the socialist community, and also the principle that Czechoslovakia's membership of that community was the 'common concern' of its allies in the WTO. The 'Bratislava declaration', which the Czech leadership signed, said much the same things, and noted the 'common international duty of all socialist countries to support, strengthen and defend' the gains made by socialism (without mentioning Czechoslovakia specifically). These were the principles which followed in the tracks of earlier formulations of 'socialist internationalism', were enunciated by the Soviet leadership after the intervention and dubbed the 'Brezhnev doctrine' in the West, and are traceable through the WTO members' bilateral treaties and party programmes of the late 1960s and 70s and in the military-political axioms on which WTO military training rests.[29] The 'common defence of the gains of socialism' also appeared in the 1977 Soviet constitution. Significantly, no real attempt was made to cite the Warsaw Treaty itself in support of the intervention, as had been done in 1956. (Although Soviet sources still claim there was a joint threat of imperialist reaction and internal counter-revolution in Hungary, the considered line on Czechoslovakia seems to be that the danger was a threat to the socialist order, rather than Western intervention as such.)

The Czech armed forces did not oppose the intervention of 21 August, not least because Dubcek's leadership had always assumed such an event would not occur and had not prepared for the contingency. Some Czechoslovakian military officers may, however, have presented a plan for resistance to the party praesidium, and the Soviet leadership may have got wind of this. If such a plan was presented, Dubcek must have rejected it. It is important to stress that the USSR did not need the military assistance of the GDR, Polish, Hungarian and Bulgarian contingents which participated. These contingents were small, and quickly withdrawn. What was important was their political complicity in the operation – indeed, the GDR and Polish leaderships were at least as concerned as the USSR about developments in Czechoslovakia, even if Kadar was less worried. (Dubcek's leadership was not formally removed until April

1969, and in view of the widespread passive resistance to the Soviet occupation, it might be argued that more organized resistance could have strengthened Dubcek's hand. As had happened earlier in Hungary, popular resistance continued beyond the re-establishment of Soviet authority at the leadership and governmental level.)

The intervention led to the renunciation of the Warsaw Treaty by Albania, which had been estranged from the Soviet Union since 1961, and the refusal by Romania to accept that the Warsaw Treaty provided grounds for the action. Although it is unlikely that Ceausescu had any sympathy with the political aspirations of the Czech reforms (for example, the abolition of censorship), he supported Dubcek on the principle of national sovereignty, and both he and Tito had visited Prague before the intervention to show their support. After the intervention, the Romanian armed forces were put on alert, an ' Ceausescu may genuinely have feared a Soviet attack on Romania. During 1969, there were military manoeuvres conducted in Soviet Moldavia, Hungary and Bulgaria, which were fairly certainly intended as warnings to Romania; in 1971 Romania resisted Soviet pressure to permit the transit of troops across Romania to Bulgaria.[30]

Although it is important to look in detail at the events of the 1968 crisis in order to understand the political workings of the WTO at that time, this does not mean that this pattern was frozen for all time. The creation of new institutions in 1969 and again in 1976 has been noted, and the question arises of the political significance of these developments. The most extreme view, of the post-1968 changes as a simple reimposition of Soviet domination to avoid possible Romanian vetos, is not convincing. In the last resort, the USSR can manage without Romania, and did so in 1968. It is more likely that the USSR recognized the dangers of its allies resenting under-consultation and of small grievances snowballing into major crises, and created new institutions so that its allies felt they had, and perhaps did have, increased political weight.

If this interpretation is correct, then the WTO evolved during the late 1960s and 1970s into something more of a mechanism for settling conflicts without the use of force, as Robin Remington argued in her book published in 1971. Remington and others have also pointed out that there were other occasions on which the USSR retreated or compromised when clashes arose.

In 1967 accommodation was reached between the USSR and Romania over strengthening the WTO and Romanian claims to independence. Throughout the 1960s, the USSR had to deal with challenges from China to its authority and legitimacy as leader of the world communist movement, a problem unforeseen in 1955. Romania in particular was able to use some of the leeway afforded by the Sino–Soviet dispute to expand its limited area of autonomy, when it became important for the USSR to have the visible public support of the Eastern Europeans.[31] (The 1971 Soviet pressure on Romania seems to have been related to Romania's endorsement of Nixon's trip to China.)

As Soviet policy towards the FRG and the West in general grew more complex in the late 1960s, tensions grew between the GDR and the Soviet leadership, echoing fears originally voiced in the pre-1955 period about a possible weakening of Soviet commitment to the GDR; in 1971 Walter Ulbricht was replaced by Erich Honecker as First Secretary of the GDR's Socialist Unity Party.[32] This problem merged with the wider questions of bloc management under conditions of emerging detente and of limiting West German influence in Eastern Europe. However, the main point to be made about the handling of these issues by the WTO is not to do with the specific solutions found in each case, but in the fact that they had to be dealt with by fudge and compromise; the invasion of Czechoslovakia represented the most extreme form of problem-solving within the bloc, but a number of other problems were resolved through a more sophisticated, and less decisive, bargaining process. This bargaining was not necessarily done in WTO institutions as such, but it added significantly to the alliance's capacity to diffuse possible conflicts between leaderships, at the same time as it reduced outright Soviet dominance.[33]

These problems did not disappear in the 1970s, for though the Helsinki process was successful in achieving a major goal of the Soviet and Eastern European leaderships, recognition of the territorial status quo (see below), it could also be argued that the relaxations of detente created a different set of problems for bloc management in Eastern Europe. Increased economic co-operation with the West helped to raise living standards, but also caused indebtedness and so helped to worsen some of Eastern Europe's economic problems, contributing indirectly to the Polish crisis at the end of the decade. Perhaps the 1976 creation of the WTO's Committee of Foreign Ministers was intended both to recognize the role played by the Eastern European leaderships during the Helsinki process, and to deal with the possible dangers of increased polycentrism. The CFM certainly did not give the USSR any way of outmanoeuvring Romania on questions like relations with China or defence spending, which continued to rumble on unresolved during the late 1970s; the China issue became even more sensitive as China moved closer to the USA and Nato, only to shift to a more equidistant position again in the 1980s.

In any case, the Polish crisis again placed severe strains on the WTO's political structures and military unity. It may well be that the alliance would not have survived another Soviet intervention, since the Polish army would probably have resisted. On the other hand, it was the Polish army itself which eventually moved to impose martial law on 13 Decem-

ber 1981, after an unprecedented period in which party authority had
collapsed and Solidarity had been legalized and played a major role in
revitalizing Polish society in spite of a severe economic crisis. As had been
the case with developments in Czechoslovakia, there was evidently concern in the Soviet leadership that there would be a 'spillover' of discontent
into the western USSR. It seems clear that the USSR made contingency
plans to invade. According to Ryszard Kuklinski, a defector from the
Polish general staff, a decision-in-principle was made in late 1980 to crush
Solidarity either by external intervention with Soviet, Czechoslovakian
and GDR forces or through internal actions, and Timothy Garton Ash has
suggested that Jaruzelski was given an ultimatum by the USSR in
December 1981: either he acted, or an invasion would be inevitable. [34] It
has also been suggested that Jaruzelski moved to pre-empt a coup against
his own leadership by harder-line elements in the Polish elite.

    Whatever the precise details of the imposition of martial law, the Soviet
handling of the crisis suggested greater reluctance to intervene than in
1968, and so perhaps a clearer understanding of the political disutility of
direct military intervention as well as its military difficulties. The Soviet
forces already stationed in Poland could not, after all, do much to prevent
the rise of Solidarity. During 1980 and 1981 a number of features of the
Czechoslovakian crisis were repeated: an *ad hoc* multilateral WTO meeting (Moscow, 5 December 1980), and a March 1981 meeting which
endorsed a 'Brezhnev doctrine' formulation; intimidatory military manoeuvres, in this case largely between Polish and Soviet forces, and some
fairly explicit threats of intervention, particularly in March 1981; a series
of bilateral meetings and visits to Poland by figures like Marshal Kulikov
and Mikhail Suslov (Kulikov was actually in the country on 13 December). There was a flurry of consultations by WTO bodies at the beginning
of December 1981 – the CFM met in Budapest, and the CDM in
Moscow. These may have been used to inform alliance members of the
impending military takeover, though there is no firm evidence of this.
What actually happened in December 1981 can also be seen as an
indication of the political success of the bilateral military integration
measures characterized by Christopher Jones. Senior Polish officers sufficiently trusted by the USSR took over the government; conservative and
loyal junior officers and security police units obeyed their orders; and the
rest of the army, however, many reservations it may have had, went along
with the takeover. The 'resolution' of the crisis, such as it was, did not
depend on the WTO's multilateral apparatus, and may have been made
easier by the previous high degree of respect for the military within Polish
society.

    George Sanford has described martial law as effecting a short-term
'symbiosis' between the central party apparatus and the military elite,
and there is evidence that the considerable expansion of the Polish Officer

corps during the 1970s was planned with domestic functions in mind. However, it is also interesting to note that much of the legislative apparatus on which martial law was based derived from a framework designed to give the Polish armed forces a partial territorial defence mission, which weakens Jones's case for a strong linkage between offensive strategies and domestic repression.[35]

The extent to which military interventions in Eastern Europe undermine officially-held views on the functions of armies in socialist states can be seen if we examine the 'defence of the gains of socialism' formula a little more closely. It has already been noted that the formula was applied in 1968 to relations within the socialist community. However, both in standard Soviet military sociology and in the latest (1986) party programme, it is claimed that the internal functions of a socialist army (such as restraining the class enemies of the socialist state from open military action) disappear once the victory of socialism has been assured.[36] These internal functions should therefore not have been relevant in post-1955 Eastern Europe, but the mere fact of the military interventions which have taken place illustrates the precariousness of Soviet ideology's grip on the political realities of Eastern Europe. Soviet sensitivity on this point would seem to be indicated by the fact that although Christopher Jones's analysis of internal control mechanisms now occupies such a central position in Western scholarship on the WTO, it has only rarely come under attack in Soviet criticisms of the Western literature, where the usual focus is on challenging Western claims about Eastern military aggressiveness.[37]

The Polish crisis also indicated the deep-rooted nature of the problems which WTO political structures have attempted to deal with. It is hard to see the system as stable in the long run, least of all in Poland itself. However, the discussion in this chapter should indicate that the WTO is not only a collection of satellites held together by the threat of Soviet military intervention. The alliance's political structures have evolved into a structure of some complexity, even if the USSR remains the ultimate military arbiter of political developments in Eastern Europe. Seeing the Soviet role purely in terms of a 'Brezhnev doctrine' is an oversimplification, though 'defence of the gains of socialism' remains significant in that it underpins political cohesion and implies a shared understanding of the limits of Soviet tolerance of political developments in Eastern Europe. These limits are probably reached if there seems to be a threat to party rule, as in Poland, or to adherence to the WTO itself, which has not been the case in Romania but was in Hungary. In Czechoslovakia in 1968 the problem was less either of these than an apparently open-ended process of political, social and economic reform, with the prospect of party supervision of internal and external security policy being taken over by the state.[38]

These distinctions between the different crises and the Soviet response in each case point to a further problem of the 'Brezhnev doctrine' analysis in its simplest form. Although such a doctrine may underline basic geopolitical realities and the fact that there are limits to Soviet tolerance, it does not in itself provide adequate guidance as to how and why particular Soviet responses were made to particular crises. Jiri Valenta has argued that the 'Brezhnev doctrine' was an *ex post facto* explanation for the USSR as much as it was for the West, and that actual Soviet decision-making on Czechoslovakia was far more complex than this conceptualization suggests.[39]

One of the most challenging prospects within the WTO by 1988 was that it was by then the Soviet leadership itself which was the most vigorous reform advocate among party leaderships. The possibility therefore arose of another period with similarities to Khrushchev's destalinization period, in which the Soviet leadership's reform policies might become too radical for the taste of some at least of the Eastern European leaderships, and Eastern European societies might be found to be more vulnerable in conditions of reform than the more stable Soviet Union. Gorbachev was presumably aware of the potential of Eastern European affairs to destabilize Soviet leaders, and in particular of the fact that Khrushchev's handling of Eastern Europe had been a factor in his downfall in 1964.[40] During the Gorbachev period Soviet spokespersons have said, when pressed, that the era of Soviet military intervention in Eastern Europe is over. Gorbachev's leadership does also seem likely to be conscious of the damage to East–West relations which would be done by any future intervention, but it is no easier today than it has ever been to predict the likelihood and shape of future political crises in the region.[41]

Foreign policy and detente

The involvement of the WTO in central question of East–West relations was implicit in the treaty itself, with its commitment to a European security settlement and disarmament. Inevitably, there have been some occasions on which the foreign policy interests of one or another Eastern European leadership have diverged from those of the USSR, and the political structures whose development has just been charted mean that the USSR cannot decide policy on its own without consulting the preferences of its allies.

It is difficult to approach these questions without trying to give an overall characterization of Soviet security policy in Europe. In the two following chapters the reflection of security policy in military organization and strategy is examined; here, an attempt is made to deal with security policy as evidenced in some areas of European diplomacy.

In the most general terms, the existence of the WTO clearly lends to Soviet foreign and security policy the added weight and legitimacy which come from being seen to negotiate as part, and leader, of a bloc, rather than as an individual state. In the early years of the WTO, the alliance's diplomacy placed great stress on the issue of Germany and then the convening of a European security conference, with the objective of gaining Western, particularly West German, endorsement of the post-war territorial and political status quo. This objective was broadly shared by the Eastern European leaderships, although, as already mentioned, the GDR was constantly alert to the danger that the USSR's search for an overarching settlement might weaken its commitment to the GDR itself.

As chapter 1 described, Stalin's pre-WTO diplomacy had indeed given the GDR some grounds for concern, in that Stalin sought to settle the issue of Germany within the scope of four-power discussions, envisaging the possibility of a reunified and neutral state. He thus saw the German issue as something distinct from the division of Europe as a whole, and so the GDR leadership had reason to be worried that the GDR's interests were not for him overriding. After 1955, with the integration of the two Germanies into their respective blocs, the German problem became for the Soviet leadership more a matter of the general European security problem. The problem obviously had to be settled on terms which were not the FRG's, and West German influence in Eastern Europe had to be limited; nevertheless, the possibility of tactical disagreements between the Soviet and the GDR leaderships still existed, and came back to the surface in the late 1960s.[42]

The late 1950s saw continued WTO diplomatic activity on the issue of Germany, including the 1958 endorsement of a GDR proposal for a German confederation. This proposal was made at the same time as other approaches on a non-aggression treaty and measures to halt the nuclear arms race, and on the possibility of a nuclear-free zone in Central Europe.[43] Particular urgency was given to these initiatives by Nato's policy of the time of introducing shorter-range nuclear weapons more widely on European territory and among the smaller European armies, in which policy the WTO saw a particular danger of West Germany obtaining access to nuclear weapons. The nuclear-free zone proposal grew out of a number of Central European demilitarization and denuclearization plans put forward by the USSR, GDR and Poland after 1956. The Polish Foreign Minister Adam Rapacki had put forward the Rapacki Plan, which envisaged the denuclearization of Poland, Czechoslovakia and the two Germanies, at the United Nations in 1957. He subsequently proposed revised versions in 1958 and again in 1962, after a degree of interest had been shown by some Nato governments (though not by the FRG, and only briefly by the USA). There were also some Western counterproposals on Central European disengagement.

Nothing came of these approaches, though they acquired extra urgency for the Eastern bloc in the early 1960s when Nato began to discuss the possibility of a multilateral force sharing European control of nuclear weapons. Poland's advocacy of the idea was interesting, in that Rapacki saw Poland as a possible bridge between East and West in solving the German problem. It has sometimes been suggested that the USSR endorsed the proposals only reluctantly, being concerned about independent Eastern European initiatives and the constraints a nuclear-free zone might place on its own plans for nuclearizing military forces and strategy. The USSR's own version, the Gromyko Plan, had been formally linked with great power responsibilities for Germany, and overall East–West disarmament negotiations. As detailed later in chapter 3, this was a period of cuts in WTO conventional forces, but simultaneous nuclearization.[44]

Poland's arms control initiatives suggested that some of the Eastern European leaderships saw a particular urgency in their own regional problems and might seek possibilities for detente somewhat independently of the USSR.[45] The 1961 Berlin crisis and the building of the Berlin wall can be seen as a counterbalancing affirmation by the GDR and USSR that the West would have to accept the status quo, and the separate existence of the GDR, before any substantial agreement could be reached. Proposals for a European security conference began to be made again more insistently from around 1964, after US–Soviet relations had recovered from the Cuban crisis and improved with the Partial Test Ban Treaty in 1963. At that particular time, differences could be detected between Polish calls for a conference which would include both the USA and USSR, and a Soviet preference for excluding the USA, though the Soviet attitude to this had fluctuated and continued to do so.

WTO bodies endorsed the calls for a European security conference, and Soviet sources tend to date the WTO's initiatives from the July 1966 Bucharest PCC meeting.[46] It should be noted, though, that at this stage the USA was regarded as to be excluded from the conference; a shift to implied acceptance of US participation was not made until the March 1969 Budapest PCC meeting.[47] A noticeable difference between the two documents produced by these meetings was that while the earlier appeal explicitly called for the removal of foreign troops and the dissolution of military blocs, by 1969 these points were no longer being stressed, implying a clearer commitment to the status quo and a resolution of the USSR's ambivalence about US involvement.

One reason for the shift to a more relaxed attitude to the US presence in Europe was that centrifugal pressures within the WTO increased between 1966 and 1969: there was Romanian resistance to Soviet policy; the Czechoslovakian crisis itself and the consequent alienation of Western

European communist parties; plus increased tension between the USSR and China. In early 1967 Romania had broken ranks with the rest of Eastern Europe and established diplomatic relations with the FRG, after which Romania was the only WTO state not to break off relations with Israel following the June 1967 Six-Day War. It is quite likely that with the unity of the WTO requiring increasingly complex management, attempts to exclude the USA from Europe were abandoned in favour of stabilizing the existing situation, and accepting the USA as a continued restraining influence on the FRG. By early 1970 it was clear that the Eastern conception of the European conference involved US participation.[48]

On the Western side, France's disaffection in regard to Nato had been accompanied by de Gaulle's floating of the idea of 'Atlantic to the Urals' detente, but this was moderated after France's shift to the right in 1968. However, an even more significant shift had to occur in the West German position before any real progress could be made. Between 1955 and December 1966, West German diplomacy followed the 'Hallstein doctrine' of not establishing diplomatic relations with any state which recognized the GDR. In December 1966 Kurt-Georg Kiesinger's 'grand coalition' of Christian Democrats and Social Democrats, with Willy Brandt as Foreign Minister, effectively abandoned this policy, thus opening the way for the establishing of relations with Romania. Reunification of Germany was still said to be the FRG's objective, the GDR was not recognized as a state, and the FRG still claimed to speak for the entire German people; this still amounted to a threat to WTO unity, since there appeared to be a danger of other Eastern European states, including Czechoslovakia, establishing relations with the FRG before the GDR was recognized. The FRG's diplomatic approaches to the East seem to be halted by the intervention in Czechoslovakia, which served to demonstrate that the USSR had to be treated as the West's primary interlocutor in expanding relations with the East. After 1968, however, the FRG's approach became more flexible; by late 1969 Brandt's new 'small coalition' of the Social Democrat and Free Democrat parties had adopted the formula of two separate German states within one nation, dropped the claim to sole representation, and offered to negotiate renunciation-of-force agreements with the Eastern European states, including the GDR.

Paradoxically, this created additional problems for the GDR. While the stated GDR demand was for full and unconditional recognition by the FRG, it became clear that the USSR and Poland were prepared to improve relations with the FRG without obtaining the GDR's maximum demands. It was from this situation of possible conflict that there arose the need for compromise and bargaining between the GDR and USSR, as already mentioned, and Ulbricht's eventual retirement and replacement by Honecker in May 1971.[49]

When the European detente treaties of the early 1970s were signed, they served to illustrate the ways in which the GDR had to go along with the requirements of Soviet detente policy even if full recognition was not forthcoming, and the GDR leadership had to make the best of the situation by insisting on the GDR's distinctness from the FRG. The treaties were the August 1970 Moscow Treaty between the FRG and USSR; the November 1970 Warsaw Treaty between the FRG and Poland; the June 1972 Four-Power Agreement on Berlin; and eventually the December 1972 Basic Treaty between the FRG and GDR. The GDR and FRG were both admitted to the United Nations in 1973. Although the GDR–USSR bargaining process continued throughout this period, a good indication of the gains perceived by the WTO as a whole is given by the PCC's December 1970 statement in its comment on the FRG–USSR and FRG–Poland treaties: 'The recognition of the existing situation in Europe, which was established as a result of the Second World War and post-war developments, the inviolability of the present borders of the European states, observation of the principle of resolving disputes exclusively by peaceful methods, not resorting to force or the threat of force – all this has great significance for the fate of peace in Europe, for the peaceful future of the European peoples.'[50]

At the same time as these European developments, the SALT negotiations between the USA and USSR had been in progress since December 1969. As far as US motivations for involvement in European detente processes were concerned, one important factor was a US desire to preclude a separate Western Europe–USSR process. Henry Kissinger's memoirs make this abundantly clear: 'While as I have indicated I had come to the view that Brandt's decision to modify the policies of his Christian Democratic predecessors was inevitable and potentially beneficial, this would be so only if it did not give the Soviets the whip hand over German and European policy. Unless we managed to get some control over the process Brandt would become more and more dependent on the Soviet Union and its goodwill for the fulfillment of German goals in the new policy.'[51] Brandt, of course, had no intention whatever of taking the FRG out of the Western political or security system, but Kissinger's response is an interesting indication of residual US suspicion not only of Soviet motives, but of Europeans in general, and of Germany in particular.[52]

Nato as a whole wanted to establish talks with the USSR on conventional force reductions, and this in turn was partly motivated by the need to control or at least get some reciprocation for unilateral US reductions of forces in Europe during the Vietnam War. In this area, the previous Soviet shift to acceptance of US participation in a European security conference was repeated in a speech made by Brezhnev in May 1971, when he accepted the idea of such force reduction talks at a crucial time for the US Senate's discussion of the Mansfield Amendment on unilateral reductions.[53] Thus there was sufficient shared interest on all sides for the Conference on Security and Cooperation in Europe (CSCE) or Helsinki process, and the Mutual and Balanced Force Reduction (MBFR) talks to go ahead from 1973.

The establishment of these new negotiating forums introduced a new element of complexity into relations within the WTO, since they simultaneously stabilized the more extreme risks of centrifugalism (in both alliances) and provided opportunities for the Eastern Europeans discreetly to articulate their own preferences. On the most basic questions under discussion, the interests of the Eastern European leaderships still coincided with those of the USSR -- the European security process offered the prospect of further and multilateral endorsement of the inviolability of borders and the other principles of the bilateral treaties with the FRG.

In other respects, however, possible divergences of interest can be identified. The CSCE process was seen as enhancing the status of small nations, encouraging East–West trade, and possibly reducing pressure for higher defence spending. Romania in particular was able to act as a relatively independent agent in CSCE forums, though the more restricted membership and bloc-to-bloc format of MBFR made this less of a feature of the conventional arms negotiations. In MBFR itself, the USSR sought to maintain acceptable ratios between Nato and the WTO, between the West German *Bundeswehr* and Soviet forces in the GDR, and between US forces in Western Europe and the *Bundeswehr*. Eastern Europeans were less keen, however, on the fourth Soviet objective which can safely be assumed, of maintaining a favourable balance between Soviet and indigenous Eastern European forces.[54]

The failure of the MBFR talks to reach agreement, largely through differences over data, is well-known; these talks are examined further in chapter 5- of this study. In the case of the CSCE, the August 1975 signature of the Helsinki Final Act was again assessed as an important achievement in confirming the status quo. As a declaration of the WTO PCC put it in November 1976: 'The [Helsinki] Conference has reflected the changes which have taken place in Europe, confirmed the territorial and political realities which took shape on the continent as a result of the peoples' victory in the anti-fascist war and post-war developments, and reflected the peoples' will to live and work together in conditions of peace and security.' However, the same statement sounded warning notes about the possibly dangerous consequences of Helsinki and detente in attacking Western use of the humanitarian 'Basket III' for what was termed interference in the WTO's internal affairs.[55] This reflected the way in which the West managed to put the WTO on to the defensive over these human rights clauses. Though Hungary and Poland were attacked less strongly than the USSR and other states, the growth of civil rights and 'dissident' groups within WTO countries in the post-Helsinki period caused problems for the individual leaderships and for the evaluation of the detente process as a whole. It may well be that the creation of the WTO's Committee of Foreign Ministers in November 1976 reflected a recognition of the need for more regular consultations in these new circumstances. Increased contact with the West also necessitated greater public insistence on ideological cohesion at home, but the survival into the 1980s of civil rights groups like Charter 77 in Czechoslovakia dramatized the way in which WTO states had taken on commitments which they had little intention of observing.

Despite these unwanted consequences of detente, the Soviet leadership remained much more explicitly committed to the concept and the process during the late 1970s, as their US counterparts gradually dropped the vocabulary of detente. Brezhnev's 1977 speech in Tula, for example, renounced any Soviet desire for strategic superiority and endorsed super-power detente, but its significance was missed by the US leadership.[56]

In examinations of detente as it developed in the 1970s, it is often argued that its breakdown can be traced to the USA and USSR's differing conceptions of the process. While there is a limited amount of truth in this, the argument is often made as if there was substantial naivety on the Western side. The attribution of naivety to Nixon, Kissinger and Brzezinski, however, is scarcely credible. The real problems with detente were the inherent contradictions in its combination of co-operation and competition, which both recognized and challenged the status quo. It should be remembered that as far as the West was concerned, peaceful political change was not ruled out in Europe, any more than the East ruled it out outside Europe; 'inviolability' of frontiers excluded only change through the use of force, and Basket 1 recognized the possibility of changing them by peaceful means and agreement. Furthermore, political parity represented a historical political gain for the USSR, but a net historical loss for the USA, which was why Kissinger tried so hard to deny it in practice, for example in the Middle East. It is quite true that there were 'losses' for the USA during the 1970s, in the sense of a series of Third World revolutions which were erroneously regarded as Soviet-inspired. Kissinger's own concept of detente, however, was partly premised on using a relaxation of relations with the USSR as a way of assisting the US retreat from Vietnam. Kissinger's critics and successors objected to the loss of US power which seemed to be involved, and this helped to produce the swing back to confrontation in the late Carter and Reagan periods.[57]

From the WTO's point of view within Europe, the growth of political dissent in the 1970s seems to have been a consequence the various governments were able to control and consider offset by the political gains already summarized. Eastern European leaderships, in turn, had opportunities for quietly 'dissident' activity. During the late 1970s there were rumours of Hungarian and Romanian disquiet over Soviet plans for the deployment of SS-20 missiles in the USSR, an indication that there might now be increased opportunities for some of the Eastern Europeans to drag their feet even over sensitive issues like missile deployment.[58] Other rumours spoke of unhappiness being voiced in 1974 with the continued notional obligation to assist the USSR with troops in the event of any future application of the 'Brezhnev doctrine'. There was also foot-dragging over military spending, and the spending burdens of some of the Eastern European states do seem to have declined during this period.

A discussion of the late 1970s and the breakdown of detente would not be complete without some examination of the Soviet intervention in Afghanistan and its effect on the WTO. While the intervention was not the sole cause of the breakdown of detente, as it was sometimes claimed to be, it was a qualitatively new commitment of Soviet combat forces outside traditional areas of deployment, and symptomatic of the wider breakdown of East–West relations. The Eastern European WTO members do not seem to have been consulted or even informed in advance, and were embarrassed by the intervention. The GDR and Hungary did release government statements endorsing the Soviet action, while Romania implicitly criticized the Soviet Union in a statement opposing foreign intervention in general. No WTO meeting seems to have paid much attention to the Afghanistan issue, and although Bulgaria, Czechoslovakia and the GDR seem to have rendered technical and economic assistance to Afghanistan and perhaps to Soviet forces, these arrangements were made bilaterally, outside WTO structures.[59]

Perhaps the most revealing events of the early 1980s were those surrounding the INF (Intermediate-range Nuclear Forces) controversy and the eventual WTO decision to station 'counterdeployment' missiles in Czechoslovakia and the GDR. A case-study of this episode provides a good view of the evolution of WTO institutions since 1955, and of the strains imposed on WTO foreign policy co-ordination by the breakdown of detente. It is presented here before some concluding remarks on WTO political structures.

The counterdeployments episode

The possibility of Soviet deployments of nuclear weapons in Eastern Europe had emerged as early as 1958, when Khrushchev raised the issue as a possible response to deployments of nuclear-capable systems with West German forces.[60] This had also become an issue during the Czechoslovakian debates on security policy in 1968 (see chapter 3), though there was no certain knowledge of whether warheads for Soviet nuclear-capable systems in Eastern Europe were stationed there or on Soviet territory. The issue came back into the limelight after Nato's December 1979 'dual-track' decision on the deployment of cruise and Pershing II missiles in Western Europe, and 1983 saw the first Soviet statements confirming the presence of nuclear-capable weapons systems in Eastern Europe.

It is possible that President Brezhnev's announcement, in October 1979, of a unilateral troop withdrawal from the GDR, was partly prompted by Eastern European pressure to try and head off Nato's plans for INF modernization. After Nato's December 1979 announcement, there was some evidence that the Eastern Europeans did not entirely share Soviet perceptions of the problem. One reason for this was Eastern European reluctance to become a site for the Soviet missiles which might be deployed in response if the Nato deployments went ahead, as well as a more general concern to limit the damage to East–West relations. Soviet statements during 1983 tended to remind the West that the USSR would take counter-measures if cruise and Pershing II deployments went ahead, while collective WTO statements attacked the Nato proposals and supported Soviet negotiating offers, but went no further.

For example, the January 1983 Political Declaration of the States Parties to the Warsaw Treaty, signed by the WTO party leaders after a PCC meeting, did exactly these things and expressed their 'appreciation' of proposals made by Yuri Andropov in December 1982, but did not mention possible counter-measures. Interestingly, a statement on the declaration made a few days later by the GDR Politburo and Council of Ministers was much more enthusiastic about Soviet proposals; the GDR 'greatly appreciates' Andropov's initiatives, but there is also a mention of the need to take 'whatever steps are required to safeguard . . . defence capacity'.[61] The GDR statement read like the contribution of a close ally but a very vulnerable one, which was well aware of the consequences for itself of further nuclear deployments in Central Europe.

Another WTO summit in June 1983 received wide coverage in the Western press because it was assumed that it had been called to issue a tough statement on counter-measures, but did not do so because of Eastern European resistance. The USSR went so far as to deny that there had been any sort of split, and it is impossible to be sure. (A Soviet government statement issued shortly before had made more specific threats about counter-measures, including placing US territory under comparable threat.) Even so, reports at the time credited Romania and Hungary with blocking calls for a tougher line, and the GDR and Czechoslovakia with backing the USSR.

The June 1983 meeting was not, technically, a WTO meeting. It was described as 'a meeting of party and state leaders' from the WTO states, [62] and was in this respect a successor to the previous extraordinary meetings held in June 1967 during the Middle East War, and, December 1980 during the Polish crisis.

A CFM meeting took place in October in Sofia, which warned against Nato's precipitation of a further round in the arms race and insisted that Nato would not be allowed to gain superiority over the WTO.[63] Marshal Kulikov attended the meeting and went further: according to an Associated Press report, he stated that if the Nato deployments went ahead, the USSR would suspend its moratorium on medium-range weapons (announced by Brezhnev in 1982), deploy additional weapons after consultation with its allies, and strengthen WTO conventional forces.[64]

In the second half of October, the West German magazine *Stern* published an interview with Colonel General Chervov of the Soviet General Staff, in which he said that Soviet tactical nuclear weapons were already in place in Eastern Europe, and would be modernized if the Nato deployments went ahead. There were then critical comments from President Ceausescu, implying that the USSR would be at least partly to blame if the Geneva INF talks broke down; a statement from an 'extraordinary' session of the CDM stating that although the WTO member states did not seek military superiority, 'in no circumstances will they allow others to gain superiority over them'; and a statement from a Comecon session, repeating the Soviet negotiating offer to destroy a number of Soviet missiles in return for the non-deployment of cruise and Pershing II.[65]

However, when official statements began to mention specific counterdeployments, the channels used were not WTO ones. In late October, separate statements on preparatory work for counterdeployments were made by the Soviet Ministry of Defence, Czech government, and GDR National Defence Council.[66] Andropov's formal statement on the break-off of negotiations and counterdeployments, made on 24 November, spoke of the measure as a decision adopted by the Soviet leadership 'on agreement with the governments of the GDR and Czechoslovakia'.[67] The measures were subsequently endorsed by the CFM in April 1984, although evidence of Eastern European discomfort over the new missiles emerged in spite of the collective display of unanimity.

The April 1984 CFM noted tersely that the Geneva talks had been broken off and counterdeployments started: 'This has compelled the Soviet Union to adopt a number of response measures. Talks on nuclear armaments have been terminated.'[68] This absence of enthusiasm contrasted with language being used in the Soviet press in early 1984, where a January article in *Krasnaya Zvezda* spoke of the 'unshakeable resolve' of Soviet missilemen stationed in the GDR.[69] It is also interesting that no PCC meeting took place between late 1983 and Mikhail Gorbachev's announcement of a freeze on Soviet counterdeployments and SS-20's in April 1985, so the counterdeployments had not in fact been endorsed by the WTO's senior body at that point. However, the illness of Konstantin Chernenko probably caused plans for a PCC meeting to be put off in late 1984.

The evidence of the counterdeployments episode suggests that the Eastern European states were concerned to limit the damage to East–West relations caused by the failure of the Geneva INF talks. They were less prepared than the USSR to stress the military counter-measures which were seen as being necessary, and even after the counter-measures became a fact of life, indications of concern about them emerged. Some reports credited Bulgaria, Hungary and Poland with having refused to take additional counterdeployments.[70] The military arrangements made were bilateral ones between the USSR, GDR and Czechoslovakia.

Even Erich Honecker and Lubomir Strougal, from the countries which accepted counterdeployments, expressed some degree of disquiet at the end of 1983, as a result of a mixture of military, political and economic concern.[71] In military terms, the counterdeployments made Eastern Europeans even more vulnerable to attack and were inconsistent with the 1982 Soviet pledge on No First Use of nuclear weapons.[72] In political terms the whole episode had damaged East–West relations and raised the spectre of domestic anti-nuclear unease. When a substantial number of the counterdeployment missiles were scheduled for removal with the signature of the INF Treaty in December 1987, the GDR and Czechoslovakian leaderships must have breathed substantial sighs of relief.

Conclusion

Once the immediate problems of managing the counterdeployment of missiles in Europe had passed, attention turned back to the future of East–West relations. Throughout most of 1984 the chill created by the events of the previous year meant there was little contact between the USSR and USA. This situation was hardly to the liking of several Eastern European leaderships, and it appeared that several of them had to be discouraged from taking independent initiatives towards Western Europe. Erich Honecker, and Todor Zhivkov of Bulgaria, abandoned plans to visit West Germany during the summer, apparently (though perhaps not entirely) under Soviet pressure. The GDR's resistance over this question testified to the growth in its leadership's self-confidence over the previous ten years, its privileged economic position *vis-à-vis* West Germany, and in a way to the fact that detente retained deeper roots in Europe than between the USA and USSR.[73] (Honecker finally made his trip to the

FRG in September 1987.)

By early 1985 there was a marked improvement in the atmosphere. Mikhail Gorbachev succeeded Chernenko as CPSU General Secretary in March; the Geneva disarmament talks began again in the same month; and on 26 April the Warsaw Treaty was renewed for a further twenty years, with an option of renewal for another ten years after that.[74] Although there were rumours of some Eastern European reluctance to renew the treaty, there is no firm evidence of any serious attempt to impede renewal. There may, however, have been some bargaining which encouraged Gorbachev to take his initiative of 8 April, when he announced a freeze on Soviet deployments of SS-20s and of counterdeployment in Eastern Europe.

The Warsaw Treaty Organization had therefore survived thirty years almost intact. What conclusions can be drawn concerning its development as a political alliance over that period? Perhaps most striking is the extent to which the alliance had evolved into a bargaining forum for defusing and resolving inter-elite conflicts of interests, at the same time as it retained the characteristics of an alliance held together ultimately by the military and political preponderance of its largest power. Although the last case of external Soviet military intervention took place in 1968, the Polish crisis underlined the continued uncertainty over the WTO's ability to resolve peacefully any social upheavals which seem to threaten either a given country's commitment to the alliance, or the authority of the ruling party in any country.

Nevertheless, within the framework of the USSR's power as the ultimate arbiter of developments in Eastern European politics, the WTO provides a fairly complex mechanism for co-ordinating foreign and military policy. Particularly since 1969, a wider range of institutions has provided Eastern European leaderships with more opportunities to discuss and influence policy, and the commonplace image of a purely 'satellite' organization is inadequate to capture the complexity of the WTO. It may even be doubted whether the 'Brezhnev doctrine' still applied in its original form by 1985, since the Polish crisis went beyond the stage where Soviet intervention would surely have been considered inevitable ten years earlier; however, the outcome of that crisis indicated that military intervention did not have to come from the USSR.

One major omission of the treatment of the WTO in this chapter has been any discussion of public opinion and attitudes towards the alliance within Eastern European societies. This would be a major study in itself, and one can only scratch the surface by commenting that popular enthusiasm for the alliance with the USSR is probably at its most lukewarm in Poland, Czechoslovakia and Romania. This creates obvious problems for the Eastern European leaderships who have been the main objects of study here. While they need to convince their domestic public opinion that they are doing their best to safeguard national interests within the alliance, they also have to reaffirm the alliance to reassure the USSR about its security interests in the region. Ulrich Albrecht has summarized these interconnections between external security and domestic political stability: 'For the smaller Eastern European countries the key question is how they can contribute to a new course in European policy that would be in consonance with their own interests but that would enhance rather than diminish the security of the Soviet Union itself' and 'The Soviet Union will only be secure if the regimes in Warsaw, Prague and Budapest are secure because they enjoy the demonstrable support of their populations.'[75]

The assessment of the Czech civil rights activist Jiri Dienstbier, writing in 1985, was that: 'If the populations of these countries were offered the status of Finland in a free referendum, they would vote for it with overwhelming enthusiasm, and would certainly prefer it to transferring their allegiance into the other camp.' The Hungarian author Miklos Haraszti has expressed a similar view: 'Neutralize these countries the Finnish way, with military guarantees – which they would happily give: guaranteed neutrality is their highest dream – and in exchange, let them become politically, culturally, economically part of Europe again.'[76] If Dienstbier and Haraszti are correct, there is obviously a substantial challenge in Eastern European public opinion both to orthodox WTO conceptions of the region's best interests, and to the widespread Western (or at least American) view of populations eager to join Nato and enjoy the fruits thereof. It is also worth noting that their formulations of an acceptable settlement do not necessarily seem to exclude a security relationship with the USSR, though they presumably would exclude an alliance, and the key point being made is that the WTO's political content would have to be removed or substantially diluted. Chris Harman's valuable study of the post-war period also shifts the focus of attention from inter-elite conflicts to intellectual and working-class conflicts with re-formed and unreformed party leaderships, and implicitly endorses this kind of analysis.[77]

In addition, there exist inter-East European rivalries such as the antagonism between Hungary and Romania over the Hungarian population of Transylvania, which flared up again in 1988. Some writers on the WTO have speculated that the USSR sees benefits in sustaining these antagonisms in order to deflect latent anti-Sovietism, but one could equally plausibly argue that the WTO would serve the purpose of making sure that they do not develop into major confrontations.

If there is a simple conclusion to be drawn, it is probably that the existing Eastern European leaderships prefer the WTO to embody a fairly lax bloc discipline. No current leadership in the area has any real desire to leave the WTO, and any variety of political regime in Eastern Europe would have to make an accommodation with the strength of the USSR. Strict discipline, however, is not in their interests because it disrupts relations with the West. For the Soviet point of view, strict bloc discipline as in the Stalinist era is no longer possible in practice or desirable in principle, and the USSR appears to have made concessions in the political machinery of the WTO which amount to a greater loosening than has occurred in the military command structure (see following chapter). The beginnings of these developments can be seen even in the WTO's foundation and early days, as was suggested in chapter 1. Nevertheless, there are times when the USSR needs to enforce a stricter discipline for specific political purposes, as in the INF counterdeployment period. If necessary, this can be done outside WTO forums. One can speculate that one reason for this is that relations with the USA remain the USSR's most fundamental concern in foreign policy, and neither Western nor Eastern Europe can ultimately be allowed to inhibit Soviet policy towards the USA. However, the enforcement of strict discipline can only be achieved for limited periods.

In Mary Kaldor's words, the WTO's institutions are essentially similar to Nato's in that they 'provide a forum for reaching agreement or consensus within a predetermined set of assumptions';[78] the WTO's major crises have occurred when those assumptions have been questioned from within. As far as relations with the West have been concerned, Soviet and WTO policy has over a prolonged period been more concerned with ensuring stability and predictability within Europe, rather than with the 'wedge-driving' strategy so frequently attributed to the USSR. A large part of the motivation for this search for stability has been the concern to retain Eastern Europe securely within a Soviet military and political sphere of influence. One of the most interesting questions to be asked about the future of the WTO, therefore, concerns the impact of Mikhail Gorbachev's foreign and domestic policy initiatives on the alliance.

Particularly in the aftermath of the INF agreement, it will be important to see whether traditional Soviet policies towards both Eastern and Western Europe are affected, and how the WTO might develop. These issues are taken up in more detail in chapters 5 and 6, and the Conclusion.

3

The Military Command Structures

The military institutions

As noted at the beginning of chapter 2, there is a certain arbitrariness in dividing the WTO's institutions into 'political' and 'military', but the same procedure is followed here as in the last section: basic data from Soviet sources, expansion and commentary. Once again, figure 1 gives a rough outline of the different institution (p. 15). In addition, some indications are given of the relationship of these WTO bodies to the central military institutions of the USSR, and of the position of Eastern European forces within the overall command structure.

Of the WTO's military institutions, the Joint Command (JC) was set up under Article 5 of the Warsaw Treaty itself. At the same time the Joint Armed Forces (JAFs) were established, together with a multinational staff to work with the commander-in-chief, to be located in Moscow (see chapter 1). The appointment of the commander-in-chief and chief of staff is vested in the Political Consultative Committee (PCC), and both posts have been filled since 1955 exclusively by Soviet officers. At the end of 1988 the Commander-in-chief (C-in-C) was Marshal V. G. Kulikov (since January 1977), and Chief of Staff General A. I. Gribkov (since October 1976).[1] The position of WTO C-in-C carries with it a position as one of the three Soviet first deputy ministers of defence.

Further institutions have been added since 1955. In a considerable reorganization in March 1969, a Committee of Defence Ministers (CDM), a Military Council (MC), and probably a Technological Committee (TC) and Military Science and Technology Council (MSTC), were set up by a PCC meeting in Budapest.[2] Soviet sources indicate that the CDM has nine members, the seven defence ministers plus the C-in-C and Chief of Staff. The Joint Command consists of the C-in-C, Chief of Staff, and deputy C-in-Cs, who are usually deputy ministers of defence or chiefs of staff. According to some accounts, the Military Council's membership would appear to be identical to that of the JC. Their functions differ in that the MC is concerned with questions of arms and military equipment, and usually meets twice a year; the JC is mostly occupied with the integration of forces into the JAFs, and is presumably in notionally permanent existence. The MC may also include a number of other Soviet and Eastern European officers with responsibility for armaments, logistics and air defence. The Command seems to have started life as part of the Soviet General Staff, though at some time it became an independent element within the Soviet Ministry of Defence, with its own staff. The date of this is slightly unclear, but John Erickson has attributed the formation of the Joint Staff as a permanent body to the same 1969 PCC meeting.[3]

This multinational JAFs staff is said to deal with all questions of the activity and preparedness of the WTO's troops and fleets, and to work closely with the allied staffs in preparing manoeuvres, meetings and training, and in carrying out the recommendations of the CDM and Military Council. In addition to the allied representatives on the Staff, the C-in-C has representatives in the allied armies to assist the national commands.[4] Representatives of the WTO Staff and other bodies serving abroad have been accorded a kind of diplomatic status by the 1973 WTO Convention.[5]

The CDM itself is supposed to meet annually, with its location and chair rotating. The MC advises the CDM, which is technically the senior body; the CDM, in turn, supervises the Joint Command's work. As with the foreign ministers, the WTO defence ministers had been meeting for *ad hoc* consultations before they were given a committee of their own; in the defence ministers' case, they had met since at least as early as 1961. It has been suggested that the formation of the CDM took place as part of a response to the 1968 Czechoslovakian crisis, and possibly in response to specific criticisms of the WTO's functioning which were voiced during 1968.

In July 1968, the head of the Czechoslovakian Central Committee's Department for Defence and Security Affairs, Lt General Vaclav Prchlik, held a press conference during which he expressed a number of criticisms of Soviet domination of the WTO. One of his criticisms was that the Eastern European defence ministers sat on the Joint Command as deputy commanders-in-chief, but were subordinate to a Soviet C-in-C who was only a *deputy* defence minister.[6] After the immediate crisis had passed, it seems that this protocol problem was sorted out by giving the defence ministers their own committee, which together with the creation of the Military Council gave the Eastern Europeans greater opportunities than previously for policy discussion. The deputy defence ministers then replaced the full ministers in the Joint Command. Another Czechoslovakian suggestion made during 1968 was for the creation of a Technological Committee, which also came about at approximately the same time.

As mentioned in the previous chapter, the significance of the 1969 reorganization has been a subject of debate. Christopher Jones has argued that the measures taken were not concessions by the USSR to make the alliance's functioning more equitable, but an attempt to use additional bodies as a way of outmanoeuvring any future resistance to Soviet policy by Romania in the PCC. Most of the observers who give the 1969 reorganization credit as a genuine attempt to provide more room for consultation and head off Eastern European discontent have nevertheless considered that there was a simultaneous move to tighten up Soviet military control of WTO forces, and that the reorganization thus worked at two different levels. The March 1969 meeting's vague statement on measures to strengthen defence organization did not give much away.

A few years earlier, Brezhnev had made a proposal to strengthen the WTO's organization, the substance of which has never become clear. That was in September 1965, and it met with resistance from Eastern Europe. In 1966, Romania countered with a series of complaints and proposals about consultations over nuclear weapons, cost-sharing, the stationing of Soviet forces and the Soviet monopoly of the commander-in-chief's position. Then came the Czechoslovakian complaints of 1968. There is some evidence that the USSR considered trying to deal with these problems by moving towards a more integrated supranational military structure, but then opted for the path of greater consultation with the creation of the additional bodies. In addition, it emerged that the military measures adopted included a revised statute for the WTO Joint Armed Forces, the text of which has not been published. Discussions of the new statute left it unclear whether Eastern European forces were assigned to the JAFs temporarily (for instance, for manoeuvres) or permanently, and this has led some commentators to suspect basic ambiguities in the document.[7]

The 1969 organizational changes do not seem to have ended the discussion since there may have been some further pressure for increased military integration in 1974 and then again in 1978, at the same time as differences (particularly with Romania) over defence spending. In any event, the CDM, Military Council and Technological Committee did constitute additional forums for Eastern European participation, even if there was no real relaxation in military command structures. Of course, the fact of the creation of the new bodies does not mean that they have functioned as the pre-1968 critics might have liked them to; nevertheless, as in the political sphere, the new bodies meant a considerable increase in the amount of consultation carried out in the 1970s.

The Groups of Soviet Forces (GSFs)

In 1955 there were Soviet forces stationed in the GDR, Poland, Hungary and Romania. Those forces in the GDR and Poland were there in accordance with the Yalta and Potsdam agreements; little is known about the precise pre-1955 arrangements elsewhere. The USSR's occupation regime in the GDR was formally ended by the Soviet–GDR Treaty of September 1955, and a section of the Soviet general staff which had previously supervised the bilateral treaty system took over responsibility for co-ordination after the signature of the Warsaw Treaty.[8] In the years immediately following 1955, more public agreements on troop-stationing were signed by the USSR and the respective countries. Treaties were signed with Poland in 1956, and with Romania, Hungary and the GDR in 1957. This may well have been done as part of a process of calming tensions after the crises of 1956 in Poland and Hungary, and in several cases (the GDR excluded) the new treaties gave the host countries more nominal control over the activities of Soviet troops.[9]

Khrushchev relates several conversations with Eastern European leaders about possible reductions in Soviet forces. According to his account, the Romanian leadership first approached him about a possible Soviet withdrawal 'Not long after Stalin's death', while in the Hungarian and Polish cases Khrushchev himself proposed Soviet withdrawal to Kadar and Gomulka. The reasons given are expense, since the maintenance of Soviet divisions in Eastern Europe cost twice as much as normal, and the desire to show that Eastern Europe was not being 'prodded along the path of socialism at bayonet point by Soviet troops'.[10] If Khrushchev is being sincere here, it is unfortunate that he was not swayed by the argument in 1956.

Khrushchev does not give any reason why the plans for withdrawal from everywhere except the GDR were not carried out, but there were still troop reductions during the late 1950s. The number of Soviet divisions in Hungary increased from two to five in 1956, and then went back down to four in 1958. At the same time, the two Soviet divisions in Romania withdrew altogether, and the situations in these two countries have remained the same since that time.[11]

The late 1950s were a period of substantial overall reductions in Soviet ground forces. There were reductions of something like 2 million men in total Soviet forces between 1955 and 1961, but the imprecision of figures available for this period makes it difficult to tell whether the cuts in GSFs in Eastern Europe were proportionate to overall cuts. It seems likely that the main savings were made in forces within the USSR itself, but the GSFG forces in the GDR do seem to have been cut and to have reached approximately their present level by 1961.[12] Khrushchev planned further reductions, but his plans were halted after mid-1961 by a combination of increased East–West tension, Kennedy's decisions on US weapons development, and resistance from the Soviet ground forces, who were unhappy about his extensive demobilizations and increasing emphasis on nuclear forces at their expense.[13]

In 1968 a further significant change took place, when five Soviet divisions remained in Czechoslovakia after the WTO occupation of that country. Their presence was confirmed in a treaty of 16 October 1968.[14] In 1979 Leonid Brezhnev announced that 20,000 Soviet servicemen and 1,000 tanks would be unilaterally withdrawn from GSFG. Some Western sources claimed that the announced reduction was in fact made up by reallocations to other units, but the IISS saw no evidence of this and confirmed the withdrawal of a tank division.[15] (It was also argued, perhaps more relevantly, that the troop withdrawal was more than compensated for by overall increases in GSFG's firepower.) The withdrawal took place at a time when Brezhnev was trying to head off Nato's moves towards a decision on new intermediate-range nuclear forces in Western Europe.

The Eastern European forces

During the late 1950s, substantial cuts were made in Eastern European as well as Soviet forces. One Soviet source gives a figure of 337,000 for reductions in Eastern European forces between May 1955 and May 1958, comprising 141,500 Polish, 44,000 Czechoslovakian, 30,000 GDR, 60,000 Romanian, 18,000 Bulgarian, 35,000 Hungarian and 9,000 Albanian troops.[16] In the case of Hungary, these reductions were in large part a consequence of measures taken after 1956, but the general and large-scale cuts were also part of a process of post-Stalinist rationalization of military establishments, as well as measures with potential diplomatic value in disarmament negotiations.[17] In addition, a process of 'renationalization' was going on, involving the replacement by natives of a number of Soviet citizens who had held posts in Eastern European armies and security establishments. This was particularly noticeable in Poland, but took place to varying degrees throughout Eastern Europe.[18]

Another feature of the late 1950s and early 1960s was that these cuts in force levels were taking place at a time of rapid developments in Soviet military doctrine, which amounted to placing increasing reliance on nuclear weapons at the expense of ground forces. At this time it was assumed that if war started, it would be nuclear from the outset, and in these circumstances the strength of a country's ground forces became less significant than formerly. Khrushchev speaks of the growth of a nuclear missile arsenal being more important than the number of bayonets, though as we now know, the kind of claims Khrushchev made on occasions at the time about Soviet nuclear superiority were groundless. Khrushchev himself has often been argued to have favoured a policy of minimum deterrence, but a recent study has shown him to have been a supporter of tactical nuclear weapons by the late 1950s.[19]

The net effect on Eastern European forces seems to have been that the initial manpower cuts of the late 50s were followed by an upgrading of forces and equipment in the early 1960s. They received some nuclear-capable equipment such as FROG and SCUD missiles, but probably had no access to nuclear warheads. They were also trained for coalition warfare in nuclear conditions, as the hitherto dormant joint command machinery began to be put to more use.[20]

One likely explanation for Soviet policy in this period is that there was an attempt to maintain and upgrade forces in Eastern Europe while making troop cuts in order to free resources and labour for the Soviet civilian economy.[21] The 1961 Berlin crisis probably also prompted increased Soviet attention to the capabilities of the Eastern European forces and it was around this time that an integrated air defence network began to be built up in the region. However, as already mentioned, Khrushchev's policies of the early 1960s were not sustained by his successors, and the USSR embarked on a more coherent attempt to obtain strategic parity (at least), while negotiating with the USA on arms control from the late 1960s. At some time in the late 1960s, Soviet and WTO priorities began to shift towards thinking in terms of conventional operations at the outset of war, partly in response to Nato's adoption of flexible response (see the detailed discussion of strategy in chapter 4).

Some more specific comments can be made on the strength and development of the forces of the individual Eastern European states (see also appendix II for figures; the IISS's figures are not universally accepted, but I am using them here only to make rough intra-WTO comparisons):

Bulgarian forces have remained approximately the same size for over twenty years. The absence of Soviet forces from Bulgaria can be seen as a reflection of Soviet confidence in Bulgarian political loyalty to the Soviet Union, and of the fact that although Bulgaria confronts two Nato allies in Greece and Turkey, relations between these two Nato countries are sufficiently poor to reduce anxieties about Bulgaria's external situation. Bulgaria's forces are large as a percentage of the population, but they do not seem to be maintained at a high level of readiness.[22]

Czechoslovakian forces suffered a sharp cut after the events of 1968, and the contingent of Soviet forces in Czechoslovakia represents the largest single fluctuation in Soviet troops in Eastern Europe during the last twenty years. Among the consequences of the 1968 Soviet (and WTO) intervention in Czechoslovakia were mass resignations of officers and purges of those who remained, while the overall strength of the Czechoslovakian armed forces fell from 225,000 in 1967–8 (ground forces 175,000, air force 50,000) to 168,000 in 1970–1 (ground forces 150,000, air force 18,000).[23]

Although the Czechoslovak armed forces have re-expanded since then, the army (though not the air force) remains smaller than it was before 1968. The Soviet Central Group of Forces more than makes up the shortfall, but the question inevitably arises of whether these forces should be considered as primarily fulfilling an external task against Nato or as fulfilling a policing function within Czechoslovakia. These two motivations should not be read as mutually exclusive, in this instance or elsewhere. There is evidence that the USSR put pressure on Czechoslovakia to station Soviet troops with nuclear weapons there before there were any worries about the internal Czechoslovakian political situation, and also that before 1968 the Soviet high command was concerned about the poor performance of Czechoslovakian forces in exercises, so it is quite consistent to view the Central Group of Forces as fulfilling both functions.[24]

GDR forces   are smaller than those of Czechoslovakia by 25,000, even though the GDR's population is larger by a million. They are also heavily outnumbered by the GSFG. However, the GDR Nationale Volksarmee (NVA) is widely considered by Western commentators to be the most efficient of the Eastern European armies, and its. six divisions are all at category 1 readiness, which makes it unique among the Eastern European armies. The relatively small size of GDR forces may result from a mixture of necessity and design. They did not officially exist in 1955, though in practice they did exist in embryo.[25] Although no distinction was made between the GDR and the other Warsaw Treaty signatories in the treaty itself, the NVA was only technically admitted to the WTO's joint command by the January 1956 PCC meeting, which also appointed the GDR defence minister as a deputy commander.[26] Conscription was not introduced in the GDR until 1962, and lasts only for eighteen months; the demands of the civilian economy have tended to leave the GDR with a labour shortage; a residual Soviet suspicion of Germany might have caused the Soviet Union to restrict GDR armed forces even if further expansion were feasible.

Hungarian forces   are numerically the WTO's smallest, and the 65,000 troops of the Soviet Southern Group of Forces are almost as numerous as the Hungarian army itself. Malcolm Mackintosh wrote in 1969 that the Hungarian army had been 'virtually disbanded' after 1956 and that in 1969 it was half its 1956 strength. The army has got smaller since then (95,000 in 1967, down to 84,000 in 1987–8), though the air force has grown from 9,000 to 22,000 between 1964–5 and 1987–8.[27] However, it is hard to see Hungary, with a population of under 11 million and no border with a Nato state, wanting or needing significantly larger forces, and the army in the mid-1950s must have been unnecessarily large on any sober calculation of the country's position. Currently, the Hungarian forces have no units estimated at category 1 readiness.

Polish forces are the largest of the Eastern European countries, in accordance with Poland's position as the largest in terms of population. In addition to five tank and three motor rifle divisions at category 1 readiness, Poland also has an airborne brigade and an amphibious assault brigade, and so has considerable and potentially versatile military strength. This level of readiness looks higher than that of the Czechoslovakian ground forces, though lower than the overall level of GDR forces. The Polish navy, though the largest of the Eastern European navies, still numbers only 19,000 men. There have been no major fluctuations in Polish force levels during the period of the WTO's existence, although the army has been presented on several occasions with a choice of participation or abstention in successive internal political crises. From the point of view of the WTO as a whole, there is a key question as to how far the national legitimacy and effectiveness of the Polish armed forces was affected by their participation in the declaration and implementation of martial law. This is a complex issue, but it appears that paramilitary forces and security police were the forces most directly involved in the physical enforcement of martial law, while the regular army largely played a secondary role.[28]

The Soviet Northern Group of Forces is the smallest, at 40,000, of the four Soviet contingents in Eastern Europe. Although Poland is obviously of vital importance for Soviet communication with Soviet forces in the GDR, one can speculate that this group of forces has been kept relatively small because a more visible Soviet presence in Poland could be counterproductive in terms of the Polish resentment it might arouse, and because Soviet forces in the GDR and in the USSR itself are more crucial to effective control of Poland. The Northern Group of Forces is in fact stationed only in the western areas of the country, the formerly German territory which became Polish in 1945.

Romanian forces The Romanian armed forces represent the lowest percentage of the population in the WTO. Only two Romanian divisions are maintained at category 1 readiness, and there have been no Soviet forces stationed in Romania since 1958. In 1964, Romania cut military service from two years to sixteen months, which resulted in a reduction in its armed forces totals. Like Hungary, Romania has no common border with any Nato state, but Romania is well-known for President Ceausescu's attempts to establish a degree of foreign policy independence within the WTO. Romanian defence policy since the mid-1960s has tended to downplay the regular army's role as compared with the concept of armed resistance by the whole population. In October 1986, Romania announced that it would implement a 5 per cent cut in forces, weapons and defence spending.[29] As argued in chapter 2, this quasi-independent stance is of less political and strategic significance than it appears at first glance; nevertheless, it is dealt with in rather more detail below.

Northern and southern tiers Some comparison between the WTO's two regional groupings of states is made in table 4 (in appendix II), and indicates that the concepts of a 'northern tier' and 'southern tier' can be quite illuminating, even though they are concepts coined by Western analysts rather than indigenous ones.

For example, the three northern tier states contain over 1.5 times the population of the southern tier, almost twice as many regular forces, about twice as many tanks and combat aircraft (forgetting for the moment the levels of modernization of this equipment), and total military budgets four times as large. Since all Soviet forces in Eastern Europe are in the northern tier countries with the exception of 65,000 in Hungary, it is clear that there is a pronounced top-heaviness in the WTO's military strength within Eastern Europe.

This bias is equally marked if we look at the degrees of readiness of divisions. All thirty Soviet divisions are estimated at category 1 readiness, while for non-Soviet divisions the figure is almost certainly less than 50 per cent (though incomplete information on Bulgaria makes this figure tentative). Of non-Soviet divisions which are at category 1 readiness, only two Romanian divisions are positively identified as being in the southern tier.

As mentioned in chapter 1, there is some evidence that prior to the formation of the WTO, the USSR considered a more limited regional alliance between itself, the GDR, Poland and Czechoslovakia. The majority of WTO exercises held between 1955 and 1976 in Eastern Europe took place on northern tier territory – the precise figure is that out of fifty multilateral exercises held during that period, forty-one took place in the northern tier.[30]

It might be objected that these figures only tell us what we know already, since Nato is also strongest in 'north-central' Europe and we know that Germany is the focus of military confrontation in Europe. However, it is useful to have these figures to hand. Of course, the imbalance alone does not entail any conclusions about the nature of the WTO's posture towards Nato – offensive, defensive, or some mixture of the two.

The Soviet forces stationed in Eastern Europe represent the highest concentration of well-prepared forces available to the Soviet Union. The IISS's readiness estimate in 1987–8 of Soviet forces elsewhere was that only about another twenty divisions and ten air assault brigades stationed in the USSR were at category 1 readiness, excluding those then in Afghanistan.[31] An assessment of forces in Europe would clearly have to take into account Soviet forces in the western USSR at some stage, though here again caution is necessary. The more alarming calculations of conventional imbalance in Europe rely on assumptions which are not universally shared about weapons performance and forces available within given time-spans to each side.[32]

'Military balance' considerations aside, however, what is significant in the WTO context is that the Soviet forces in the western USSR underline the relative weakness of the Eastern European armed forces. If we add together Soviet divisions in Eastern Europe and the European USSR Military Districts (that is, Baltic, Byelorussian, Carpathian, Kiev, Leningrad and Odessa), they comfortably outnumber the fifty-eight non-Soviet divisions in Eastern Europe, even before readiness comes into the calculation.[33]

It is at least clear that in terms of personnel, Eastern European forces in the WTO play a less significant role than the USA's Western European allies play in Nato. A calculation of ratios within the alliances reveals a proportion for all armed services of almost 4:1 for Soviet to allied personnel in the WTO, and of approximately 2:3 for US to allied personnel in Nato. These figures may be a result of conscious political choices, but they also reflect the fact that the USA's Nato allies are stronger than the USSR's allies by almost any standards of measurement – population, economic strength, military traditions and potential.[34] This is not to say that Eastern European forces, which are still numerically substantial, can be disregarded in 'balance' calculations; just that their weight within the WTO is different from that of the Western Europeans within Nato.

WTO Command and Eastern European forces

The question of integration of Eastern European forces into WTO structures is an area of particular difficulty for anyone analysing the WTO from open literature. Uncertainties surrounding the 1969 reorganization have been noted. The *Soviet Military Encyclopaedia* records that: 'The Joint Armed Forces comprise forces and resources which are earmarked according to agreements between the WTO participants for joint actions, and joint military bodies which are formed in accordance with Article 5 of the Treaty.'[35] The joint bodies referred to here are the Military Council, Staff, etc. As for the military units involved, a number of Soviet sources state that those forces which comprise the JAFs remain under national command at all times, that is, the WTO is not a supranational military command any more than the PCC deprives the treaty signatories of any national sovereignty.[36] Since the national commanders are technically the respective ministers of defence (or perhaps heads of government), and the deputy defence ministers sit on the Joint Command, it is presumably through this mechanism that national command is formally retained.

The most likely Eastern European units to be permanently incorporated into the JAFs would seem to be some or all of those calculated to be at category I readiness, which would include forces from the GDR, Poland, Czechoslovakia, and possibly Bulgaria. Among these would be specialized elite units such as the Polish airborne division and amphibious assault division, and perhaps also the Polish and GDR navies, which would form part of a United Baltic Fleet together with the Soviet Baltic Fleet. Indeed, national command seems to be non-existent in the case of the GDR, where the 1964 USSR–GDR Treaty places the NVA under WTO command at all times, and the commander of Soviet forces in the country can conduct manoeuvres and troop movements without consulting the host government.[37] The particular importance of the GDR is also underlined by the fact the the C-in-C of the Group of Soviet Forces, Germany, is identified as a *glavnokomanduyushchii*, which gives him a status equivalent in this respect to the WTO C-in-C himself, and superior to the commanders of the other groups of Soviet forces.[38]

It is difficult to arbitrate between the different accounts given of WTO command structures. In the version given in the past by the IISS, the Joint Command has been seen as exercising peacetime authority over Soviet forces in Eastern Europe and the western USSR, with the Eastern Europeans themselves only remaining under national control until war broke out.[39] Command of air defence networks has been assumed to be centralized in Moscow, but this would not apply to those parts of Eastern European air forces supporting ground troops. This control of air defence might not be operated through the Joint Command, since air defence forces have a separate existence in the Soviet system (this is taken up further below). John Erickson has also suggested that there are permanent WTO commands for navies, air forces and special troops.

Other sources have questioned the IISS view of Eastern European forces falling under the Joint Command once war broke out. Some have argued that the Joint Command would have no wartime function, and on the outbreak of war command would pass into the hands of the Soviet supreme commander, who would exercise it through his own headquarters and general staff. Viktor Suvorov argues that once the transition to wartime conditions had taken place, no Eastern European unit larger than a division would be commanded by a national officer, and Soviet command would operate at Corps, Army and Front levels, and Ryszard Kuklinski has stated that a 1979 statute places up to 90 per cent of Polish forces under direct Soviet command in case of emergency or war.[40] The essence of this argument is that, whatever the functions of the WTO's military structures, these bodies would become redundant once war had broken out. This would limit their functions to training and standardiza- tion concerns, discussion of policy and supervision of manoeuvres.

Inevitably, there can be little firm evidence for either view. In 1968, however, although preparations for the occupation of Czechoslovakia were made via WTO channels, the operation itself was commanded by General Pavlovskii, who did not hold a WTO post, but was Commander-in-Chief of Soviet Ground Forces.[41] The WTO also lacks its own bodies for administering mobilization or logistics, and does not itself seem to plan exercises, as distinct from supervising them; all these functions would seem to be carried out by Soviet bodies. It does therefore seem likely, from what little evidence is available, that the Joint Com- mand has an intermediate role, whereby command passes through it at times of threat or crisis, but is passed on to Soviet bodies when WTO forces go into action, as in Czechoslovakia or in a possible conflict with Nato. Similarly, the WTO Staff's functions would appear to be entirely, or almost entirely, peacetime ones.

Chapter 2 has already introduced the argument of Christopher Jones, to the effect that the WTO's military organization is designed to pre-empt any Eastern European state organizing an armed defence of its own territory. For the specific purposes of a discussion of command structures, Jones's argument is that Eastern European formations are in practice, even if not in theory, detached from national control; bilateral mechan- isms tie allied forces to the Soviet military; and combined training and exercise programmes serve to drill a multinational force suitable for intervention purposes within Eastern Europe.[42]

While the maintenance of technical national command could serve as a device to disguise the absence of effective national control of forces, Jones is not entirely convincing in arguing that this feature of WTO command mechanisms is the key to understanding the political essence of the alliance. This is not to deny that the insight is illuminating. The system of multinational exercises and the creation of the 'greater socialist officer corps' are certainly of great use to the fostering of political cohesion, but these mechanisms do not of themselves mean that there are no more traditional 'security' considerations involved. If the USSR feared military attack from the West, or contemplated attacking Western Europe, but was worried about the weakness and/or unreliability of its allies in the region, these measures of military integration would also make perfectly good sense. It is true that Jones explains WTO mechanisms partly in terms of deterring Western intervention in Eastern Europe, but this is seen as being essentially an Eastern European problem, not something which could equally well arise from a more basic East–West military confrontation in Europe. One could equally well argue that if the Soviet leadership considers that it might, *in extremis*, have to go to war with Nato for any reason, there is no point in giving unwilling Eastern European allies any way of blocking the effective implementation of a vital military decision.

The WTO's multinational exercise programme dates from 1961, when it was instituted by the then Commander-in-Chief, Marshal Grechko. Its initiation at that time may have been related to the revival of ground forces in response to Khrushchev's attempted downgrading of them, and to recent events such as the Berlin crisis and Kennedy's decision to expand Nato's conventional forces, as well as to the more general concern to bind Eastern European forces into Soviet structures. Confirmation that the purposes of WTO exercises are at least partly intimidatory and cohesive can be seen in the fact of increased numbers of exercises in 1968 and 1980–2, at the times of the Czechoslovakian and Polish crises.[43] Apart from the ground force exercises, joint exercises of Soviet fleets with ships from the GDR, Poland and Bulgaria probably also have as much political as military significance, given the comparative weakness of these Eastern European navies. At the same time, however, multinational exercises have been observed by Western analysts to keep pace with developments in Soviet thinking on the relationship between preparation for nuclear and non-nuclear operations, which undermines the argument that their purposes are purely internal.[44] The figures quoted earlier, on relative numbers of exercises in the northern and southern tiers from 1955–76, also indicate differentiated degrees of attention being paid to different regions. Since both the Czechoslovakian and Polish crises occurred in northern tier states, the continuation of the geographical imbalance in the later distribution of exercises is unsurprising, and can be readily seen from Jeffrey Simon's documentation of exercise locations.

It is worth mentioning again at this point the significance of the bilateral Soviet–East European treaties and troop-stationing agreements, which were outlined earlier. The Warsaw Treaty itself, it will be remembered, provides for consultation in the event of the threat of an armed attack on any of the signatory states, and 'In the event of an armed attack in Europe . . . immediate assistance . . . by all the means (considered) necessary, including the use of armed force' (Article 4 – see appendix I). The bilateral agreements which additionally provide for the stationing of Soviet troops in the GDR, Czechoslovakia, Poland and Hungary differ in the obligations which they place on local Soviet commanders. The Polish and Hungarian treaties require the host government's agreement before

Soviet troop movements can take place, but these requirements are absent from the GDR (1957) and Czechoslovakian (1968) treaties. In the case of the GDR, the Soviet commander is also in command of the national armed forces and has the right to declare a state of emergency independently of the GDR government. In the light of these special provisions for the WTO's two frontline states, it looks unlikely that the GDR and Czechoslovakian governments would technically have been able to veto the 1983 introduction of nuclear counterdeployments, even though separate agreements were said to have been reached with them (see previous chapter).

Despite the original treaty's limitation of the obligation of mutual assistance to the event of an armed attack 'in Europe', the latest round of bilateral treaties signed since 1967 does not limit the allies' mutual assistance obligations with any geographical qualification.[45] WTO meetings have regularly commented on issues beyond Europe (for instance, Vietnam), but the most likely explanation for the treaty wordings is that the USSR attempted, in the late 1960s, to extend its allies' commitments to include defence against China. The years 1969–73 were the period of Soviet military build-up in the Far East, following increased tension and the Soviet nuclear threats made against China in 1969. It has been suggested that there was a specific Soviet attempt to pressurize the Eastern Europeans at the 1969 Budapest PCC meeting.[46] If this pressure was applied, it does not seem to have been very successful at that time, though some reports did later emerge about the presence of Eastern European advisers or forces in Afghanistan.[47] As long as Sino–Soviet relations do not go into another decline, however, the obligation should remain technical rather than of immediate political saliency.

Military intervention and the question of Romania

As chapter 2 has already argued, past instances of military intervention in Eastern Europe have revealed as much about the WTO as a political organization as from a military perspective, but some more narrowly military observations can still be made.

The 1953 Soviet intervention in East Berlin was very brief, and indeed seems to have taken place only after the crisis had largely subsided.[48] In 1956 the Hungarian crisis was accompanied by a similar crisis in Poland, which was resolved without military conflict and with the appointment of Gomulka as party leader. One key factor which defused the situation in Poland was Khrushchev's calculation that a significant part of the Polish army would resist any Soviet armed intervention, as well as the assessment that Gomulka could, on the whole, be trusted by the USSR. In

Hungary Soviet forces did intervene, and met resistance from some Hungarian army units and armed civilians, though Khrushchev could not, presumably, have been sure in advance of the likely extent of resistance.[49]

In 1968, the Czechoslovakian leadership had these precedents to go on. Dubcek's approach seems to have been to assume that the Soviet leadership could be persuaded that political developments in Czechoslovakia did not threaten Soviet interests, and that there was no need to consider military defence against possible intervention. One can argue that Dubcek was naive, but one can also argue that if he had prepared the army to support his leadership, the intervention would have come sooner, rather than been deterred. This may have been the reason why the rumoured preparations by some military officers of plans for resistance made no headway. At any rate, the Czechoslovakian army had no orders to resist, and did not do so.[50]

It has been suggested that one purpose of the WTO manoeuvres during the pre-intervention period was to reduce the Czech army's stocks of live ammunition, in case resistance was considered. The intervention itself was swift and relatively efficient (it is sometimes cited as an instance of Soviet attainment of 'strategic surprise'), though the occupiers were surprised by the extent of the civil disobedience they encountered. This may have been because the Soviet leadership held the genuine belief that if Dubcek's leadership was removed, a grateful population would welcome the Soviet occupiers. One comes across regular references in the literature on the WTO to morale problems in the occupying allied armies, particularly among the Russians and Germans.[51] Other rumours from 1980 and 1981 suggest that something similar would have happened had an intervention in Poland been attempted, to say nothing of the risk that the Polish army would have resisted.[52]

These reports are only straws in the wind, and such events did not substantially affect the ability of the USSR to occupy Czechoslovakia, or of the Polish armed forces to impose martial law. However, they do suggest that 1968 represented a kind of 'high point' of the USSR's ability to impose crisis solutions by military means. While the events in Poland do indicate that the mechanisms described by Christopher Jones have succeeded in sustaining an Eastern European officer elite which can perform this function, anyone looking coolly at Eastern Europe from the USSR must surely be aware of: (a) the limited utility of direct Soviet military intervention to resolve political crises; and (b) the fragility of any 'solution' imposed by domestic military forces, as in Poland.

The discussion of intervention leads naturally to some further consideration of the most unorthodox member of the WTO, Romania. Mention has already been made in chapter 2 of Jones's arguments concerning Romanian non-participation in a number of WTO structures which serve to lay the foundations for possible Soviet intervention in Eastern Europe. Here, the nature and significance of Romanian unorthodoxy are looked at in rather more detail.

Soviet troops have not returned to Romania since they left in 1958. Romanian troops are believed to have participated in no multilateral WTO exercises since 1963, though Romanian officers may attend manoeuvres elsewhere on a staff basis or as observers, and staff map exercises have taken place in Romania. (Soviet sources give varying accounts of the extent of Romanian participation.) Romanian forces are therefore untrained to participate in joint operations under a common Soviet–WTO doctrine, and Romania does not even permit the transit of foreign troops across its territory – a fact which has prompted the USSR and Bulgaria to pay particular attention to their sea links between Odessa and Varna.[53]

In place of the shared doctrine adhered to by the rest of the WTO, Romania has substituted a doctrine similar to Yugoslavia's, characterized as 'homeland's defence by the entire people'. Although the process of Romania's self-distancing from the rest of the WTO began before 1968, the heretical revision of military doctrine can be traced to the 1968–9 period. Romanian doctrine rests jointly on the defence of national territory and sovereignty, and the notional involvement of the entire people in the defence of the nation. This doctrine was formalized in a law on the organization of national defence adopted by the Grand National Assembly in 1972, and subsequently updated in a 1978 law and presidential orders. Although potential enemies are not openly specified, there seems to be little effort made to conceal that the doctrine amounts to an attempted deterrent against Soviet intervention as much as any other threat.[54]

Such a commitment to defence by the entire population implies and entails a heavy reliance on reserves and on low-level military training throughout society, involving women as well as men. It should probably be classified as a 'high entry price' alternative defence strategy, rather than one which would hope to maintain total territorial integrity in the event of war. The prospect of military/political stalemate is intended to deter any aggressor from attempting occupation of the country. (At the same time it assumes a preparedness on the part of the population to sustain high casualties in fighting a much stronger and better-equipped opponent.) As far as the rest of the WTO is concerned, there remains a tension between Romania's treaty obligation to render assistance to its allies, and the implications of the rest of the military doctrine that deployment of troops outside the country's borders is not contemplated. Technically, at least, Romania is still committed to assisting its allies in defence against a Nato attack, though not in any aggressive campaign.[55] This distinction has been overlooked by some Western commentators, who would assume that a Nato attack is inconceivable, and it may not have any real significance for Romania either, given the absence of any border with a Nato state. The Warsaw Treaty's assistance clause, it will be remembered, is not automatic, and depends on consultation and the view taken of what is 'necessary'. Even so, Romania's participation or non-participation in the WTO air defence network would be significant, and the situation in this area is not entirely clear.

The Romanian press agency, Agerpress, specified in 1978 that Romanian forces would remain under national command in wartime, thus implying that this was not the case for the other Eastern European armies.[56] It seems likely that this 1978 episode was a response to a Soviet attempt to reform the WTO command structure to Romania's disadvantage. As already mentioned, this had happened before, Romania having reacted sharply to proposals put forward by Brezhnev in 1965.[57] Soviet publications dealing with Romanian defence affairs tend, understandably, to downplay these Romanian departures from the norm, though mention is made of the 'war of the entire people' concept, and on some occasions of the limited Romanian contributions to WTO manoeuvres.[58] Conversely, Romanian publications tend to play down the extent of Soviet–Romanian co-operation in the pre-1968 period.

The policy described here reflects a number of military, political and economic concerns. In practical strategic terms, unduly close Romanian integration into the WTO would serve few Romanian interests. Given that Romania's geographical position makes it relatively unimportant as a target in itself, the country has nothing to gain through being dragged into a Central European conflict through the remaining technical commitment to the collective defence of Central European WTO territory.

However, the stated Romanian doctrine also assumes a high degree of popular support for the present political leadership in order to be successful in practice. Paradoxically, it could be said to fit Jones's model of WTO military doctrine in so far as it protects the existing regime, but this is done by preventing any domestic faction appealing to outside forces for assistance; there is no basis on which a domestic faction could assert that it was acting in any interest wider than 'the nation'. Rumours concerning the Romanian military tend to relate to more pro-Soviet 'dissident' groups, opposed perhaps to Ceausescu's personal rule rather than to military policy *per se*; these reports have surfaced in stories of possible coup attempts in 1971 and 1983.[59] As noted, Romania does not participate in the WTO system of training senior officers at Soviet military academies.

Earlier chapters of this study have already given some indications of the ways in which a broader foreign policy stance lies behind this phenomenon of Romania's distancing itself from WTO military command structures. Measures of dissent over the twenty-five years have included the 1964 reduction of military service from twenty-four to sixteen months and the 1986 defence cuts; the defence spending issue and Romania's diversification of its sources of military equipment; the maintenance of good relations with China during the worst period of the Sino–Soviet split; non-participation in and condemnation of the intervention in Czechoslovakia, and the specific phrasing of the 1970 Soviet–Romanian Treaty to give no grounds for legitimizing intervention; and periodic calls for mutual bloc dissolution (though this has also been a common WTO position).

Romania's unorthodoxy also had important economic roots, since it evolved in the early 1960s partly as a result of opposition to Soviet pressure for a particular conception of the division of labour within Comecon.[60] This issue was also revived in the mid-1970s. However, although Romania's quasi-independent posture has thus extended beyond the sphere of military command and control, the country's domestic politics have never been liberalized in any way which would have caused Soviet alarm. The term 'Stalinist' continues to be applicable to Romanian politics in a way which has become inaccurate for the rest of the Eastern bloc since the mid-1950s. Furthermore, Romania's peripheral strategic position makes it of minor concern to the USSR, and Romania has not tried to suggest that its military doctrine should be a model for any other WTO states. Romania may have genuinely feared Soviet intervention in 1968, but there is no evidence that Ceausescu has ever contemplated withdrawal from the WTO. It is likely that he has had an astute awareness of the limitations of his position, and would not risk the uncertainties attendant on attempted withdrawal.[61] Independent Romanian gestures also tend to become less interesting for the West in periods of greater initiative in Soviet policy, as has been the case since 1985. (Paradoxically, in the Gorbachev period the earlier situation has been reversed; now the Soviet Union is less concerned about Romanian foreign policy, and more worried about the absence of domestic political/economic reform.)

Romania's continuing economic difficulties also leave the country, now an importer of Soviet oil, in a weak position to assert itself internationally. The 1986 defence cuts probably reflected these problems, and accounts of Romanian life in this period painted a grim picture of the country's population enduring energy shortages and general economic and social crisis, as the leadership tried to deal with heavy foreign debt through domestic austerity and an export drive.[62] It seems reasonable to speculate that any post-Ceausescu leadership in Romania may be forced to seek improvements in relations with the Soviet Union, in which case military policy might also be affected, and indeed there were rumours that this process of moving back closer to the USSR and WTO was already beginning in 1987–8.

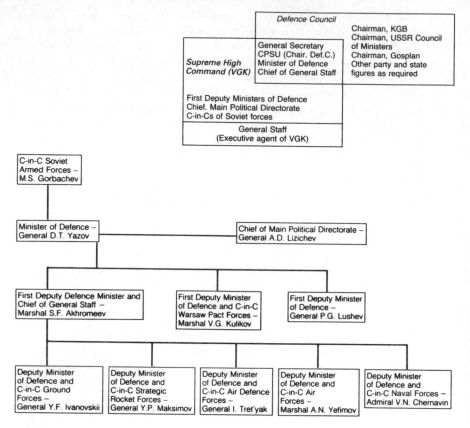

Figure 2   Stavka (headquarters) of the Soviet Supreme High Command (as at early 1988)

(Sources: Soviet Military Power 1987, US Department of Defense, updated from *Air Force Magazine* v 71 n 3, March 1988)*

Soviet defence organization

In order to get a clearer picture of the position of the Eastern European armed forces in the European military system, it is necessary to give a rather more detailed account of the USSR's own command structures. This is of particular importance because these structures have been going through a recent period of reorganization.

As of late 1988, the WTO Commander-in-Chief was Marshal Viktor Kulikov. His position within the Soviet high command is illustrated in figure 2. The personnel occupying these command posts have changed rapidly in the last few years, through a combination of death (Ustinov, succeeded as Defence Minister in 1984 by Sokolov), enforced retirement (Gorshkov's replacement by Chernavin in 1985, Yepishev's by Lizichev in 1986), and transfer (Ogarkov's replacement by Akhromeev in 1984). In May 1987 came Mathias Rust's incursion into Soviet airspace and landing in Red Square, which resulted in the replacement of Sokolov by General Yazov, and of Koldunov by General Tret'yak.

The Defence Council exists in peacetime, technically as a state rather than a party body, though it may in effect be a joint state and party body, since it is chaired by the party general secretary. In the event of war, the Defence Council would probably become the supreme state body with authority over the high command. The peacetime equivalent of the high command is the Main Military Council or Collegium of the Defence Ministry, which probably supervises the Soviet military establishment from day to day and is chaired by the Minister of Defence.[63]

As far as the WTO C-in-C himself is concerned, he would seem to be at best an advisory member of the Defence Council, while the Chief of the General Staff may be a full member. It is not easy to be certain about the relationship between positions occupied in the Soviet leadership and membership of bodies like the Defence Council and Politburo. For example, when Sokolov succeeded Ustinov as Minister of Defence, he did not inherit Ustinov's Politburo seat, becoming only a non-voting or candidate Politburo member, but he must nevertheless be assumed to have taken over Ustinov's seat on the Defence Council. Yazov also became a candidate Politburo member at the June 1987 Central Committee plenum, shortly after his appointment as Defence Minister, and presumably he is also now a member of the Defence Council. The relationship between WTO and purely Soviet structures also needs to be examined with care.

In 1977, Kulikov and Nikolai Ogarkov were appointed simultaneously to their posts as WTO C-in-C and Soviet Chief of Staff. Kulikov had previously been Chief of Staff himself, and though the post of WTO C-in-C had formerly outranked the Chief of Staff, it gradually emerged during 1977 that Ogarkov was now senior, and that Kulikov had in effect been demoted *vis-à-vis* Ogarkov. Differences over detente and negotiations policy, as well as sheer factionalism, seem to have lain behind this episode.[64] Since no particular changes within the WTO itself have been identified at this time, once can only assume that these events were related more to debates within the Soviet leadership than to developments which affected Eastern Europe directly. Presumably Kulikov remained subordinate to Akhromeev, Ogarkov's successor, although Ogarkov's own transfer to other duties in September 1984 raises further questions about command structures. The most convincing account that has been given of

Ogarkov's transfer is that he took command of a new grouping of Soviet forces in Eastern Europe and the western USSR, which would be a command requiring close integration, and perhaps competition, with Kulikov's WTO command.[65]

It has already been mentioned that the C-in-C's peacetime supervision of WTO forces is not thought to extend into an operational command function. The picture traditionally painted has suggested that, if war broke out, Soviet groups of forces in Eastern Europe would be transformed into Fronts or groups of Fronts, into which Eastern European divisions would be integrated, but under Soviet command at Front and Army level. (A wartime Front consists of several Armies, an Army of several divisions – thus the larger-than-average GSFG would split into more than one Front.) This Soviet command would be exercised via orders from the Stavka/Supreme High Command, a process which would presumably involve the WTO C-in-C in some capacity, but without the kind of pre-eminence which his title seems to imply. He might, at this stage, carry no more weight than the five service chiefs who are technically his subordinates.

Air and naval units would be organized slightly differently. The relative unimportance of the Eastern European navies makes it possible that they would fall under the authority of the C-in-C Soviet Naval Forces even in peacetime, and Chernavin may act as WTO naval commander in addition to his main duties. Presumably this does not, however, apply to the Romanian navy in the Black Sea.

There is a need for more caution in describing air force structures, as these have been considerably reorganized since 1980–1, and most of the comments made on the reorganization have applied to the Soviet air forces as a whole rather than to the participation of the Eastern European forces. The generally agreed account of these structures before 1980–1 was that the entire WTO air defence system was centralized in Moscow at all times, under the control of the C-in-C of Soviet Air Defence Forces, known then as the *PVO-Strany*. (Even if there was a technically distinct WTO air defence command, presumably the WTO and Soviet commanders were in practice the same person.) This would have meant that Eastern European air forces would have fallen under more than one command: air defence interceptor elements under the Moscow-centred command, and ground-attack and battlefield support elements under a more local command. This local command would have been closely integrated with locally-stationed Soviet air armies (in Czechoslovakia, Hungary and Poland), but not necessarily part of the Soviet structure, except in the case of the GDR. Romania may have been, and may remain, outside this structure altogether.

As figure 2 indicates, Soviet air defence and air forces have firmly-established identities as separate services. The air defence forces formerly included not only interceptor aircraft, but also Surface-to-Air Missiles and Anti-Ballistic Missiles. The two major components of the Air Force proper (the *VVS*) were Long-Range Aviation (bombers) and Frontal Aviation (for ground support and strike missions). Frontal Aviation aircraft were assigned to Soviet forces in Eastern Europe, where they were known as Air Armies, as well as to Military Districts within the USSR.[66] One aspect of this system which is unclear is the question of whether Soviet interceptor aircraft based in Eastern Europe would have fallen under the *PVO-Strany* or under Frontal Aviation, that is, under a Moscow or a local group of forces commander.

At any rate, this system was made more cumbersome by the existence of Ground Forces Air Defence Troops, operating anti-aircraft artillery and surface-to-air missiles (in both Soviet and Eastern European armies). Its reform in 1980–1 formed part of a more general overhaul of the Soviet command-and-control system, but may also have been accelerated by the impending deployment by Nato of cruise missiles in Western Europe. Air defence has always been a key concern of the USSR in Eastern Europe, and one could predict that the advent of modern cruise technology would prompt renewed emphasis on traditional air defence.[67]

Recent reorganization measures

Accounts of the reorganization of Soviet air forces have now appeared in a number of sources, and they have been accompanied by further accounts of a more general restructuring of Soviet forces in the western USSR and Eastern Europe. The essence of the reorganization of the air forces appears to be as follows:[68] The former *PVO-Strany* has changed its name to *Voiska-PVO*, or Air Defence Forces. There are some differing interpretations of the changes, but it appears that the *Voiska-PVO* operate at theatre and army/front level, and include the interceptor element and also anti-aircraft rocket forces. In addition the *Voiskovaya PVO* (Troop PVO) comprises anti-aircraft rocket and artillery forces, and provides ground anti-aircraft defence at division level. This means that Frontal Aviation forces have been reduced in size while retaining a separate identity, and have also lost other aircraft to a new command identified by some sources as 'Aviation Armies of the Soviet Union', replacing Long-Range Aviation for air strike missions. At the same time, however, other sources speak of Long-Range Aviation now forming part of 'Strategic Nuclear Forces', thought to be a new command incorporating all strategic nuclear delivery systems (land-based missiles, submarine-launched missiles, and nuclear bombers) which was set up by Marshal Ogarkov when we was Chief of Staff.[69]

This reorganization of air defence forces is related to a more general restructuring of command systems. The command of the integrated *Voiska-PVO* force just described no longer follows the previous pattern which mixed a national Soviet command system with more local command of Frontal Aviation by commanders of groups of forces or (in wartime) Fronts in Eastern Europe. Instead, the *Voiska-PVO* forces would be be in the hands of commanders of Theatres of Military Operations in wartime, and possibly in peacetime as well. Air force commands now correspond to these Theatres of Military Operations.

The reorganizations of Soviet nuclear forces and Theatres of Military Operations (the Russian acronym is TVD) appear to have been conducted simultaneously. Evaluation of these recent changes is difficult, since some of the Western analysts who have given accounts of them have relied not only on open Soviet sources, but also on privileged information which includes lecture materials obtained from Soviet military academies, by what means the outside observer can only speculate. (During 1988 some lecture materials from the Voroshilov Academy, delivered in 1973–5, began to be published in the West.) In the account which follows, I have tried to pick out the elements common to recent Western analyses without taking sides where disputes occur, or endorsing the more far-reaching strategic conclusions which have been drawn. Fortunately, there are a number of central points which do not seem to be in dispute.

Firstly, it is suggested that the new strategic nuclear command has, at some time over the last ten years, grouped strategic nuclear forces into a single command which has taken them away from their original service commanders. This would mean that the lowest organizational rung illustrated in figure 2 gives a rather misleading impression, in that the new command reflects a division of missions between intercontinental and theatre commands, as opposed to the traditional division of roles between land, sea and air forces. Further suggestions made about this reorganization have included the idea that Marshal Ogarkov carried it out and placed the command initially in the hands of his then subordinate, Akhromeev; and that one reason for Admiral Gorshkov's dismissal in 1985 was his reluctance to see the navy's missile-carrying submarines removed to the new command.[70]

In some accounts it is suggested that recent changes have also given the Soviet high command and staff an expanded peacetime role at the expense of the ministry of defence, the minister, and his collegium.[71] Whether or not this interpretation is correct, there is widespread agreement that the reorganization also established an intermediate command level between the staff and frontal commands, at a level which would seem to integrate land, sea and air forces as well as, presumably, theatre and shorter-range weapons which do not form part of the strategic nuclear command.[72]

There are a number of divergences in the terminology used to identify these intermediate commands in the different accounts available. In the US Department of Defense's version, which seems to be largely shared by the IISS, the USSR has introduced the concept of three theatres of war (Far Eastern, Southern and Western), of which the Western is sub-divided into North-western, Western and South-western Theatres of Military Operations or TVDs (Other TVDs are the Atlantic, Arctic, Southern, Far Eastern, and Pacific.) According to this scheme, Eastern Europe is divided between the Western and Sout-western TVDs along the northern-southern tier divide (though the TVDs also cover Soviet territory and Military Districts). Viktor Suvorov favours a different terminology, identifying a Western TVD which covers all of Europe, but is sub-divided into Strategic Directions. Hines and Petersen prefer TSMA, for theatre of strategic military action, but again divide Europe into three, which corresponds to the DoD's TVD scheme. TSMAs/TVDs should be understood as regions identified for a certain type of military action, rather than command organizations *per se*; the corresponding command structures are termed High Commands of Forces (HCFs or HCOFs).

The confusion which may be engendered by these different accounts should not, however, obscure the main point. These intermediate command structures are thought to exist in peacetime, and to have an existence distinct from the persisting WTO and military district organizations. It is presumed that in wartime they would form an additional, and crucial, link between the Soviet high command and front commanders. Marshal Ogarkov was variously identified as C-in-C of the Western TVD (plainly the most important, covering Central Europe), or of the whole Western theatre; in either case, he would be occupying a position which appears to be of greater importance than that of the WTO C-in-C himself.

These intermediate regional commands are not new features of Soviet military organization, and much of the material from which their existence and constitution have been pieced together relates back to operations carried out in the Second World War. The *Soviet Military Encyclopaedia* dates the concept from the writings of Jomini in 1815, and traces its importance through the Russo–Japanese War and the Second World War into the nuclear era.[73] The significance of their reintroduction from the mid-to-late 1970s onwards has generally been taken to be related to a Soviet reassessment of the possibility of prolonged conventional conflict, involving deep conventional strikes, and/or a presumed attempt to establish (via the concurrent nuclear reorganization) a back-up capacity for effective nuclear war-fighting. However, it would be a mistake to draw immediate conclusions about the import of this reorganization (assuming it has been described correctly) before closer attention has been paid to the evolution of Soviet strategy itself, and also to evolving Soviet arms control and disarmament policy. For the time being, the only deductions that will be attempted concern Marshal Ogarkov himself, and the likely relevance of the reorganization as described to the WTO.

If Ogarkov was indeed put in charge of one of these newly-created commands, he was clearly not removed altogether from high-level decision-making, but nevertheless lost his former pre-eminence. His transfer may have been prompted by an assertive call he made in 1984 for more investment in conventional weaponry; some analysts have suggested that it may have been caused by his attempt to adhere to a belief in the winnability of nuclear war in the preceding few years. If Ustinov and Ogarkov, regarded as twin architects of the general strategic reorganization, came to differ on a fundamental point of military policy, this gives us a good reason for caution in attributing any clear, unambiguous set of goals to the measures which they undertook. The very diversity of the analyses which have been offered of Ogarkov's views and position suggests that even if there was firm agreement on the goals of the reorganization in 1976–7, this was not necessarily still the case by the mid-1980s.[74] The curious 1985 flurry of rumours that Ogarkov was about to return to the limelight as defence minister, or WTO C-in-C, or both, is another oddity which has not been explained.[75]

As far as the WTO itself is concerned, the Soviet command restructuring would seem to have involved a reallocation of air force and air defence units, and a presumed but unclear effect on the WTO C-in-C's position in the chain of command. It has been suggested that Eastern European forces, in particular ground forces, are now in the process of being restructured and more directly integrated into the TVD/HCOF structure, or at least will come under increased pressure to be subordinated to a single command authority. *Soviet Military Power 1988* identified a new command and control arrangement set up in the 1980s to permit the integration of Eastern European forces without national approval, and also reported a Western TVD headquarters as falling under WTO control, but did not explain the latter's relationship to Soviet structures.[76] (By early 1989 Ogarkar, Akhromeev, and Kulikov had all been replaced, with Kulikov being succeeded by General Lushev in February.)

Conclusion

This survey of the WTO's military command structures has suggested that, over the period 1955–88, there were some appreciable moves away from strict Soviet control of decision-making and discussion forums, at least in peacetime. The involvement of defence ministers and their deputies does seem to give the Eastern European defence establishment extra opportunites for participation, so that whatever public opinion in the various countries may think about the Soviet alliance, the military and political establishments seem to have benefited from the evolution of the WTO since 1955. Robin Remington has pointed out that the need to professionalize Eastern European armed forces required that their importance be recognized institutionally.[77]

At the same time, however, these relaxations do not seem to have been extended to the sphere of likely wartime command, and there is no evidence to suggest that major Soviet strategic reorganizations have been elaborated or even discussed in detail in WTO forums. If anything, Soviet control over Eastern European armed forces seems to have become tighter during the 1980s. Nor has WTO decision-making been put in the hands of potentially 'disloyal' elements, and here Christopher Jones's work is useful in outlining the way in which a conservative 'greater socialist officer corps' has been nurtured throughout the armed services and defence establishments of Eastern Europe. Like any major international organization, military or otherwise, the WTO doubtless creates and sustains its own bonds of elite loyalty, even if Soviet fears of latent Eastern European anti-Sovietism remain.

The picture of Soviet command structures which has emerged in this section leaves us with a view of the WTO C-in-C as enjoying an imposing title, but a much less imposing practical role in wartime. This does not mean that the WTO is superfluous to Soviet security concerns, but it does underline the fact that the organization in itself is as important politically as militarily. One should be careful, however, in drawing out the implications of what appears to be the relative insignificance of the Eastern European nations in the Soviet military command system. It would be a *non sequitur* to argue that this implies that Eastern Europe is not a militarily important area for the USSR. The Soviet problem in the region is that it is militarily important and has remained so throughout successive phases of Soviet military thinking, but the WTO allies have not been seen as either strong enough, or reliable enough, to ensure Soviet security interests independently of a Soviet-dominated defence organization.

One has only to recall the early post-war importance of the area for the USSR, when one of the major threats to Soviet security came from US bombers based in or easily transferable to Western Europe, to see that effective air defence in an Eastern European 'buffer zone' has long been vital in Soviet eyes. The relationship between offensive and defensive concepts and uses of this 'buffer zone' is examined in chapters 4 and 6, and though it might seem to have diminished in importance once the era of strategic missiles arrived, it has in some respects regained importance in a period when the emphasis has shifted back towards low-flying cruise missile technology, and towards planning on both sides for conventional military operations which may not involve (in theory at least) the use of nuclear weapons.

The USSR's military concerns in the region can perhaps be summed up as a need to encourage the Eastern Europeans to maintain their military establishments at an adequate level, and so to share the burden of defence costs, but without allowing the most crucial areas of military command out of Soviet hands. Simultaneously, the USSR has to guard against the danger of its allies perceiving themselves as mere instruments of Soviet policy, and it seems that it is this tension that WTO institutions have attempted to resolve.

4
Strategy and Politics

Sooner or later, any study of the WTO or of Soviet security policy has to address some of the questions most basic to European security: what are the essential features of Soviet military doctrine and strategy in Europe, what political considerations have influenced them, and in what directions are they currently developing? This chapter addresses these questions in three stages. Firstly I examine the development of Soviet doctrine and strategy, and set this alongside an examination of the Western debate in an attempt to clarify what that debate is 'about'. Secondly, I look briefly at the involvement of Eastern European forces in the Soviet military posture in Europe. Finally, I look at recent debates concerning the balance in Soviet thinking between nuclear and conventional strategies. In chapter 5, these developments are related to recent shifts in Soviet policy on disarmament and in the wider sphere of East–West relations.

Soviet strategy and Western debates

Much of the course of the Cold War since 1945, or at least its public presentation in the West, rests on a perception of a post-war desire on the part of the USSR to expand further into Western Europe, or to use its military strength in Eastern Europe as a political lever against the West if military action was too risky. Nato's retention of broad support in Western Europe rests on the acceptance of this view, and the participation of the smaller WTO states in this Soviet posture is taken to be that of countries originally occupied by the USSR, and then trained to take part in offensive operations against Western Europe as a way of strengthening the Soviet hand.

A discussion of the validity of this analysis is inevitable in any examination of WTO military strategy. Its validity or otherwise became a renewed focus of attention after the December 1987 signature of the INF Treaty, which was widely presented as reviving the spectre of a Western Europe threatened by superior Soviet conventional forces. In some respects this may have been a productive development, since it returned the European security debate to its most basic controversies, and provided an opportunity for them to be considered anew.

Since I will be arguing against what I shall term the 'orthodox analysis' of Soviet policy, I will try to characterize it as fairly as possible. One will not find in standard Nato statements any claim of a Soviet urge to military conquest of Western Europe, despite the power of this conception as a popular image. Rather, the orthodox argument rests on the claim that in the absence of adequate Western military strength, Soviet political leverage (sometimes in the form of 'nuclear blackmail') will be exerted against the West. The cruder version of the argument may be more prevalent in the USA than in Western Europe, but it is not heard from Nato's public spokespersons. It can be heard in something close to its basic form from British government figures, which perhaps says something about the peculiar difficulties of explaining British policy. One would, however, be hard pressed to find many significant Western European political figures in the late 1980s who would attempt to present any serious case for hostile Soviet military intentions in the region.

The more sophisticated argument from political leverage raises two problems:

(a)   it needs support in the form of evidence that the Soviet Union does in fact seek to exert this leverage, and in particular it requires some kind of specification of *how* exactly 'nuclear blackmail' or other leverage based on military strength might work;

(b)   it needs to support the discussion of Western military requirements (hardware and strategy) in terms which are something other than a retreat to the cruder version on the argument.

If there is one concept which seems to unite orthodox and revisionist analyses of Cold War history, it is probably the notion of Eastern Europe as a 'buffer zone' in Soviet security thinking. However, this is only the start of the problem; different analysts can accept the 'buffer zone' thesis but go on to present widely-differing analyses of the objectives of the Soviet posture. The historical controversy rests partly on differing analyses of the post-war purposes of Soviet forces in Eastern Europe. Orthodox analysts are likely to argue for an actual Soviet military threat to the West at that time, but there is a good deal of evidence that, whatever the precise role of Soviet forces in the area from 1945–8, they were not preparing to invade Western Europe, and also that they were smaller than Western governments claimed at the time.[1] Behind this military controversy lie the long-running disputes between different schools of Cold War historians, from orthodoxy into revisionism and 'post-revisionism', on the post-war development of US and Soviet foreign policy and the establishment of the two blocs in Europe.[2]

While this is not the place to re-fight these battles, it is worth noting once again the diversity of the accounts offered of Western policy: from the traditionally revisionist work on the global role of US 'atomic diplomacy' and the need to establish a liberal world economic order in conditions of extreme West European economic weakness, to more recent work on the British preoccupation with preserving Britain's great power status in an era when the USA was the new hegemonic Western power, and on the need for domestic US political consensus.[3] For many of the revisionists, the assumption of an immediate post-war Soviet threat is seen as acting as a rationalization for policies needed to keep the USA and Western Europe in alliance for these quite different reasons, and also as serving to obscure ways in which US and Soviet interests coincided, in particular in the suppression of German nationalism.

A problem common to most Cold War historiography has been the comparative unavailability of source material on Soviet policy, and the consequent imbalance in the literature. Nevertheless, the issues contested by the historians can be fairly easily stated: how far was the Cold War inevitable given Soviet interests in Eastern Europe and domestic politics, and how far did Soviet policy evolve in response to allied policy in Germany, the Truman Doctrine, and the Marshall Plan?[4]

In competition with more traditional revisionist accounts of Soviet policy as essentially reactive is an analysis of Stalin imposing ideological consolidation, and closing the USSR off from the West almost immediately after the war, for primarily internal reasons. From this account one can build an alternative analysis involving analogies with revisionist accounts of Western policy, of the emerging Cold War serving Stalin's purposes in strengthening internal discipline at a time when the USSR was recovering from its own wartime devastation.[5]

Eastern Europe itself was primarily affected by the conflict between the principle of post-war national self-determination, as asserted in the 1941 Atlantic Charter and the 1945 Yalta 'Declaration of Liberated Europe', and the USSR's insistence on friendly governments in the region. John Lewis Gaddis has argued that Roosevelt never really appreciated the contradiction, while Gian Giacomo Migone, in a stimulating re-reading of the period, has suggested that US policy was never in practice concerned with the status of Eastern Europe, but far more preoccupied with the USA's own priorities in the West. However, there was more to Soviet concerns than the need for a purely military buffer zone. In the historical circumstances described, the Eastern European states could clearly form an important buffer zone against a Western political/economic system on the verge of revival under US hegemony, as well as against any future attempt to invade Russia from the West: hence the Soviet pressure on Poland and Czechoslovakia to refuse Marshall Aid. Stalin was content to see the Western powers resolve the post-war affairs of Greece and Italy to their own satisfaction as long as the Soviet security zone was not threatened (though Germany, as outlined in chapter 2, was always a special case). In the simplest terms, the political demarcation line in Central Europe marked approximately where the eastern and western armies halted in 1945, though Vojtech Mastny has argued that during the war itself, Stalin had no fixed design for establishing Soviet control over the whole eastern area. The consolidation of the Soviet-dominated zone into the Stalinist system took place gradually and at different rates in different countries between 1945 and 1953, though the question of whether this occurred autonomously or partly in response to Western policy is one I have to leave to one side.

I will not dwell further here on these historical disputes, and will simply point out that they encapsulate an entire ongoing and unresolved debate between interpretations of the Cold War as either a clash between competing social systems, or a device for managing intra-bloc relations in the respective camps. Perhaps the most promising direction for reinterpretations of post-1945 Europe lies in Mary Kaldor's critique of the different schools. The orthodox historians, she argues, were bound as realists to focus on Soviet military power, while the more economically-minded revisionists were bound to focus on US economic power, but neither of these approaches on its own could do justice to the complexity of the evolving post-1945 bloc structure. Any satisfactory synthesis will need to reconceptualize the specific forms which capitalism and the states system took after 1945.[6]

In purely military terms, the 'orthodox analysis' of Soviet policy tends to underestimate the significance of the American nuclear monopoly which prevailed until 1949. One recent study has made an assessment that the Soviet armed forces did not have any deliverable nuclear weapons until 1954. We do not know for sure whether these first warheads could be used against the USA itself or against Western Europe. Although the latter may seem more likely, it has also been argued that there was little Soviet interest in tactical nuclear weapons, for use on a European battlefield, until around 1953.[7] US intelligence at the time considered that the USSR had usable weapons before 1954. However, the USA had stationed nuclear bombers capable of striking the Soviet Union in Britain as early as 1948, and it is partly in the light of these considerations that the evolution of the Soviet posture should be assessed. It is true that the US deployments took place during the Berlin crisis, but it is debatable whether they were genuinely a reaction to Soviet policy.[8]

In a period of US monopoly, or when the USSR could retaliate against Western Europe but not the USA, it would have made strong military sense for the USSR to threaten conventional and/or nuclear retaliation against Western Europe, if it saw itself threatened by the USA. To point this out is not to concede the assumption in the 'orthodox analysis' of an immediate post-war Soviet military threat; the posture evolved as one factor in worsening East–West relations, not as the root cause of that breakdown. It was not spelled out at first, though by 1956 Bulganin was using the nuclear threat quite explicitly against Britain and France at the time of Suez. There is also a published account of Stalin planning an attack on Western Europe in 1951, provided by an exiled Czech historian, Karel Kaplan, but this account in itself could not be said to settle the basic political dispute.[9]

The above argument may appear to be a digression, but I hope it makes the point that anyone's analysis of the evolving Soviet and WTO posture in Europe since 1955, and of the military roles assigned to WTO forces, depends on one's assumptions about the controversial preceeding period. It is undeniable that Soviet strategy evolved into an 'offensive–defensive', or hostage-taking, posture against Western Europe, as will be argued below. No one can say for sure that this would not have happened whatever US post-war policy had been, but the posture did not appear in an international system which was otherwise *tabula rasa* and in which the USSR alone was taking initiatives.

I would add one further point about the 'orthodox analysis'. It assumes that the Soviet military posture has been helpful to the USSR by intimidating Western Europe politically even if no blow is ever struck, but even this is questionable. It is far from clear that the appearance and/or reality of a Soviet military threat to Western Europe has helped Soviet foreign policy more than it has hindered it. Western Europeans as a whole might be more inclined than the USA to reach agreements with the USSR because they are less convinced of the reality of 'inherent Soviet expansionism', not because they are more intimidated. Soviet foreign and military policy have not, in my view, been as smoothly aligned with each other as the USSR or its Nato opponents have traditionally argued. This point is developed further in chapter 6.

Having entered these caveats about the problems of discussing Soviet strategy, it is possible to turn to a more substantive treatment of the issue. The first important point is to recognize the weight of military tradition and recent history in influencing Soviet military thought. The experience of the Second World War was bound to create or strengthen a Soviet preference for fighting any future war outside Soviet territory; in the post-1945 situation, this inevitably meant as far to the West as possible, in or beyond the newly-acquired 'buffer zone'. This preference is not wholly a product of the Second World War, however, since the theory of large-scale mobile operations pre-dates 1941 and even 1914, and can easily be explained by a tradition of Russian thinking in terms of mobile offensive–defensive operations to combat foreign adversaries on a flat and open

terrain, where positional defence made little sense. A glance at the output
of the main military publishing house, *Voennoe Izdatel'stvo*, or at any
issue of the Soviet Ministry of Defence's journal *Voenno-Istoricheskii Zhurnal*
(Journal of Military History), will provide eloquent evidence of both these
influences.[10]

In many ways, therefore, it is easy to see how the concept of forward
defence, involving rapid incursions on to enemy territory in the event of
conflict, became a cornerstone of Soviet military strategy in Europe.[11] The
relationship between this strategy and nuclear weapons has varied. In the
1950s and early 1960s, Soviet thinking seems to have assumed that war in
Europe would be nuclear from the outset, or would very rapidly become
nuclear. During this period, the possibilities of victory in nuclear war and
pre-emptive nuclear attack could be found in Soviet military writings, but
from the late 1960s onwards more attention began to be paid to the
possibility of conventional operations at the outset of a future war. In this
period, the emphasis shifted towards viewing Soviet nuclear weapons as a
deterrent to the use of, and if need be a means of pre-empting, Nato's own
after a period of conventional conflict. The increased attention to conventional operations developed in parallel to, or perhaps in response to,
Nato's own shift away from massive retaliation towards flexible response.
At the same time, the possibility of nuclear 'victory' began to be phased
out of publicly-available Soviet writings. Since about 1980, close observers
in the West have detected refinements of these developments in Soviet
thinking, in the shape of particular forms of conventional operations, as in
the much-discussed Operational Manoeuvre Groups. These latest debates
are reviewed in detail in the third section of this chapter.

One does not have to rely solely on Western interpretations to draw up
this picture of certain essential features of Soviet military thinking. Many
of its components are made clear in basic Soviet texts, although important
distinctions are made between the concepts of 'military doctrine', 'military art' and 'military strategy'. (Among the Western interpreters there
are also important differences of view, to which I shall return shortly.)

'Military doctrine' has traditionally been defined as 'the established
views of the state at a given time on the aims and character of a possible
war, on the preparation of the country and armed forces for war, and also
on the methods of waging it'. There are two sides to military doctrine, the
political and the military-technical, of which the political side is 'leading',
and it is said that 'Soviet military doctrine takes an exclusively defensive
direction, and its chief feature is the defence of the socialist fatherland.'
On the military-technical side of doctrine, however, the importance of
carrying the war on to the opponent's territory is recognized, and it is said
that: 'Together with the offensive as the decisive form of military actions,
[Soviet doctrine] also recognizes the legitimacy of the defence at the

strategic, operational and tactical level. However, Soviet military doctrine considers the defence to be a temporary and enforced form of military actions, which can be used . . . when . . . it is necessary to win time for . . . the creation of conditions for the subsequent transition to a decisive offensive.'[12]

'Military science' is the 'system of knowledge about the character and laws of war and the methods of conducting it'. 'Military art', a subheading of 'military science', is the 'theory and practice of the preparation and conduct of military actions on land, at sea, and in the air'. Soviet military art is described as having developed with the use of deep operations, encirclement and rapid breakthroughs; in addition, 'the offensive' is characterized as 'the basic form of military actions', while 'the defence' is only 'a form of military actions'.[13]

These concepts have been widely and publicly acknowledged; in early 1987, the English-language edition of *Soviet Military Review* carried a 'tactical glossary' describing offensive battle as the main way of achieving victory, with defensive combat considered as suitable for providing conditions for going over to the offensive.[14] They also seem to have been preserved through successive phases of Soviet thinking on the use of nuclear weapons, though Soviet texts have not always tried to make such a clear distinction between a defensive doctrine and offensive military concepts. The most widely-quoted text remains Marshal Sokolovsky's *Military Strategy*, whose successive editions in 1962, 1963 and 1968 shifted slightly towards consideration of conventional operations, but which posited a requirement for Soviet superiority over the potential aggressor, and argued that victory could be achieved through the actions of mass armies even in a nuclear war. Offensive operations are considered here to be of greater importance than defensive operations, though the purpose of preparation for nuclear war is its prevention, following the classic paradox of 'nuclear deterrence'.[15] (The book also claimed that the USSR *had* superiority, which Sokolovsky and his contributors must have known to be false.)

Another text from the same period, Sidorenko's *The Offensive*, also attributes decisive significance to the offensive, while distinguishing this from any aggressive intention to attack the West. The book paints a horrifying picture of the need to prepare for combat involving high manoeuvrability and on broad axes in conditions when nuclear weapons are being used.[16] Indeed, it is noticeable that both Sokolovsky and Sidorenko go out of their way to stress the continuing importance of all branches of the Soviet armed forces in nuclear combat; one can perhaps see this as part of a continuing response to the attempts in the Khrushchev period to downgrade the other services at the expense of the Strategic Rocket Forces.

The assumption of the possibility of victory grew weaker during the 1970s, and more attention was paid to conventional operations (albeit with continued stress on the dangers and possibility of nuclear escalation). This switching of attention towards conventional operations can be traced both through theoretical writings and through the evidence of Soviet and joint WTO exercises, from around 1969 onwards.[17] Even so, the Soviet commitment to large-scale mobile operations did not disappear. Here is Marshal Nikolai Ogarkov writing in 1981, in what has been interpreted as a reference in keeping with the command structure reorganization examined in chapter 3: 'In this connection, not frontal operations, but a wider-scale form of military actions, the strategic operation in a theatre of military action, should be examined as the basic operation in a future war.' The Soviet armed forces are said to be capable of conducting 'not only defensive, but also modern offensive operations on the ground, in the air, and at sea'.[18] In Ogarkov's 1985 'comeback' pamphlet, *Istoriya uchit bditel'nosti* (*History Teaches Vigilance*), he again spoke of offensive combat and deep operations within a defensive military doctrine as important parts of Soviet military tradition.[19]

The controversial Ogarkov was not alone in continuing to elaborate these concepts, though he is perhaps the most frequently cited. After Ogarkov's transfer, his successor, Marshal Akhromeev, repeated the gist of Ogarkov's remarks about the increased importance of conventional weaponry, though without linking this point explicitly to offensive operations.[20] Colonel-General Gareev, a Deputy Chief of General Staff, has argued that while technological superiority is not important, superiority in military art is (perhaps by way of admitting the impossibility of technological superiority over the West): 'But a defensive military doctrine, far from precluding, also presupposes high combat readiness for retaliatory strikes and offensive, decisive actions of our armed forces should an aggressor decide to attack us. We do not strive for superior military technology, but we will do everything, as during the Great Patriotic War, so that we not only do not give way, but ensure the superiority in military art of our military cadres and in the combat skills of our personnel. This is one of the inexhaustible sources for increasing the fighting efficiency of the army and navy without any additional material expenditures.'[21] In his 1985 book on Frunze, Gareev summarized the defensive–offensive relationship as follows: 'The defensive character of [Soviet] military doctrine does not exclude either a high level of military preparedness in the Armed Forces, or active offensive actions against an aggressor, should he carry out an attack on our country or its allies.'[22]

The object of outlining traditional formulations of Soviet strategy in this way is not to offer direct support for any particular Western interpretation of Soviet political objectives. This basic summary of certain key aspects of military thinking seems to me to be consistent with a number of analyses of conceivable Soviet aims, and the next task is to assess the relative plausibility of these options. The traditional Soviet understanding of the relationship between offence and defence seemed to be placed in question from 1986 onwards, and these developments are discussed in chapter 6. For the time being, however, I am concentrating on the range of alternative explanations offered for the historical development of post-1945 Soviet thinking. There would seem to be five contending interpretations in the Western literature:

1 Invasion and occupation of Western Europe, or the use of such a threat to 'Sovietize' or 'Finlandize' the region.
2 War-avoidance, and deterrence of the USA from attacking the Soviet Union by means of a threat to retaliate at an early stage against Western Europe; this posture was maintained after the Soviet Union was able to retaliate against the USA itself, and maintained its importance as the focus shifted towards conventional strategies.
3 Deterrence of West Germany or other European powers from intervention in Eastern Europe.
4 Maintenance of Soviet control of Eastern Europe, and the prevention of territorial defence by Eastern European states.
5 No identifiable goal beyond the sheer inertia of Soviet military institutions, which are unable to shake off the traditional adherence to the offensive.

These possibilities are obviously not alternatives in the sense of being mutually exclusive, and one might even support them all simultaneously as contributions to Soviet policy. One does not have to attribute total coherence to Soviet policy; it could be over-determined, confused and/or inconsistent, the product of competing internal and external influences.

Even so, the weight given to these different possibilities will depend on the interpreter's preconceptions, most importantly about both the nature of the Cold War, and the legitimacy of Soviet fears of the West. Perhaps the most central contenders in the Western debate are descriptions (1) and (2). I propose to examine them by taking Christopher Donnelly and Michael MccGwire as the two main protagonists, and hope thereby to shed some light both on Soviet policy and on the nature of the Western debate.

Christopher Donnelly has become one of the principal commentators on the development in Soviet conventional strategy identified as the Operational Manoeuvre Group (OMG) concept, while Michael MccGwire has developed his alternative analysis of Soviet military objectives as part of a more general critique of Western security thinking and its reliance on 'nuclear deterrence'. They write, of course, from differing institutional bases; Donnelly from the Royal Military Academy at Sandhurst, and MccGwire from the Brookings Institution. Thus one is writing primarily for a British and Nato military audience, and the other from a civilian think-tank on the liberal wing of the American debate. There is therefore a reversal of the more familiar divergence between American 'hawk' and European 'dove', though MccGwire, as a European liberal intervening in the US debate, may see himself in the first instance as challenging prevalent American ideas rather than those of a British military analyst like Donnelly.

Since Donnelly and MccGwire might not accept that their respective views are as opposed to each other as I am suggesting, I will sketch out what I take to be their essential arguments.[23] They share an awareness of the importance of Soviet historical experience, and draw from this the conclusion that the avoidance of war, and especially of nuclear war, is a top priority for the USSR. From this it is seen to follow that *if* a war between East and West *is* fought, the USSR needs to ensure a speedy victory in Europe, by conventional means if possible. Donnelly describes the OMG development as an attempt to work out a strategy which can defeat Nato conventionally, before Nato can respond to a Soviet attack by using nuclear weapons. Donnelly would not, I think, rest his case solely on the operational capabilities of OMGs for conventional deep-strike operations, but would add arguments about combined arms operations and the Soviet need to ensure surprise by various deception techniques. MccGwire also sees a Soviet hope of defeating Nato in Europe, as the first phase of a possible two-phase war with the West. (In both cases, the strategy is understood to be put into operation only if war becomes inevitable, though there are differences over what this amounts to.) MccGwire's account of a hypothetical attempt to defeat Nato in Europe is described as an attempt to establish a Soviet 'defense perimeter',[24] which would deny the US a bridgehead in Europe, and seek to avoid provoking nuclear attack on the USSR itself by not attacking North America.

So far the two accounts have identifiable similarities, and they both imply that the existing Nato strategy of flexible response does give the USSR some slender expectation of being able to carry out the strategy. MccGwire says this explicitly, but as part of his general critique of 'nuclear deterrence' rather than as an argument for, say, returning to massive retaliation. He also characterizes the Soviet strategy as having emerged as a response to Nato's flexible response planning. Donnelly does not say it in so many words, but one can, I think, read between the lines a certain dissatisfaction with flexible response as it has existed. The important difference between the two accounts lies in their divergent views of the wider political context in which Soviet military strategy should be seen.

For Donnelly, the unquestioned long-term Soviet foreign policy goal is taken to be the communization of Europe by stealth. The military strategy is seen as a kind of back-up to this policy, and the question arises of precisely how the military strategy relates to the political goal. Donnelly's 1985 pamphlet expresses the point as follows: 'The Politburo, therefore, is pursuing a policy of communizing Europe at the moment by peaceful means: subversion, espionage, political manoeuvring and pressures, economic activity – that is, anything which falls short of armed hostilities';[25] and: 'War and peace, to any communist leader, are only alternative tools for achieving all-important objectives of a policy, and to any communist leader the all-important policy is and remains the establishment of communism (of his own particular brand) throughout the world. No ideological or pseudo-intellectual argument, however well-meaning, must be allowed to obscure this essential point. Equally vital is to understand that, to a true communist, the triumph of communism is inevitable, and can only be hastened or delayed, not prevented.'[26]

Now, this may or may not be correct. In my view it is a superficial treatment of East–West relations, and the assertion that any disagreement is 'pseudo-intellectual' is disturbing. The immediate question to be answered, however, is the relationship of these arguments to Donnelly's characterization of Soviet military strategy, and here there seems to be a crucial gap in his case. It is not clear whether the offensive features of the military strategy are to be taken as evidence *for* the offensive nature of Soviet foreign policy in general, or whether, since the offensive foreign policy is a given, the offensive military strategy must support it. Presumably the latter argument is what Donnelly means, since he does say that though the WTO does not want a war, the existence of a strong military force is in itself intimidatory. (In this sense Donnelly is not a straightforward advocate of the 'invasion or occupation' variant of my option (1).) But this in turn is problematic, partly because he assumes the offensive foreign policy but does not argue for it, and partly because the connection is not self-evidently true. Has Soviet military strength been a factor which has intimidated Western Europe into submission or into opposition? As likely as Donnelly's argument is the suggestion that Western European states do *not* see the USSR as inherently politically expansionist (at least, not in the way that many in the USA do), but will continue to co-operate in military opposition to the USSR as long as it is the major Eurasian military power. Conceivably the Soviet leadership may believe, or have believed, along with Donnelly, in the intimidatory potential of their military power for communizing Europe, but it is by no means clear that they would have been right to do so. If the military posture *is* a back-up to the political strategy, then one has to be able to identify political means of wielding the threat convincingly, or it is no more than a bluff.

Donnelly's reply to my criticisms would, I suspect, be that his discussions of operational military planning, OMGs, etc., do not require or entail any particular set of political assumptions, and that I have placed too much emphasis on a nonexistent link between two distinct arguments. In reply, I would say that while it is perfectly true that there is no entailment from the one sphere to the other, that is precisely the problem, since the passages from Donnelly I have quoted do seem to make that connection. It is true that the paper I have quoted is untypical among Donnelly's writings in its more detailed analysis of Soviet foreign policy, since most of them do stick more narrowly to military questions – but, once again, that fact makes the relationship between the two arguments all the more important to pin down.

Similar problems exist with other analyses which follow the same general pattern as Donnelly's. P. H. Vigor's analysis in *Soviet Blitzkrieg Theory* appears to be careful to limit itself to dealing with likely Soviet strategy in the hypothetical event of a Soviet decision to attack Nato, but at no stage does he offer any substantial account of the political circumstances which might produce such a decision.[27] At one point he even seems to be arguing that there could be no Soviet political action which could count as evidence that the USSR was *not* intending to attack Nato, thus invalidating his own general caution.[28] This tendency to focus on Soviet operational planning at the expense of political objectives or intentions is not confined to Donnelly and Vigor, but can be found more widely in mainstream Western literature.[29] It has come under criticism not only from radical critics of Nato, but also from Michael MccGwire, to whose critique I will now turn.

As has been seen, MccGwire does not take issue with a Donnelly-type analysis of Soviet operational thinking *per se*. His challenge is to Western strategic analysis in a wider sense, since he is concerned to question the assumption of a Soviet urge to expand into Western Europe by means of military conquest, and to expose the contradictions in Western deterrence theory which this basic mistake has led to.[30] Against this, he sets his alternative analysis of Soviet strategic objectives as concerns motivated by the goal of war-avoidance if possible, and the avoidance of defeat and nuclear attack on the USSR if war seems inevitable. Up to a point, it could be argued that Donnelly is not MccGwire's primary target, since Donnelly could reply that he does not postulate a Soviet war of conquest in Western Europe, merely a politically expansionist disposition backed up by an offensive military strategy, and would agree that the latter is only to be used if war looks inevitable.

Even so, MccGwire is clearly challenging Donnelly along with others in a methodological sense. He writes: 'That mindset [i.e. deterrence theory] encourages us to ignore Soviet political-military doctrine about the restricted circumstances in which a conflict might justifiably be initiated (none of which can be met by a premeditated attack) and to focus instead on Soviet operational doctrine about how such a war might be fought and won.'[31] This misleading focus he identifies with the 'colonel's fallacy', the carrying out of threat assessment at the wrong level of analysis. (He also points out that the hope of not losing if war is inescapable is shared by the West, but the fact is not a very reliable guide to political intentions.) Such a charge does seem to be a challenge to Donnelly, given the latter's insistence on the importance of the operational level of Soviet military planning as one to which Western military establishments have paid insufficient attention. MccGwire observes: 'NATO military planners are required to ask not "Is there a threat?" but "Where is the threat?".'[32] Donnelly, fairly certainly, falls within the category which MccGwire calls 'the keepers of the threat'.

There would also be substantive disagreements between MccGwire and Donnelly over the source of the danger of war. MccGwire associates himself fairly clearly with the Soviet view that there is a danger that war could arise from an uncontrollable chain of events as much as from a deliberate decision to attack, which he contrasts with a US view 'that war could only come about through some Soviet initiative that the West had failed to deter'.[33] Donnelly, one can surmise, would lean towards the US view here, and there is no evidence that he would accept MccGwire's injunction to 'avoid the assumption that US intentions are self-evidently benevolent'.[34]

This cautionary comment on US policy is of course fairly mild in tone, and falls well short of the analysis which would be offered by a Soviet commentator or many more radical critics of US policy. MccGwire's own thesis rests on his identification of a clear shift in Soviet assumptions in late 1966, away from an assumption that war would inevitably lead to a nuclear attack on the USSR, to a view that it might be possible to deter the USA from initiating a nuclear exchange.[35] This was accompanied by a gradual reassessment which began earlier, and saw the danger to Soviet security lying less in premeditated Western attack than in the risks of nuclear escalation from a conventional conflict. (MccGwire shares with a number of others a general view of significant shifts in the late 1960s, but his own account is very specific.) From this he derives his account of the objective of establishing an 'extended defense perimeter' including Western Europe in the event of war, clearly in the context of a policy of war-avoidance though still within a theory of a struggle between two competing social systems. The role of nuclear forces is described as that of deterring Nato's own use of nuclear weapons, in part by insisting publicly that any US nuclear attack on the Soviet Union would result in retaliation against the USA itself. This Soviet posture is not seen as entirely ruling out the possibility that a nuclear war might need to be fought, but it does carry the implications that (a) nuclear pre-emption by the Soviet Union is not contemplated, and (b) as long as strategic reductions are balanced on the US and Soviet sides, cuts in nuclear weapons can benefit Soviet security.[36]

MccGwire's analysis suggests a downwards revision of the Soviet assessment of the threat from the West, due to increased Soviet strength. However, any view which took seriously Soviet views of a security threat from Western nuclear weapons, particularly in terms of the mid-1980s deployments of cruise Europe, could quite easily accommodate MccGwire's account of Soviet strategy as having evolved in reaction to an external threat rather than as an intimidatory instrument.[37] One of the weakest points of Donnelly's analysis is the exclusion, almost by definition, of the possibility that the operational developments he describes so thoroughly might be reactive as well as, or rather than, assertive. One could also argue that the more threatened the USSR feels, the more reason it has to devise military options on the lines Donnelly identifies, but that this does not in itself carry implications about political intentions.

There have been other analyses supportive of MccGwire's general line of argument which have emerged in recent years from mainstream writers on strategic affairs, in addition to the more radical challenges to Nato policy. Among those who have followed MccGwire in distancing themselves from more alarmist work are Michael Howard and (at times) John Erickson. Howard has usefully refocused attention on to Soviet political concerns in a way which, I would suggest, is not too far removed from the more radical work of the Alternative Defence Commission.[38] The difference between them is that Howard is unwilling to challenge nuclear deterrence as such, but his analysis of the USSR's chief political concerns is not very different from the ADC's. In the case of John Erickson the position is a little more complicated. In 1978 Erickson was writing about the USSR's 'drive for control of the Eurasian land mass',[39] but he then apparently reacted against the hair-raising rhetoric of the first Reagan administration by presenting a more doveish view of Soviet nuclear thinking.[40] A 1985 article seemed to be a rather uncomfortable mixture of the two approaches,[41] while a 1986 publication saw a return to a fully-fledged 'colonel's fallacy' treatment.[42]

It is clear that MccGwire has contributed already to a wide-ranging reassessment of Soviet policy, and that that reassessment brings with it an implicit debate about the Cold War as system. Nevertheless, MccGwire's analysis of Soviet strategy and policy is not entirely convincing and unproblematic.

The documentary evidence which MccGwire adduces in support of his location of the shift in Soviet planning at December 1966 is painstakingly presented, but not overwhelming.[43] No doubt there will be detailed responses to his argument, but it is not clear that his evidence is strong enough to support the argument's entire weight. A more general problem seems to be the high degree of rationality and coherence which he attributes to Soviet planning.

MccGwire is disposed to accept a straightforward rational actor model of decision-making in the Soviet Union, with planners reassessing the global military confrontation and coming to clear and rational decisions. But do we really know this to be the case? It is obviously quite possible that Soviet policy-making is more reactive and clear-cut than the West's, but MccGwire seems to rule out any real possibility that factors akin to bureaucratic politics and inter-service rivalry operate in the Soviet Union. MccGwire himself says he has chosen to concentrate on why certain decisions were made rather than how, but this begs the question. For example, since one of the elements in the policy MccGwire describes seems to be a renewed and reinforced emphasis on the status of the Ground Forces, and since there is evidence (reviewed below) of continued conflicts of view over questions like the military utility of nuclear weapons, his implied picture of smooth, streamlined decision-making and consequent unanimity looks oversimplified. He does deal briefly with inter-service rivalry with reference to the Soviet navy, but not really in such a way as to convince the reader that the issue as a general problem has been adequately considered and ruled out. There is, perhaps, something of a parallel here with MccGwire's earlier work on Soviet naval policy, which made many of the same basic assumptions about rationality.[44] The one-dimensional nature of his decision-making model in *Military Objectives in Soviet Foreign Policy* was legitimately criticized by reviewers of the book, though they did not always summarize all his views accurately.[45]

Another problem lies in the practical difficulties of actually fighting the sort of war MccGwire describes. The likelihood of escalation to intercontinental nuclear exchanges from any conflict is not only a fear voiced frequently by Soviet sources, but a fact of life, as the Western literature on nuclear command and control demonstrates.[46] One of the most clearly identifiable threads in Soviet statements on disarmament during recent years has been the fear that decision-making on war and peace will pass out of the hands of politicians and over to automated systems, which can surely be considered a genuinely Clausewitzian position in the nuclear age. Furthermore, if Soviet planners have been keeping up with US naval literature, as they surely have, they will know that the USA's forward naval strategies of the 1980s imply early attacks on Soviet strategic missile-carrying submarines, and thus little chance of keeping these forces out of the early stages of a war. Even though the US Navy itself may not have the forces necessary to *carry out* its maritime strategy, its dangers even on the drawing-board are all too apparent.[47]

It is therefore hard to see how Soviet planners could rationally believe the strategy described to be practicable, though illogicality can hardly be considered a proof of the non-existence of a given military strategy. MccGwire can partly meet this criticism by saying that however impracticable the strategy he describes may appear, its basic impulse (avoiding nuclear attack on the Soviet Union) is such a high priority that even a faint chance of success is better than nothing. Another problem, however, is that he pays comparatively little attention to European political factors, since he concentrates on the global military confrontation. This has not been the case in all his writing, in the sense that some of his articles have added to their critique of 'nuclear deterrence' some perceptive remarks about the domestic political role of the concept. He has written: 'It [deterrence doctrine] has become a buzzword, a political pacifier that can be used to explain all kinds of policy, to justify any weapons program or operational deployment, and to stifle all dissent'[48] and 'deterrence theory has had a lasting and damaging effect on domestic attitudes. This is the sphere in which its effects have probably been most pernicious.'[49]

Some of the weight and potential of these comments was lost in *Military Objectives in Soviet Foreign Policy*, and the comparative neglect of European politics was one consequence. His treatment in that book put to one side the possibility that 'deterrence' may not really be 'about' the Soviet Union at all, but 'about' domestic or intra-alliance politics, and he concentrated instead on the revision of analyses of the Soviet Union. But in so doing, he filtered out a whole range of important factors like the role of 'deterrence' in sustaining transatlantic relations between the USA and Western Europe,[50] and on the other side not only the influence of Germany and Eastern Europe on Soviet approaches, but also the possibility of examining whether the political functioning of deterrence doctrine has any counterpart on the Soviet side. (Interestingly enough, the downplaying of these arguments in MccGwire's 1987 book softened the contrast between his views and Donnelly's.)

MccGwire's work has certainly served an important purpose in challenging more orthodox conceptions. There remains, however, a risk that a geostrategic approach like MccGwire's may miss some of the subtleties of European security politics and of Soviet institutional specificities, and in so far as that is the case, his account shares a weakness with numerous others written from within the US debate, on both right and left. Perhaps the root of the problem is that MccGwire has set out to challenge a prevailing view of the USSR as rational and malevolent, and has done a fairly successful job of challenging the malevolence claim, but in doing so has held the rationality assumption constant, which is less convincing. For the purposes of the discussion which follows in chapter 6 of this study, it is worth recording MccGwire's concluding comment on the role of offensive operations in the Soviet posture: 'one can conclude that NATO has no alternative to living with Soviet forces that are structured for offensive operations against Western Europe, but that the assertiveness of the threat will diminish as the Soviets think war less likely.'[51]

The Eastern Europeans

The need to focus principally on Soviet forces in explaining WTO military strategy should not result in the complete neglect of Eastern European military roles and views of Soviet strategy. Near the beginning of his book on the Warsaw Pact southern tier, Ivan Volgyes makes a daunting comment which refers to the roles of the Eastern Europeans throughout the WTO: 'Perhaps for no other component can we find so little evidence as for the military doctrine regarding the mission of the armed forces within the Warsaw Pact as a whole.'[52] However, piecing together information about the likely roles in wartime of the various WTO armed forces is not entirely a lost cause. Evidence can be gathered from exercises, from the nature and quantity of equipment in the forces' inventories, and from military publications monitored extensively by Western experts and intelligence services. The results need to be interpreted with care, but there is enough material to make the attempt worthwhile.

We have already seen how Eastern European units appear to be closely integrated with Soviet forces at a fairly low level of command, and how the lack of access of Eastern Europeans to the highest command levels makes it doubtful whether they can exercise much influence on the most important questions of strategic organization, in spite of their increased role in policy discussion since 1969. The role of the Eastern European forces in the WTO military posture has always been a secondary one. At the time of the 1960s equipment modernization programme and initiation of training in 'coalition warfare', the Eastern European armies were equipped with some nuclear-capable weapon systems (Su-7s, SCUD and FROG missiles), and trained for warfare in nuclear conditions. Some Western commentators have considered that they were trained to use nuclear warheads as well as to fight in nuclear conditions, but majority opinion has doubted that they have ever possessed nuclear warheads for these weapons or would be given them in wartime. If this is correct, it indicates a sharp difference between the WTO and Nato, and a clear subordination of the WTO to Soviet strategy and doctrine on the possible use of nuclear weapons. A representative Soviet source comments that 'It is also important that the armies of the allied countries should be guided by the same military and strategic concepts, the same principles of military development.'[53]

As far as the command structure is concerned, the overall picture seems to be that Eastern European units in Central Europe would support Soviet operations as part of Soviet commands, and the relative degree of responsibility borne by the different armed forces seems to be indicated by their readiness levels. One of the main tasks of Soviet military representatives in Eastern Europe is thought to be the precise assessment of the role each unit can be allotted in the event of war. In one or two cases, however, it is worth picking out certain respects in which official Eastern European security thinking has sought to distance itself from the prevailing Soviet concepts.

The clearest example of this was in Czechoslovakia during the mid-1960s, when shifts in thinking among the military were influenced by a number of considerations: leanings towards detente with the FRG as the Cold War ebbed; discontent with Soviet political domination of the WTO machinery; and a general concern that Soviet strategy in Central Europe had scant regard for Czechoslovakia's own interests. Some of these concerns were similar to sentiments voiced by Romania in the mid-1960s. The Czech concerns emerged in mid-1968 in the shape of the Gottwald Memorandum, drafted by officers at the Gottwald Academy, and the press conference given in July by Lt-General Prchlik, the head of the Central Committee military affairs department. The content of the Gottwald Academy's proposals included the development of a specifically Czechoslovakian national defence doctrine, a Central European security system which might involve agreements with the FRG and conceivably neutrality, and a call for public discussion of Czechoslovakia's security needs. In addition, reforms proposed within the army would have reduced party supervision and increased governmental control. Some of these ideas were included in the unpublished Action Programme intended for the 14th Party Congress. Along with Prchlik's very specific complaints about Soviet domination of the WTO and the unwanted presence of Soviet troops supposed to be 'manoeuvring' on Czech territory, such developments seem to have alarmed the USSR and added weight to the arguments in favour of military intervention.[54]

It is not really clear whether Czech worries included concern about actual Soviet strategies. Alexander Alexiev argues that Czech military circles were worried about Soviet strategy involving limited nuclear options in Central Europe, but quotes a commentary from the period which looks more like a worry about the Soviet security guarantee not being good in a crisis, reminiscent of de Gaulle's query about the US guarantee to Western Europe.[55] In any case, worries about vulnerability in any form would be quite understandable for a small Central European state like Czechoslovakia. The USSR, with no forces in Czechoslovakia prior to 1968, had encountered resistance from the Czech leadership earlier when it had tried to impress on them the need to fill the gap in the WTO defences. This indicates that the Czech fears were not simply a product of the liberal Dubcek leadership, but were quite rational fears for any Czech to entertain. One Czech source has claimed that this Soviet pressure resulted in the stationing of some nuclear weapons on Czech soil at some point in the 1960s, under the command of the Strategic Rocket Forces.[56]

Although Czechoslovakia's experimental thinking was interrupted in 1968, it seems likely that fears of being turned into a particularly vulnerable nuclear target area may have been reawakened by the 1983 Soviet counterdeployments of Soviet missiles in the country. This would account for the muted expressions of concern which were mentioned in chapter 2.

The history of Polish involvement in WTO military doctrine indicates some degree of specialization. The Polish Army seems to have had responsibility, in theory at least, for an external front with a mission against northern German and Denmark – though the recent reorganization into TVDs may have affected this. In addition, part of the Polish army has traditionally been designated as 'Defence of National Territory' (OTK) troops, a role which involves a combination of air defence, civil defence, resisting enemy penetration and internal security.[57] Johnson's view is that there has been a considerable gap between the theory of OTK and the practical preparation for it, but one can see why Poland might develop such a concept. Poland is not as vulnerable as the GDR, but it is nevertheless a clear target for extensive Nato nuclear and conventional bombing in the event of war, a consideration as strong today as it must have been in the 1950s. However, the OTK concept was developed as part of a strategy for securing a strategic rear area, rather than purely as a territorial defence and, as mentioned in chapter 2, provided much of the legislative apparatus for the declaration of martial law in December 1981.[58]

In Poland's case, the awareness of vulnerability and concern for self-protection comes out in the 1958 Rapacki Plan, which was also referred to in chapter 2. Rapacki seems to have seen it as a way of using Poland to bridge the gulf between the Soviet Union and Germany, and to have been motivated by the same concerns about the vulnerability of Central–Eastern Europe which prompted the Czechoslovakian would-be reformers a few years later. It is curious that while most Western writers consider that the plan would have served Soviet interests by establishing a nuclear-free West Germany (as well as GDR, Poland and Czechoslovakia), others

argue that the Soviet Union had mixed feelings about it because it would
have restricted Soviet freedom of action and prevented a nuclearization
which the Soviet Union also planned. Since the Western governments
rejected the Rapacki Plan, we may never know, but it remains a monu-
ment to the perilous situation of the Central European states on either side
of the bloc divide.

Enough has been said already about Romanian defence policy to
indicate that it does not fit the standard WTO pattern, and that Romanian forces are in practice not available to the WTO command. The
structure of the Romanian armed forces also supports a fundamentally
territorial concept of defence, but investment in the air force and navy
seems to have been at the expense of spending on the army, and Romania's military strength as conventionally measured has never been great,
and so has been no great loss to the WTO.[59]

To get some idea of the limitations of Eastern European forces within the
WTO, it is worth identifying some of the military roles allotted to Soviet
forces in the European theatre which Eastern European forces clearly
have no part in.

They would play no part in Soviet operations in northern Scandinavia,
which can be seen as partly strategic operations in view of the importance
of the Kola peninsula to Soviet strategic nuclear forces. The Eastern
European forces have only a limited naval capacity to support the three
Soviet fleets based in the western USSR. The Eastern Europeans have no
long-range bombers which could bomb.British or French ports and carry
out the mission of cutting Western Europe off from the USA, and they
almost certainly have no nuclear bombs or warheads for the systems in
their inventories which *are* nuclear-capable. Their chief contributions to
the WTO consist of air defence capacity, in which area only Romania's
role is questionable, and conventional ground force strength, to which the
three northern tier states in particular make valuable contributions in
spite of a significant lag in modernization of equipment. These are not
negligible contributions to the WTO's military division of labour, and
should not be overlooked, even though this study has not gone into the
question of political reliability in any detail.

As in the sphere of command structures, changes in WTO military
strategy would seem to implemented at a level above that at which
Eastern European forces play a major role. However, it seems likely that
the strategic importance of Eastern territory has, if anything, increased
again in the period described by both Donnelly and MccGwire as involving renewed attention to conventional operations in the 'European
theatre'. There is some evidence that Eastern European forces, as well as
Soviet ones, have been trained and exercised in Operational Manoeuvre

Group-type formations, in particular in exercises held in 1982 in Poland and Bulgaria,[60] but their more likely role in wartime would be for 'holding' operations behind front-line Soviet forces.

This can be seen as an illustration of a long-term military development visible in both East and West. Once the problems of making a posture based on the immediate use of nuclear weapons look credible became apparent, military thinking on both sides turned back towards earlier concepts of mobility and deep strike operations. These plans may be quite irrational, given the enormous number of nuclear weapons in the inventories and the likelihood of their being used, but at the planning level that irrationality can be pushed to one side. Following the renewed emphasis on mobile operations, possession and capture of territory regained some of the importance it was in danger of losing in the period of assuming immediate nuclear use, and so the Soviet position in Eastern Europe retained its major military as well as political importance.

In terms of an assessment of the purposes of the WTO, it becomes clear from an examination of military strategy that an analysis purely on the internal lines summarized earlier as alternative (4) (see page 77) is inadequate. WTO strategy as it affects Eastern Europe may well prevent territorial defence, but it does more than that. Through a variety of devices, some of which give a degree of notional commitment to national defence (as in the case of Poland), WTO military strategy docs try to organize Eastern European forces into effective support in areas of vital importance for Soviet military operations. The next question which needs to be addressed is how far current Soviet strategy admits the possibility of nuclear operations, or whether that possibility has been entirely ruled out in favour of conventional strategies.

Nuclear and conventional developments

Strictly speaking, the debate over Soviet nuclear and conventional planning should be conducted as a sub-argument within that over the 'colonel's fallacy', since a shift from nuclear to conventional planning would be compatible with either Donnelly or MccGwire's general accounts of Soviet political objectives. A discussion of these developments can, however, be useful as a background to Soviet disarmament policy and the possibility of alternative security concepts, which are the concerns of chapters 5 and 6.

It has already been argued that the past fifteen years (at least) have seen major shifts away from Soviet claims about the possibility of victory in a nuclear war, and that military planning has paid more attention to conventional operations since the late 1960s. It was also argued within the

Western debate that the Soviet commitment to No-First-Use of nuclear weapons, made in 1982, was tantamount to a further acceptance of Mutually Assured Destruction and a signal that the Soviet Union had no interest in nuclear war-fighting. However, it is also still argued either that a nuclear war-fighting strategy is retained 'in reserve', or that the political consensus against war-fighting is not shared throughout the Soviet military establishment.

In its simplest form, this debate has been presented as being over whether the Soviet Union now 'accepts' Western conceptions of deterrence, and it has all too often been conducted in terms which suggest that the nature of Western 'deterrence' policy is commonly agreed and unproblematic.[61] Setting that difficulty aside, the most convincing accounts written during the early 1980s led to the conclusion that while the Soviet Union was well aware of the paradoxes and problems of deterrence, it had no more coherent view than the West on the relationship between war-prevention and the preparations for fighting wars which war-prevention was seen as requiring.[62]

The Pentagon's published view of Soviet planning in 1988 was that 'Soviet military doctrine now recognizes that neither strategic nuclear nor conventional forces are by themselves "decisive", but that they only achieve their maximum effectiveness in concert. The Soviets have spent great resources to modernize and expand their conventional forces, while continuing to expand their strategic nuclear and offensive forces, stressing their ability to fight under both nuclear and conventional conditions.'[63] Other treatments have debated recent Soviet planning by focusing on the views and role of Marshal Ogarkov, with various arguments to the effect that he was dismissed for continuing to insist on the possibility of nuclear war-fighting in defiance of Ustinov; that he did not abandon his belief in victory in nuclear war; and that he (and others) have genuinely moved the focus of their attention towards the option of fighting a possibly prolonged war with advanced conventional weapons. One of the texts most frequently cited as evidence for Ogarkov's belief in the possibility of victory in nuclear war is his contribution on 'Military Strategy' to volume 7 of the *Soviet Military Encyclopaedia*, and this passage is certainly uncompromising in its assertion of the possibility of victory.[64] A close reading of Ogarkov's often-quoted 1985 publication, however, suggests that though he was unwilling to abandon the dictum that 'victory is possible' in war, he saw it as *militarily incompetent* to think that war could be fought effectively with limited nuclear strikes, a charge which could conceivably be aimed at Soviet as well as Western opponents.

Some of his key passages from 1985 read as follows: 'Military actions will be conducted simultaneously across wide areas, and distinguished by unprecedented destruction, will have a high-manoeuvre, dynamic character and will continue until complete victory over the enemy'; 'The military-technical content of Soviet military doctrine . . . envisages the conduct of active, decisive military actions involving the military might of the state and its armed forces until the complete rout of the aggressor, if he attempts to encroach upon our country'; and, referring to US plans described as being for a limited but decapitating strike, 'Such adventuristic, militarily incompetent reasoning is completely groundless. The purveyors of such ignorant conceptions must be unmasked. They are dangerous.'[65]

One should not put undue emphasis on Ogarkov's views alone or assume that they are internally fully coherent, but it is still worth noticing that:

(a) his insistence that a disarming first-strike is impossible seems to imply that he does not regard SDI as a first-strike threat (or didn't in 1985 – he does not mention SDI in this pamphlet);

(b) he makes a number of comments on the possibility of prolonged conventional war, and calls for heightened capacity, and so could well be interpreted as maintaining his earlier insistence on the need for higher spending on conventional weapons.

If Ogarkov's new argument about the military disutility of nuclear weapons was a genuinely-held belief, he was fully in tune with Gorbachev's disarmament diplomacy on this point. He may, however, have been polemicizing with internal opponents in military circles. The political leadership evidently took very seriously the statement made by Reagan and Gorbachev at Geneva in November 1985, that nuclear war could never be won and must never be fought. This statement seems to have been considered of equivalent weight to the 1972 Statement of Basic Principles of Mutual Relations between the USA and USSR.[66]

There is certainly evidence that there is not total agreement on this view in the Soviet Union, and that Ogarkov may have been challenging domestic opponents who may have included Colonel-General Gareev, author of the book on Frunze mentioned earlier, or Marshal Kulikov, then WTO C-in-C.[67] Again, these debates are not hidden from view, and are hinted at even in publications such as the Soviet Peace Committee's English-language journal. In a 1986 interview with Nikita Moiseev, an academician involved in Soviet work on the nuclear winter hypothesis, the interviewer said: 'Even in our country not everyone – alas – yet understands the inevitability of universal demise in the event of conflict.'[68] An outspoken attack on unnamed parties who still insisted that socialism could defeat capitalism in a nuclear war was published in early 1987, by G. A. Trofimenko of the US–Canada Institute, and similar exchanges took place in early 1988.[69]

If one accepts something like MccGwire's description of a two-tier strategy which retains nuclear forces but does not envisage using them early on, if at all, then clearly the basic dilemmas will not disappear as long as the USA and Soviet Union (or anyone else) possess nuclear weapons. However, the existence of Soviet military thinkers who are more reluctant than Ogarkov to accept the principle of military disutility of nuclear weapons is something distinct from the risks of nuclear escalation attendant on *any* conflict between nuclear-armed powers. The balance of evidence, though, does suggest that a shift in thinking towards conventional strategies has indeed taken place.

Brezhnev's declaration of the Soviet commitment to No-First-Use of nuclear weapons, made in 1982, lends further weight to the argument. In amplifications of the move which sought to convince the West of its sincerity, Marshal Ustinov and Mikhail Mil'shtein described it as accompanied by a tightening of control over nuclear weapons to ensure against unauthorized release, and other changes in military planning.[70] In one way this was convincing, since it was consistent with the kind of command structure changes described earlier. If control over strategic nuclear weapons had been given to a central strategic command, then Ustinov could have been referring to a genuine attempt to keep nuclear forces out of the early stages of a war. On the other hand, these explanations left something to be desired in that they (a) were inconsistent with the subsequent 'counterdeployments' of nuclear-capable shorter-range systems in Eastern Europe at the end of 1983, and (b) refocused attention on to conventional strategies. Furthermore, the problems of operating command-and-control systems adequately even in peacetime conditions were dramatized by the September 1983 KAL 007 incident and the May 1987 Red Square light aircraft incident.

The 'counterdeployments' represented a challenge to the No-First-Use declaration in that the forward deployment of such highly visible and vulnerable nuclear-capable systems would invite pre-emption and increase the pressures towards first use in a crisis on both sides.[71] One could argue that the counterdeployments were a primarily political move which might have conflicted with purely military developments, and that if up until that time the Soviet Union had been sparing in its deployment of nuclear weapons within Eastern Europe, it was signalling to the USA that it did not consider a nuclear war limited to Europe as a possible option. On the other hand, one could ask why the Soviet Union had developed short-range nuclear systems at all if it did not consider limited nuclear conflict a possibility, as the Czechs may have asked themselves in the 1960s. Stephen Meyer's analysis argues that, in that period, Soviet strategy worked on the assumption that war would *start* with intercontinental nuclear strikes, and then continue at the theatre level, and it seems clear that this is no longer the case.[72]

Nevertheless, the Soviet Union has evidently not abandoned dual-capable short-range systems, and it remains quite possible that the new preference for conventional operations is still entangled with a strategy which envisages the widespread use of nuclear weapons if it appeared that Nato was about to use its own nuclear forces.[73] Such a strategy also raises questions about the role of intermediate-range nuclear forces, particularly SS-20s. It is in fact possible to give a fairly satisfactory account of the development of SS-20s and of planning for their use which sees them as having been not a new threat to Western Europe, but the preservation of a capacity to retaliate against US forward-based systems and the regional nuclear powers, Britain, France and (by no means least) China. They can also be seen as broadly consistent with the No-First-Use declaration in that one of their main purposes would have been to deter the use of Nato's own theatre nuclear forces, though pre-emption may not have been entirely ruled out.[74] The elimination of the SS-20s themselves under the terms of the INF Treaty has now rendered this issue a largely historical one.

Throughout this discussion of the relationship between nuclear and conventional forces in Soviet thinking, one is faced with the problem of relating it to its political context, and of asking whether a Donnelly-type of MccGwire-type account is more convincing. This becomes a particular challenge when looking at the more detailed accounts of forces and strategies believed to be at the centre of Soviet thinking, notably the Operational Manoeuvre Group (OMG) concept. The most succinct description of OMGs would be of groups of Soviet (and possibly Eastern European) forces which would attempt to break rapidly through into Nato rear areas in the event of conflict in Europe, in order to capture or destroy Nato's airfields, communication centres and nuclear weapon sites. The object would be to win a quick conventional victory before Nato can use nuclear weapons, thus preventing Nato from dictating (notionally) the terms of nuclear escalation. Air and airborne forces would be closely involved in such operations, and it was argued that 'counterdeployment' missiles used in a conventional mode would also play an important part. OMG operations are designed to fit into the organizational innovations of TVDs, and to be co-ordinated with naval and amphibious operations on the flanks. Their first appearance in exercises has been traced to the Soviet 'Zapad-81' exercises in September 1981, a few months after the appearance of the Ogarkov *Kommunist* article cited earlier.[75]

What one makes of these analyses, however, depends very much on one's view of the Donnelly–MccGwire debate and, once again, on one's view of Soviet threat assessments. Much of the conventional analysis sticks very closely to the model of taking Soviet developments as a given to which the West must find a response,[76] but there is far more than that to the debate about OMGs and analogous Western developments like Air-Land Battle and Follow-On Forces Attack (ALB and FOFA). First, one should consider the genuine Soviet fear of Nato forward-based systems against which the Soviet strategy seems in large part targeted. Secondly, Soviet commentaries on Western developments treat them as measures prompting Soviet responses – predictably, perhaps, but one should not dismiss reaction in both directions.

In my own view, both the Soviet and Western developments should be seen as products of two long-term trends: the military search for escape routes from the apparent cul-de-sac created by the self-deterring nature of nuclear weapons, and the technological impetus of rapid developments in 'conventional' weaponry which have seemed to reopen the possibilities of prolonged (and possibly mobile) conventional combat. The former influence can be seen in the Western attempts to embellish flexible response with further conventional options, and in the Soviet strategic revisions documented by both Donnelly and MccGwire. The second factor appears in the form of a general shift of military-technological competition towards conventional means, and in particular in the Soviet fear of US military-technological superiority (partly achievable via the SDI programme, perhaps) and in increasing Western attention to the possibilities of strategic conventional weapons, as advocated in the 1988 'Iklé report', *Discriminate Deterrence*.[77] Concepts of limited nuclear use may not have been replaced by these developments, and the USA's AirLand Battle concept in particular seems to integrate nuclear and conventional battle-field war-fighting capabilities. In some respects, however, limited nuclear use concepts have not necessarily been the most alarming of recent strategic developments. There is, of course, a further question as to whether either side can seriously hope to devote the resources seen as being necessary to the full development of these conventional capabilities. A habitual optimist might hope to see the progressive entropy of conventional war-fighting capacities through financial stringency.

It is worth commenting that Western analysts are on occasion quite open about having drawn on Soviet operational concepts in elaborating AirLand Battle and associated ideas, in a kind of 'Sovietization' of Nato strategy. While the standard Soviet response has been to criticize the new Western developments as involving dangerous shifts towards offensive conventional war-fighting, this response has not been universal on the Eastern side. Colonel-General Gareev, for example, noted with a certain smug satisfaction that the USA was by the early 1980s acknowledging the existence of 'operational art' as a distinct category, after several decades of levelling criticism at Soviet military theory for making supposedly unnecessary distinctions.[78]

Further questions and a note on 'balance'

Two key questions emerge from this discussion. The question to be answered by the orthodox analysts of Soviet military affairs is *why* these new conventional options must be construed as an increase in the threat; if they are premised on war-avoidance and especially on avoidance of nuclear war, they could be part of an overall policy which is more concerned with ensuring 'security' through political means and disarmament treaties, rather than an additional option for political pressure. In the following chapter I review the evidence which suggests that the former explanation is closer to the truth.

The question to be answered by the Soviet political and military leaderships concerns the function of an offensive–defensive military strategy within a defensive doctrine. If, as I have tried to suggest, an offensive–defensive strategy need not be considered as inherently aggressive, it still raises the question of its political impact on the other side. It is hard to believe that, within Europe or anywhere else, the Soviet Union could really consider its forces capable of effectively pre-empting Nato nuclear weapons by a conventional attack, though, as already argued, to challenge a military strategy on the grounds of irrationality is not to dispute the possibility of attempts to implement it. But unless Soviet military strategy is accompanied in Europe by the kind of superiority which WTO forces do not possess, then the offensive elements of that strategy have been little more than a dangerous bluff. In chapter 6 I examine the evidence that this point is now appreciated, at least by the Soviet political leadership, and that in certain important respects the historical debates reviewed in this chapter may have been left behind by events.

Some further brief comments on 'military balance' are unavoidable at this point. Chapter 3 of this study has already questioned the prevalent view of WTO superiority. The most frequently-quoted view which challenges the notion of 'overwhelming Soviet conventional superiority' has been that of the London International Institute for Strategic Studies, though it has sometimes been rather misrepresented by some radical critics of Nato, since its essential point has always seemed to be an attempt to vindicate flexible response, rather than an argument about a conventional balance existing regardless of nuclear weapons: 'Our conclusion remains that the conventional balance is still such as to make general military aggression a highly risky undertaking for either side . . . there would still appear to be insufficient overall strength on either side to guarantee victory. The consequences for an attacker would still be quite unpredictable, and the risks, particularly of nuclear escalation, remain incalculable.'[79]

This is not to say that the IISS has always been right and Nato's radical critics wrong, since it is quite possible to argue that the conventional balance has in some respects been shifting in Nato's favour, and that the WTO still has good reason to be alarmed by the potential interventionary strength of the US army and the *Bundeswehr*.[80] In 1987–8, in fact, the IISS tried to distance itself from what it felt were misrepresentations of its 'military balance' analyses in a number of quarters, omitted its previous overall assessment, and stressed the limitations of its own statistical approach.[81]

The main point for my present purposes, however, is that it is very hard to see Soviet or WTO forces as possessing the current capability to carry out the strategy traditionally attributed to them, or to use the threat of military force for political gain in Europe. While Soviet forces in Eastern Europe are plainly larger than would be needed for effective policing of the region, if that were their only mission, they would also be in the wrong place if global territorial expansion were the Soviet aim. MccGwire points out that in that event they would have been more use stationed on the borders of countries like Iran or in the Horn of Africa.[82] There is therefore a good chance that the Soviet Union would be prepared to resolve European security problems through negotiation, but there is also a genuine political and military problem which stems from the traditionally offensive elements in the Soviet military posture in Europe.

5
Arms Control and Disarmament Policy

In chapter 2 of this study I examined the history of the European detente process, and the role of negotiated agreements in the Soviet and WTO approach to political 'security and stability' in Europe. My concern in this chapter is to investigate the relationship between these primarily political negotiations and the more narrowly military policies discussed in chapter 4, and to see how this relationship has been reflected in policies for arms control and disarmament. I have focused on the negotiations which have most directly concerned the WTO and the European security system, without going into strategic negotiations in any detail. However, broader questions of Soviet foreign policy have to be addressed, and I have also explored some of the keywords of the Gorbachev foreign policy period, notably 'New Thinking' and 'reasonable sufficiency'.

It is almost a commonplace of discussions of Soviet security policy to point out that Soviet conceptions of the East–West 'balance of forces' cover much more than a military balance. Factors like the economic achievements and potential of the USSR and its socialist allies, the strength of peace and workers' movements in the West, and Third World national liberation movements, have traditionally been considered to act as restraints on Western policy, in addition to the USSR and WTO's own military strength. They have also been considered to shift the 'correlation of forces' towards the ultimate victory of socialism. However, close observers of Soviet writings on international relations over the last thirty years have seen Soviet theory evolving away from earlier class-based approaches to pay more attention to the primacy of politics and the states system, and to the complexity and indeterminacy of a system in which the earlier US hegemony has declined substantially.[1]

In drawing inferences about Soviet approaches to disarmament negotiations, some Western writers have seen the USSR as a follower of a rigorously self-interested policy: aiming at the avoidance of war if the desired ends can be achieved without it, and favouring only measures of disarmament which will not undermine areas of Soviet strength and advantage. A good representative of this school of thought is P. H. Vigor, who sees a shift from Soviet support for General and Complete Disarmament before 1937 to support for measures of partial and nuclear disarmament after 1945, when Soviet strength *vis-à-vis* the West was greater but general disarmament would have affected conventional forces.[2] This analysis can be seen as fitting in closely with the views of Soviet military strategy advanced by Christopher Donnelly, and by Vigor himself.

A more nuanced school of writing is less convinced that Soviet policy has rested so squarely on the search for advantage, and also treats the Soviet Union as less of an awesomely-logical Clausewitzian-Marxist-Leninist monolith.[3] These writers would point to factors in Soviet arms control and disarmament policy which have amounted to Soviet acceptance of security as dependent on the potential opponent as well as one's own strength, and the acceptance of treaties which might have fallen short of the optimum demands of the Soviet military. For example: the acceptance of mutual vulnerability in the ABM Treaty; the explicit disavowal of superiority as a goal; the exclusion of US Forward-Based Systems from the SALT agreements when the military might have preferred to include them. There is a recognition of substantial debates taking place in the Soviet Union during the 1970s over issues like the value of security through consultation and, more broadly, how far Soviet trade and diplomacy should co-operate with the capitalist world. Though differing accounts are given of the resolution of these debates, the very recognition of their existence is beyond the framework of the Vigor school of thought.

Conventional arms control

The disarmament negotiations of most direct relevance to the WTO's role in European security over the last twenty years have been the Mutual and Balanced Force Reduction talks on conventional forces, from 1973 onwards, and the Intermediate Nuclear Forces talks of the 1980s.

Chapter 2 showed how the MBFR talks came to be set up in the context of moves towards the wider CSCE process; the main task of the historical analyst is to account for their failure, as so frequently bemoaned, to reduce the two blocs' forces in Central Europe by a single rifle or soldier. The MBFR negotiations area covered forces in the GDR, Poland, Czechoslovakia, the FRG, Belgium, the Netherlands and Luxemburg. The most notorious obstacle to progress at MBFR was the failure to agree on a common data-base for force levels from which reductions would start.[4] This fundamental disagreement can be pointed to as the prime example of the failure of political detente in Europe to be developed into 'military detente', which has been taken on both sides to have been the desired outcome of MBFR.[5]

However, this traditional analysis overlooks the inherent limitations of MBFR, and the fact that there were certain things which this negotiating forum was never intended to achieve. As Jane Sharp has shown, Nato wanted the negotiations to stabilize force levels in Europe or obtain reciprocation for unilateral US reductions, and to open up WTO territory to inspection. The USSR sought to constrain Nato's nuclear and conventional technological superiority and, as outlined in chapter 2, to maintain a complex set of numerical ratios: between Nato and the WTO; between the *Bundeswehr* and GSFG; between US forces in Europe and the *Bundeswehr*; and between Soviet and Eastern European forces. With so many intricate concerns at stake, it is no great surprise that progress was slow, and the data discrepancy issue was a symptom of deeper problems as well as a stumbling-block in itself. The Eastern European leaderships, for their part, did not necessarily share the Soviet objectives, being particularly concerned about the size of Soviet and East German forces.

Although the two sides' positions on a number of the vexed technical problems of MBFR moved closer together over time, the USSR never came close to accepting any measures which would have threatened either its political position in Eastern Europe, or its apparent wish to maintain offensive conventional capabilities in the region. This apparent unwillingness to negotiate constraints on these capabilities caused considerable damage to the USSR's credibility, and the circumstantial evidence available on Soviet weapons procurement during the 1976–81 period supports the analysis that whatever self-imposed constraints there were on strategic forces, there was much less of a throttling-back on theatre nuclear and conventional forces.[6]

It is all the more interesting, therefore, to observe the way in which some of the longstanding Soviet MBFR positions seemed to be implicitly revised from 1986 onwards, though in different forums. The USSR had responded positively to a 1983 French suggestion for a separate security forum within CSCE, seeing this as a way of taking security issues out of the human rights polemics of the existing discussions. This resulted in the Conference on Confidence and Security-Building Measures and Disarmament in Europe, which started meeting in Stockholm in January 1984. Although progress here was also slow, this forum was able to make use of work done earlier in MBFR on confidence-building measures, and 21 September 1986 saw the signature of the Document of the Stockholm Conference on Confidence-and Security-Building Measures and Disarmament in Europe.

The Stockholm document's provisions on on-site inspection of exercises, covering the Western USSR as well as Eastern Europe, were an innovative and significant contribution to confidence-building and to the reduction of the fear of surprise attack. They went beyond the optional observation regime agreed in Helsinki. The Stockholm agreement made it more difficult to prepare for offensive operations under the guise of manoeuvres, and generally enhanced the 'transparency' of military activities, albeit without doing anything to restructure the forces involved, and with exceptions for alerts and mobilization activities.[7] It also further delegitimized intervention within blocs, at least technically, with its commitment of the signatories to refrain from the threat or use of force against any state, 'regardless of that State's political, social, economic or cultural systems and irrespective of whether or not they maintain with that State relations of alliance.'[8]

Movement towards the Stockholm agreement coincided with other Eastern initiatives on forces in Europe. Gorbachev proposed a package of European force reductions in a speech in East Berlin in April 1986, and on 11 June 1986 this became a formal proposal from the WTO Political Consultative Committee, the 'Budapest appeal'. This proposed reductions of manpower and equipment across the whole Atlantic-to-the-Urals region, of 150–200,000 men in the first stage, and later cuts of 25 per cent on each side in the early 1990s; tactical air forces and short-range nuclear weapons would be reduced simultaneously, and the forum could be either an expansion of MBFR or a further CSCE forum. The appeal also, and perhaps more importantly, said that: 'In the interests of security in Europe and the whole world, the military concepts and doctrines of the military alliances must be based on defensive principles.'[9]

A complementary proposal was put forward in early May 1987 by Poland's General Jaruzelski, entitled 'Plan of nuclear and conventional arms disengagement in Central Europe'.[10] This differed from the WTO proposal in that it covered only Central Europe, and weapons and equipment rather than manpower, but it dealt with both nuclear and conventional disengagement and with the evolution of 'strictly defensive' military doctrines. A degree of scepticism in the response to the 'Jaruzelski plan' was understandable, given its self-proclaimed intention of bolstering the Polish government's international standing, but the proposal fitted well enough within the framework of the WTO proposal and of the Rapacki tradition of concern for Central European disengagement (see chapter 2).

The references in these statements to defensive military doctrines broke important new ground, and will be discussed in detail in chapter 6. Even the quantitative parts of the Budapest appeal, however, suggested that the USSR and WTO were moving from positions taken in MBFR. It appeared that substantial troop cuts were no longer ruled out, and although the sceptical side of the Western response suspected that Gorbachev was trying to snuff out any remaining hopes of agreement in MBFR, a more charitable interpretation saw evidence of a genuine desire to start afresh, with an alternative to MBFR seen as necessary to get away from the unproductive nature of that forum (and from Soviet positions which could not easily be reversed within the same forum). Part of the sceptical response was due to the fact that the principle of asymmetrical reductions had been accepted in MBFR in 1978, and the 1986 proposals appeared to return to unrealistically high figures for symmetrical cuts. However, the 1986 initiatives were also accompanied by suggestions of mutual asymmetrical cuts in areas of advantage. Overall, one can perhaps see a progression from MBFR via Stockholm to the proposed new forum, in the sense that the Stockholm negotiations indicated serious WTO interest in Western proposals for confidence-building measures, and the new forum could hope to build on this by addressing force cuts once again in the wider geographical area, and even doctrines.

For the new forum, Nato preferred a bloc-to-bloc approach rather than CSCE, although this did not please France. The so-called 'Group 23' of Nato and WTO states began informal consultations in Vienna in February 1987, and inevitably began to dispute the mandate of the proposed negotiations. Nato was concerned to exclude short-range nuclear missiles and nuclear-capable aircraft, particularly after the signature of the INF Treaty. One significant development in early 1988 was a published admission by General Yazov of a 20,000 WTO tank superiority in Europe. Nevertheless, by mid-1988 there had been little progress, and the USA showed little interest in a Soviet plan put forward at the Moscow summit which envisaged a trade-off between Soviet tanks and US aircraft. Further public Eastern suggestions for the Vienna mandate followed in July, in statements by Gorbachev himself and by the WTO's PCC, meeting in Warsaw.[11]

The important question of defensive military doctrines will be taken up again later; for the moment, it is important to set arms control negotiations in the context of more general Soviet foreign policy approaches during the 1985–8 period.

'New thinking'

The umbrella term used to describe developments in Soviet foreign policy over the past few years has been 'new thinking', though 'new thinking' is not supposed to apply only to the area of foreign policy. The use of the term seems to stem from a quotation from the 1955 Russell–Einstein Manifesto, incorporated into the title of a book published in 1984 by Anatolii Gromyko and Vladimir Lomeiko, *Novoe myshlenie v yadernyi vek* (*New Thinking in the Nuclear Age*).[12]

The Soviet account of 'new thinking' has been usefully summarized by Margot Light under six headings:

1 the interdependence of survival in the nuclear age, which necessitates a new approach to problems of security;

2 the need for a reduction in the level of military confrontation, while
  retaining the principle of equality and equal security;
3 security as a political, not a military-technical, problem;
4 national and international security are indivisible;
5 the need for a more flexible foreign policy and a readiness to compromise in negotiations;
6 the need for a comprehensive view of international security, covering
  the military, economic, political and humanitarian spheres.[13] (The
  ecological sphere is also much emphasized, though Light herself does
  not mention it; global issues and all-human values are sometimes said
  to override inter-state and ideological differences.)

One problem with the early Soviet treatment of 'new thinking' was that
it was not always easy to tell whether it was supposed to be a continuation
of past policies or a break with them; thus the extent to which a critique of
Brezhnevite foreign policy was involved was not at first made clear with
any consistency. In Gromyko and Lomeiko's book the impression was
given that the Soviet Union had been guided by New Thinking since 1945,
but they later spoke of the need for a 'fundamentally new approach' as a
reflection of proposals made in 1986, but not before.[14] In fact the truth of
the matter was probably somewhere in between, since the themes of 'new
thinking' can be identified in policy debates, if not in diplomatic practice,
stretching back into the Brezhnev and even the Khrushchev periods.
Nevertheless, their crystallization in material published under Gorbachev, and reflection in the General Secretary's own speeches and writings
after March 1985, does make it possible to speak of a phenomenon of the
Gorbachev period itself, and clearer criticism of the previous policies
gradually emerged.

The range of Soviet commentators who contributed to the literature on
'new thinking' included academic policy advisers, government ministers
like Vladimir Petrovskii, and the new Central Committee international
secretary Anatolii Dobrynin.[15] Mikhail Gorbachev himself used the concept as a basis for a number of diplomatic initiatives and policy statements
during the 1986–8 period, including his book *Perestroika*.[16] It should also
be mentioned that the advisory and executive personnel and organization
of Soviet foreign policy was quite extensively refurbished during this
period, with a range of measures including the replacement of Andrei
Gromyko by Eduard Shevardnadze as Foreign Minister; the setting up of
arms control advisory units within the Foreign Ministry and Central
Committee apparatus and the encouragement of civilian participation in
arms control analysis; and a reorganization of the geographical responsibilities of Foreign Ministry advisory bodies.[17] Among the objectives that
could plausibly be inferred from these measures were a strengthening of

party control over foreign policy at the expense of the Foreign Ministry itself (though Shevardnadze himself emerged as quite a substantial figure in his own right), and the increased provision of advice on arms control from groups other than the professional military. (I have not, however, tried to deal here with the precise mechanisms by which advisers' ideas find their way into the General Secretary's speeches.)

Some of the themes of the 'new thinking' literature fit in well with the conclusions of Western debates stretching back over long periods, on issues such as global economic relations and Soviet relations with the developing world.[18] In some ways, the new concepts offered cannot be said to break out of the familiar paradoxes of detente and peaceful coexistence, with their continued attention to inter-systemic competition as well as co-operation. In the 1986 CPSU Programme the reality of inter-systemic competition was still asserted, with the words: 'The most acute struggle between the two world outlooks on the international scene reflects the opposition of the two world systems – socialism and capitalism.'[19] However, there is certainly also a recognition of the con-tradictions of traditional concepts of coexistence, as in Gorbachev's own notable remarks about 'groping in the dark' for a new understanding of the phenomenon of global interdependence.[20] Moreover, the new ap-proach is clearly more than a simple reaffirmation of old concepts of detente in that it sets out explicitly to downgrade the nuclear and military elements in relations between states and systems, downgrades (almost to the point of invisibility) the role of class forces in inter-state and inter-systemic political and economic relations, and tends towards prioritizing co-operation rather than competition (sometimes in terms of 'national interests', and sometimes in terms of 'all-human' interests).

In the areas of 'new thinking' most directly related to the arms race and security policy, some valuable Western studies have already been pub-lished which provide pointers to the basis on which Gorbachev's early disarmament diplomacy was built. In two particularly useful papers, Pat Litherland identified a school of Soviet civilian writers on the arms race which he identified as the 'mutualists'. Since the late 1970s, these analysts had been putting forward an analysis of the arms race which recognised it as an interactive process posing problems of control for politicians on both sides. Their analysis contained a questioning of whether 'balance' in nuclear weapons could ensure security and stability, as traditionally argued, conceded that Soviet actions might contribute to the continuation of the arms race, implied scepticism about the meaningfulness of 'superi-ority' in nuclear weapons, and also implied greater leeway for flexibility and unilateral steps within the framework of negotiations. These 'mutual-ists' included a number of those who were most prominent in early writing on 'new thinking', and Litherland's conclusion (writing in November

1986) was that 'mutualist' themes had clearly influenced Gorbachev's statements on the arms race, though he had not endorsed those views entirely.

An equally valuable study published in 1987 by Stephen Shenfield also focused on Soviet analyses of the arms race, and did full justice to the variations between different schools of thought, including military writers.

Shenfield argued that Soviet analysts had come to see the danger of catastrophic nuclear war as placing in doubt the inevitability of humanity's communist future, and that the decline of detente around 1980 challenged the belief that peace would be strengthened as the 'correlation of forces' changed to the advantage of socialism. In the ensuing ideological debate, Shenfield continued, international interdependence had been proposed as the crucial factor working in favour of detente; 'peace' had been prioritized over 'socialism' as the goal of foreign policy, which implied a need for greater restraint; assessments of capitalism's capacity for peaceful coexistence had become more optimistic; and non-military factors in the 'correlation of forces' had attained increased weight.

Shenfield's study suggested that these tendencies had gradually become more influential in Soviet foreign policy analysis, though he also identified groups and individuals who had resisted their progress, and pointed out nuances in the positions of different writers. Like Litherland, he connected his discussion of recent debates with the arguments of the 1960s and 1970s over the possibility of 'victory' in nuclear war.[21]

By mid-1988, in the period immediately preceeding the 19th All-Union Party Conference, much more explicit comments were appearing in both official statements and academic commentary to the effect that mistakes could be made and had been made in Soviet foreign policy. Taken collectively, these comments amounted to an initial stage in the application of *glasnost'* to foreign policy, albeit much later than the phenomenon had appeared in spheres such as economic and cultural policy and Soviet history. Oleg Bogomolov published a 1980 memorandum from the Institute of the Economy of the World Socialist System, criticizing the intervention in Afghanistan. Professor Vyacheslav Dashichev published in *Literaturnaya Gazeta* a remarkable article which criticized Soviet policy in Eastern Europe and the Third World, and indeed did so in a quite unnecessarily self-flagellatory way which virtually absolved the USA from having played any significant role in the decline of East–West relations in the late 1970s and early 1980s.[22]

It became clear that these were not isolated contributions when the Central Committee's Theses for the 19th Party Conference were published, and followed by Gorbachev's speech at the conference itself. The Theses criticized Soviet foreign policy for failing to use opportunities to ensure Soviet security by political means, and for allowing the country to be drawn into an arms race which affected its social and economic progress and international standing.[23] A number of press commentaries published around the time of the conference then took up these themes, including a piece by Aleksandr Bovin which applied the concept of 'peaceful coexistence' to relations *within* the world socialist system.[24] (This came shortly after the signature of the Soviet–Yugoslav declaration of March 1988, which is examined in chapter 6).

Gorbachev's main conference speech repeated some of these points at rather greater length:

> Nevertheless, while drawing lessons from the past, we have to acknowledge that command methods of administration did not spare the field of foreign policy either. It sometimes happened that even decisions of vital importance were taken by a narrow circle of people without collective, comprehensive examination or analysis, on occasion without properly consulting friends either. This led to an inadequate reaction to international events and to the policies of other states, if not to mistaken decisions. Unfortunately, the cost of this to the people, and the implications of this or that course of action, were not always weighed up.
>
> In response to the nuclear challenge to us and to the entire socialist world it was necessary to achieve strategic parity with the USA. And this was accomplished. But, while concentrating enormous funds and attention on the military aspect of countering imperialism, we did not always make use of the political opportunities opened up by the fundamental changes in the world in our efforts to assure the security of our state, to scale down tensions, and promote mutual understanding between nations. As a result, we allowed ourselves to be drawn into an arms race, which could not but affect the country's socio-economic development and its international standing.
>
> As the arms race approached a critical point, our traditional political and social activities for peace and disarmament began, on this background, to lose their power of conviction. To put it even more bluntly, without overturning the logic of this course, we would actually have found ourselves on the brink of a military confrontation.
>
> Hence, what was needed was not just a refinement of foreign policy, but its determined reshaping [. . .]
>
> In the course of our analysis of the fundamental changes in the world we are overcoming many stereotypes which limited our options and, to a certain extent, supplied arguments to those who indulged in misrepresenting our real intentions.[25]

The conference debates themselves and the resolutions which resulted paid surprisingly little attention to foreign policy, being largely taken up with domestic issues, including constitutional reform.[26] Shortly after the conference, however, the trend towards more open discussion of foreign policy was authoritatively confirmed by Foreign Minister Shevardnadze in a speech to ministry staff and diplomats, in which he called for a 'pluralism of views and evaluations' of foreign policy. An almost immediate response then came from Egor Ligachev, who challenged Shevardnadze's disavowal that peaceful coexistence was a special form of class struggle with the words: 'We proceed, comrades, from the fact that international relations are particularly class in nature, and that is of fundamental importance.'[27] This was a sharp challenge to Gorbachev and Shevardnadze in view of the lenghts to which they had gone to avoid such formulations over the previous three years. It may have contributed to Ligachev's apparent downgrading by the Central Committee plenum at the end of September, though there was no immediate evidence to that effect. (It was immediately after this that Gorbachev assumed the Soviet presidency.)

'Reasonable sufficiency' and disarmament

In the sphere of public diplomacy, the implications of 'new thinking' became visible in the use of the concept of 'reasonable sufficiency', which largely replaced 'parity' as the favoured criterion for measuring the Soviet defence effort. Gorbachev's own use of the term is dated by Soviet commentators from a speech he made during his visit to France in late 1985.[28] Earlier uses of the terms 'sufficient defence' and 'sufficient security' (by Chernenko) have also been pointed out.[29] Gorbachev himself, in making his report to the CPSU Congress in February 1986, specified as one of the principles of his proposed international security system 'a strictly controlled lowering of the levels of military capabilities of countries to limits of reasonable adequacy' (*razumnaya dostatochnost'*).[30] After that, 'reasonable sufficiency' became the more standard translation.

The practical implications of this new formulation were not self-evident from the context, though it was certainly a verbal shift away from the traditional commitment to 'parity and equal security'. The new party programme, as adopted at the same congress, was ambivalent about 'parity'. On the one hand it spoke of the Soviet attainment of parity as a 'historic achievement of socialism', thus placing constraints on the ideological elbow-room available for any critique of 'parity'.[31] On the other hand, it revised the formula used to describe the party's commitment to the provision of resources for defence. Previously (most notably in the 1977 Soviet constitution) the wording was: 'The state ensures the security and defence capability of the country, and supplies the armed forces of the USSR with everything necessary for that purpose.'[32] In the 1986 Programme, the party committed itself only to maintaining forces 'at a level ruling out strategic superiority of the forces of imperialism', which was clearly a weaker formulation and suggested a possible retreat from numerical parity.[33]

These new formulations followed on from Gorbachev's January 1986 statement in which he spoke of the need to repudiate the 'notorious logic' of the arms race, and outlined his three-stage plan for complete nuclear disarmament by the year 2000. In his February speech, Gorbachev also spoke of parity as a factor of declining efficacy in ensuring military-political restraint, a concept which clearly owed much to the 'mutualist' analysis identified by Litherland. The relationship between these comments and the disarmament proposals seemed to amount to an acceptance that the level of nuclear overkill involved in the existing 'parity' permitted deep cuts to be made without damage to Soviet security, and even that unilateral cuts were possible on the Soviet side. These points became clear both from publications which elaborated the new approach, and from Gorbachev's subsequent disarmament diplomacy.

Some of the commentators with responsibility for explaining these developments spelled out the declining significance of numerical parity, while others spoke of 'approximate parity' in terms which made it clear that what they were talking about was maintaining a retaliatory capability while cuts took place – in effect, an advocacy of minimum deterrence and mutually assured destruction at decreasing level of nuclear forces.[34] (There also appeared to be implications in 'reasonable sufficiency' for conventional forces, which are taken up in chapter 6.)

There were some notable ironies in the Soviet negotiating position during this period. Although a thoroughgoing critique of nuclear deterrence on strategic and moral grounds was being presented under the banner of 'new thinking', in practice Soviet negotiating policy was asserting the continued need for nuclear deterrence in its simplest form, in the sense of preserving the ABM Treaty from the Reagan administration's assaults on it and plans for the Strategic Defense Initiative (SDI). Soviet scholars produced elaborations of Gorbachev's schematic (in the third phase, highly schematic) plan for deep cuts, and on occasions went out of their way to distance themselves from the suggestion that 'reasonable sufficiency' entailed perpetual minimum deterrence rather than complete denuclearization. This seemed to be part of a debate between different groups of scholars and diplomats, some of whom took the aspiration to a nuclear-free world very seriously, while others regarded it as misplaced or naive, particularly in view of the existence of third-party nuclear systems.[35] At the same time, 'reasonable sufficiency' seemed to cover the possibility of the USSR making an asymmetrical or 'semi-symmetrical' military response to SDI, if negotiations failed to block the project.[36]

If one implication of 'mutualism' and 'reasonable sufficiency' was that the USSR was secure enough to take unilateral steps in an effort to start a disarmament process, then Gorbachev was not the first to make the attempt. It was under Brezhnev that the No-First-Use declaration was made, and a 1982 moratorium on new SS-20 deployments, as part of a series of unsuccessful attempts to forestall Nato's plans for the deployment of cruise and Pershing II. Andropov's proposals in 1982–3 also came to nothing, and given Nato's determination to deploy there may have been little that could have been done at that stage; even so, the final Soviet position of willingness to reduce SS-20 numbers to the level of British and French warheads did represent a significant step back from the previous claims that an INF balance already existed.

Negotiations at Geneva were about to recommence by the time Gorbachev became General Secretary in March 1985. His first initiatives were a new SS-20 and counterdeployments moratorium in April 1985, followed by the moratorium on nuclear testing announced on 1 August 1985, and later extended until early 1987 despite the absence of a serious US response.[37] In October 1985, during his visit to France, Gorbachev made another set of proposals which included a reduction of SS-20s in the European zone of the USSR and the possibility of a separate INF agreement.[38] After the November summit with Reagan in Geneva came the January 1986 statement, which included acceptance of the principle of on-site verification for the third stage.[39]

In the course of his February 1986 Congress speech, Gorbachev made the notably 'mutualist' comment that 'in the military sphere we intend to act in such a way as to give nobody grounds for fears, even imagined, about their security.'[40] This seemed to amount to an admission that earlier military build-ups had been excessive. At this stage it appeared that a separate Euromissile agreement was possible independently of negotiations on SDI and long-range missiles, but this position was abandoned at Reykjavik in October 1986. Here, a Soviet offer of major cuts, including the zero–zero INF deal, in exchange for constraints on SDI, was blocked by US insistence on the highly dubious 'broad interpretation' of the ABM Treaty. This Soviet position was reversed again in early 1987, perhaps with encouragement from the Eastern Europeans, and the 'zero option' once again became a possibility.[41] Comments by the 'mutualist' journalist Aleksandr Bovin openly queried the wisdom of the original deployment of Soviet SS-20s, and by the end of the year as the Washington Summit and the INF Treaty signature approached, Deputy Foreign Minister Aleksandr Bessmertnykh endorsed Bovin's view with the words: 'a number of decisions have clearly not been optimal.'[42]

The INF Treaty

After much uncertainty during the summer of 1987, especially over the role of Pershing-Ia missiles operated by the FRG with US warheads, the INF Treaty was finally agreed, and signed during Gorbachev's visit to Washington in December. The adjustments to the Soviet position which were made during the course of that year served to expose Nato's disarray and embarrassment at the Soviet acceptance of a 'zero option' proposal which had never been considered a serious negotiating offer when first put forward by the USA. Indeed, the conclusion of a 'double zero' agreement covering two categories of land-based missiles amounted to a substantial unilateral cut on the Soviet side, and testified to the adventurousness of the policies licenced by 'new thinking'. Existing overkill capacities and retargeting capabilities may not have entailed actual reductions in Soviet warheads targeted on Western Europe (or vice versa), but the treaty was undeniably an instance of disarmament as distinct from 'arms control', and represented a significant shift from the previously established notions of 'parity'.[43]

On the Nato side, the perceived requirements of flexible response came under much discussion as a consequence of the treaty, which reflected the way in which Gorbachev had called the West's bluff in the negotiations. It is true that the treaty appeared to threaten declared Nato strategy more directly than Soviet strategy, even if the more extreme lamentations about the perceived danger of a denuclearized Europe were grossly overstated.[44]

In terms of Soviet military strategy, the INF Treaty fitted in with the kind of planning described by MccGwire and/or Donnelly, in the sense that even a limited denuclearization of Europe might reduce the risks of intercontinental nuclear escalation and attacks on Soviet territory in the event of war. It was also consistent with Soviet support over the previous few years for a variety of disengagement plans in parts of Europe: the 'Palme corridor' proposal for a nuclear-free corridor along the inner-German border; negotiations between the West German SPD, the East German SED and the Czechoslovakian party for a nuclear- and chemical-free zone; Nordic and Balkan nuclear-free zone proposals.[45] These plans, as well as the INF Treaty itself, were all very welcome to the Eastern European leaderships, who had fretted at the immobilism of Soviet diplomacy in 1984 and early 1985.

The argument that this Soviet diplomacy was closely calibrated with the requirements of military strategy has been put with some force by a number of commentators.[46] There is some justification for this, at least in the sense that the nuclear agreements concluded and proposed presented no threat to the 'conventionalization' of Soviet strategy which chapter 4 examined. However, a number of caveats should be entered.

Firstly, Gorbachev's diplomacy during this period was extremely innovative, and major concessions were made – the exclusion of British and
French systems from INF calculations; on-site inspection in the Stockholm and INF agreements; delinking INF from SDI. At one stage, a
sympathetic American observer commented that if Gorbachev made any
more concessions, he would come close to accepting the Reagan 'arms
control' agenda in its entirety.[47] This flexibility also seemed to cause
domestic problems for Gorbachev, for as early as mid-1986 there were
reports of military unhappiness in the USSR about his persistence with
approaches to the West in the face of US indifference, particularly over the
moratorium on nuclear tests. It was even being suggested, reportedly, that
Gorbachev had illusions about the US administration.[48] The decision to
pursue the INF deal may have been a finely-balanced one, given the
possibility that the USA may have hoped to use the deal to safeguard
SDI and speed its deployment.

Secondly, it is not clear that the INF Treaty had no impact on Soviet
planning, in spite of the nuclear retargeting options available. As Dennis
M. Gormley put it: 'the elimination of over 400 SS-20 launchers and 1,500
nuclear warheads will impose unwanted constraints on Soviet nuclear
contingency planning for an escalating conflict.'[49] The 'counterdeployment' missiles to be removed from Eastern European territory were also
among the weapons which had earlier been identified as playing an
important role in Soviet conventional planning, since some of them were
dual-capable.[50]

Finally, it was quite clear from mid-1986 onwards that the Soviet
leadership knew very well that if and when an INF treaty was signed,
attention would shift on to conventional forces in Europe. The 1986
Budapest appeal was a recognition of this, and discussions in the Soviet
press of 'reasonable sufficiency' as a criterion for conventional forces
supported the evidence from public diplomacy. As mentioned, this will be
the subject of chapter 6.

Public discussions of the treaty in the USSR can also be adduced as
evidence in the examination of 'new thinking' and its military applications. There were a number of instances when the Soviet press mentioned
public expressions of concern about the unbalanced nature of the treaty,
after the rather belated admission that the USSR would have to destroy
more missiles than the USA.[51] There was a temptation in the West to
dismiss these as window-dressing. However, even though the military
leadership fell into line behind the treaty, there was evidence that concern
extended beyond the professional military who might have been expected
to have reservations. Sceptical currents in public opinion had been
expressed well before the signature of the treaty, when an early 1987
opinion poll published in *Kommunist* echoed some familiar Western views

about nuclear disarmament: 30 per cent of those questioned thought denuclearization would heighten the risk of conventional war, and 22 per cent thought the complete liquidation of nuclear weapons was impossible because they could not be 'disinvented'.[52]

In their public explanations of the treaty's terms, the military leadership and civilian leaders and commentators made a number of points related to the apparent imbalance: arithmetical calculations were less important than making a first step towards disarmament; approximate parity remained in force both strategically and in Europe; it was especially important to get rid of Pershing-IIs because of their short flight-time; the number of *modern* missiles to be destroyed was very close on either side. Foreign Minister Shevardnadze made a particular effort to address concerns he said had been expressed by the public. The Supreme Soviet finally ratified the treaty just before the Moscow summit, in late May 1988.[53]

Explanations

It may be helpful to consider these aspects of the INF Treaty against the background of a range of explanations for the emergence of 'new thinking' as an element in Soviet foreign policy. The general formula used by Gorbachev and Shevardnadze was to say that Soviet policy should seek to shape an external environment favourable to internal development. However, the formula needs unpacking to see how precisely it was considered to apply to the mid-1980s, and what was considered to have gone wrong in the immediate past.

At the more sceptical end of the spectrum, one could argue that Gorbachev's reassessment of policy was grounded in a view of the Soviet Union as being in serious danger of losing the East–West competition. Brezhnev's policies may have given the country strategic nuclear parity, but by the late 1970s it was in serious relative decline technologically and economically, and Brezhnev and his immediate successors were incapable of the sustained diplomatic initiative needed to prevent the USA from exploiting its economic-technological superiority and regaining significant military advantages, particularly through the SDI project. According to this line of argument, Gorbachev's denuclearization policies were intended to give the USSR a breathing-space which would enable the USSR to shift resources to the civilian economy and provide a basis for more efficient competition with the West. In the military sphere denuclearization is not a disadvantage since the Soviet Union would be almost invulnerable in a denuclearized world. In addition, Soviet military-technological capacities can be seen as being enhanced in the long term by a stronger and more advanced economy (this is in fact an argument regularly used by military writers themselves), so the country would be better able to meet the future challenges of exotic conventional military technologies.

If this explanation takes the competition side of peaceful coexistence more seriously, a more charitable view would allow more weight to the co-operative aspects in Soviet thinking. According to this view, Gorbachev can be seen as taking on board the 'mutualists'' view of the arms race, recognizing the fact that neither Soviet nor global security had been enhanced by past military build-ups, and seeing the futility of the pursuit of 'parity'. If Shenfield's reading of Soviet ideological trends is correct, then an increasing awareness of the global nuclear predicament had led to the conclusion that the conflict between capitalism and socialism could not be pursued by any methods which ran the risk of nuclear or even conventional war, though the new trend did not immediately establish itself entirely securely.

A third alternative might be the increase in self-confidence which characterized Gorbachev's leadership, with an argument running something like this: Brezhnev's leadership was at root too insecure to find alternatives other than an attempted military solution to a problem like the Afghanistan crisis; Gorbachev, on the other hand, felt secure enough to seek political solutions more determinedly, and knew that the Soviet Union could make arms control/disarmament concessions without damaging its security in the short term.

Posing these lines of thought as stark alternatives is doubtless an oversimplification; they may all be present to some degree in recent Soviet policy. There is support for the first strand of analysis in much that has been said by Gorbachev himself and by important commentators like Evgenii Primakov, Director of the Institute of World Economy and International Relations. Once he was firmly established in office, Gorbachev obviously felt able to be increasingly blunt about the state of the Soviet economy (or perhaps he had only then found out how bad things really were). He began to describe the late Brezhnev period as having been a 'pre-crisis situation', and his own formulations made it clear that the impending crisis had been a socio-political as much as an economic-technological one.[54] Doubtless the Solidarity period in Poland caused serious alarm in the Soviet elite over the possibility of mass unrest arising out of economic stagnation. Even so, it is worth remembering that for approximately the first year of his general secretaryship, Gorbachev seemed far more intent on economic efficiency than political democratization, and that his appreciation of the need for both seemed to be a gradual realization rather than a pre-planned strategy. By 1987, Gorbachev and Primakov were both being very explicit about the need to remedy socialism's technological lag behind capitalist development.[55]

A problem which arose for Soviet commentators using these arguments was that they were undeniably vulnerable to the charge that 'new thinking' amounted to an admission of Soviet weakness relative to the West. Both Primakov and General Lizichev, head of the Main Political Administration in the armed forces, sought to refute this charge, but, it must be said, without much conviction.[56] What was really needed to make the intellectual case for 'new thinking' more convincing was not only the argument that the new approach was only common sense in the nuclear age (which was said), but also a relatively relaxed view of the USA's ability to turn economic-technological advantages into military/political power.

Some commentators did take this line, though not altogether consistently. V. V. Zhurkin, S. A. Karaganov, and A. V. Kortunov co-authored a series of articles in which they argued that the USA could not effectively use military force for any action larger than the invasion of Grenada, but also that the imperialist threat had in general shifted towards the Third World. Their analyses still contained a strong underlying note of alarm that a US strategy of seeking economic 'victory without war' might have a good chance of succeeding, but this may have been a way of saying that the real threat to Soviet great-power status was from scientific-technical development in general, which was a threat from the West as a whole and from Japan, as much as from the USA specifically.[57] In addition, the argument could be seen to imply that Soviet allies in the Third World could expect less Soviet support, as long as the USSR itself was not threatened. (What one thinks of these Soviet analyses depends to a large degree on one's view of the USA's relative decline within its own, Western sphere of economic-political hegemony. Some might argue that the Soviet alarm was exaggerated; others that the US decline had been much less steep than the USSR's.)

In diplomatic terms, these analyses can be related to the parallels between the situation in 1987–8 and that in an earlier period of detente. In 1972, the USA hoped that arms control negotiations with the USSR and summit diplomacy would make it easier to withdraw from Vietnam as defeat loomed there. In 1987–8, the USSR was hoping that the INF Treaty would contribute to an atmosphere in which withdrawal from Afghanistan would be easier.[58] By the late 1980s the USSR, the 'incomplete superpower', was in the process of withdrawing from its strategic overextension at a time when the USA had almost as much economic reason to do the same, but seemed unable to match the sort of reappraisal which Gorbachev and his advisers seemed to have made.[59]

None of this, however, means that the co-operative aspects of Gorbachev's reassessment were insincere or secondary to their more 'hardheaded' geopolitical aspects. They have been stated clearly enough, and on the basis of sufficiently wide-ranging background discussion, to be credible on their own account, whatever may be the domestic and foreign obstacles to their implementation.

In tying together the loose ends of this chapter, it is useful to look again at the objections which were raised in Western Europe to the measures of denuclearization involved in the INF deal: that it would leave Western Europe exposed to attack by Soviet conventional forces, and 'decouple' Western Europe from the USA. There was a good deal of truth in the argument that the deal left gaps in flexible response – but the contradictions and problems of flexible response are extremely deep-rooted, and had certainly not been resolved by the original deployments of cruise and Pershing II. It is also true that denuclearization measures alone would, for obvious geographical reasons, coincide with certain Soviet military interests. However, the Nato objections only made sense if one accepted: (a) that the claimed overwhelming Soviet conventional superiority did in fact exist; (b) that Donnelly's account of Soviet political objectives, rather than MccGwire's, was nearer the truth; and (c) that a denuclearized Europe and moves towards it were *per se* undesirable, and Soviet disarmament proposals entirely self-interested. There are serious grounds for doubt about each of these propositions. I have argued against some of their central points in this chapter and the previous one; my view that a nuclear-free Europe would be desirable for numerous political reasons will have to be left unargued for separately, but in many respects it follows from a rejection of these propositions.

However, the last two chapters have also left some important questions unanswered. Even if (a large if) the European security system could be extensively denuclearized, would Soviet military planners who might support Gorbachev on denuclearization be prepared to accept any more thoroughgoing demilitarization of international relations? The weight of offensive thinking in Soviet military tradition remains a very real problem, though defensive doctrines have been mentioned since 1986. Moreover, denuclearization is not a sufficient condition for the construction of an alternative security system in Europe. Chapter 6, therefore, will examine possible Soviet and WTO interests in alternative defence and security concepts in Europe, their relationship to bloc politics in the dual sense of West–West and East–East relations, and the important question of Soviet military-political relations.

6
Alternatives

The Western debate

In this chapter, I look at the alternative defence debate from both West and East, and examine possibilities for radical restructuring of the European security system. These questions bring the WTO itself back into the centre of the discussion, and I examine the potential challenges to traditional WTO functions which might be posed by alternative defence concepts.

The alternative security debates of the 1980s have had to grapple with several apparently intractable strategic facts of the post-war era. In purely military terms, the USA's main strengths since 1945 have lain in the combination of a nuclear arsenal with strong air and sea forces and an extensive overseas base system. The USSR, despite its development of a comparable nuclear arsenal, has remained much more of a traditional land power, for which the control of territory in East-Central Europe and the security of the western USSR have been crucial.

This is not to say that territory has been unimportant for Nato, since its central rationale has been to ensure the territorial integrity of the Federal Republic of Germany and its neighbours. However, there has been an important asymmetry of threat perceptions within Europe. The Soviet Union has feared nuclear devastation arising from escalation from a smaller-scale conflict, or perhaps accident, even if the fear of premeditated attack has declined. The West has principally feared Soviet conventional forces, or some political use of them, as outlined in chapter 4. In fact, Soviet control of territory in East-Central Europe could not by itself ever have *prevented* Western attacks with nuclear missiles, but it has undeniably made a contribution to the Soviet military posture, as chapter 4 explained. More importantly, perhaps, it has provided a buffer against the political threat to 'existing socialism' from 'democratic capitalism' (for want of better terms).

The alternative defence and security debates in the West have tended to take both sets of fears seriously, as political 'brute facts', even if not as entirely justified fears. Up to a point, however, the geostrategic facts of life from which much of the alternative debate has started have been specified independently of any conception of the Cold War as an ideological conflict, in something like these terms: the USA remains undeniably the world's strongest single military power, but is geographically isolated from its main alliance partners; the USSR is the strongest single Eurasian military power, and is bordered almost entirely by suspicious and/or hostile regions and powers which may be collectively stronger, but would each individually be weaker than the USSR itself.

In putting forward proposals to reduce the fears of East and West in the light of these seemingly intractable facts of geopolitics, proponents of alternative approaches have mostly concentrated on Soviet conventional strategy and on conventional alternatives to the nuclear emphasis in Nato's existing flexible response doctrine. My main purpose in this chapter is to examine the Soviet and WTO responses to these alternative ideas, but a certain amount of exposition of the Western concepts is necessary before the Eastern responses can be properly assessed.

On the Western side one can identify a spectrum of positions ranging from 'Atlanticist reformers' and advocates of 'common security', through a variety of concrete military proposals for 'alternative defence', to the more radical anti-bloc and pacifist proposals of a number of groups and individuals in the peace movements.

At the establishment end of the spectrum have been the 'Atlanticist reformers', figures like the *Foreign Affairs* 'gang of four' who in 1982 advocated No-First-Use of nuclear weapons in the course of an attempt to re-establish a transatlantic consensus in the face of challenges from the Western European and US peace movements.[1] In the international sphere, Olof Palme's global initiative brought together establishment figures to advocate 'common security' in 1982, with the participation of Georgii Arbatov from the USSR.[2] The Palme Commission proposed a Central European zone free of chemical and battlefield nuclear weapons, but did not go as far as addressing non-offensive conventional strategies or advocate bloc dissolution, and was criticised from the left for its state-centred model and reluctance to challenge 'deterrence' head-on.[3]

In the 1970s and early 80s, groups and individuals in Western Europe, particularly in the FRG, were putting forward alternative models for the conventional defence of Western Europe, with minimum or no reliance on nuclear weapons. These researchers and writers were the heirs to previous attempts on similar lines, including the unsuccessful attempt of the League of Nations in the 1930s to reduce all nations' capacity for offensive war, and further attempts in the FRG in the 1950s.[4] There was considerable variety in the models put forward for 'non-provocative defence', but a succinct definition has been offered by Egbert Boeker and Lutz Unterseher: 'The build-up, training, logistics, and doctrine of the armed forces are such that they are seen in their totality to be unsuitable for offence, but unambiguously sufficient for a credible conventional defence. Nuclear weapons fulfil at most a retaliatory role.'[5]

This formulation avoids the difficulties involved in attributing defensive or offensive characteristics to individual weapons systems, and allows for considerable flexibility. Among the models put forward under this general rubric is Anders Boserup's formulaic advocacy of 'mutual defensive superiority' as a criterion for stability, which is designed to prevent a decisive outcome on the battlefield and ensure that crucial decisions remain in the hands of the politicians.[6] A wide variety of more specific models have also been put forward, some closer than others to the existing Nato posture. In the FRG the debate inevitably became entangled with relationship of some of the alternative proponents to the SPD.[7]

In the UK, the Labour Party's espousal of the principal tenets of alternative defence was not accompanied by such a range of debate, in spite of the Alternative Defence Commission's work (see below), and this contributed to the low electoral profile accorded to the issue in 1987.[8] Elsewhere in Europe, some of the most notable work was done in Denmark, where the University of Copenhagen's Centre of Peace and Conflict Research provided a forum for the work of Anders Boserup and Bjorn Moller.[9]

It can be dangerous to generalize about such a diverse body of work, but many of the alternative defence modellers did not want to appear to be posing a fundamental challenge to the existing European security system, in the sense that they tended to accept, if only for the sake of argument, establishment views about the likely form of a possible Soviet/WTO conventional attack on Western Europe. This was done partly because convincing existing military institutions of the value of alternative approaches was seen as important, and the argument used was that WTO reciprocation was desirable, but not a condition for Western restructuring. However, they certainly sought to challenge alarmist views about the likelihood of premeditated Soviet attack, and saw the dangers to crisis stability in Europe as lying in the existing mutual threat postures, exemplified in the first instance by Nato's nuclear first-use posture and WTO conventional forces.

One can draw a distinction between some of these writers and more radical currents within Western peace movements, which either took up 'civilian defence' or pacifist positions, or argued explicitly not only for European nuclear disarmament, but also for European disengagement from the US nuclear 'umbrella', and for the dissolution of both Nato and the WTO.[10] The alternative military modellers also insisted that military planning had to be seen as part of a detente policy rather than as an autonomous sphere of activity, but within the peace movements there has always been a certain wariness between proponents of the two approaches. Although it can certainly be argued that the alternative military modellers have points in common with both the Atlanticist reform currents and the anti-bloc radicals, the underlying tensions between the different political agendas can be seen clearly in any comparison between the views of the reformers and the radicals. The former were explicitly trying to re-establish an Atlanticist consensus, while many of the latter were challenging that very concept and tended towards explicitly anti-imperialist views of both the USA and the USSR. A failure to come to terms with these very different agendas has led some centrist academics with broadly alternative sympathies into unconvincing attempts to find a non-existent consensus.[11]

In Britain, the general principles of alternative defence were taken up by the Alternative Defence Commission in its 1983 report, which also aimed positively at the decoupling of US strategic nuclear weapons from Western Europe.[12] In its second report, the ADC presented a more fully articulated anti-bloc argument which moved it further from the alternative military modellers' approach.[13]

Within the Western debate, the advocates of bloc dissolution often had a stringent critique of Soviet policy, particularly in Eastern Europe.[14] There was also a limited amount of innovative writing on Soviet military policy in general, but by and large the examination of Soviet military policy was not taken up by alternative writers concentrating on detailed military plans.[15] Criticisms voiced from the left of alternative military modelling included not only the charge that it did not challenge the bloc structure, but also that it was compatible with arguments for continued high defence spending (as happened with the British Labour Party), and that its language could all too easily be turned back against the peace movement (as clearly happened in Reagan's 1983 SDI speech). From the right, meanwhile, came charges that the alternative military models were not effective, and would leave gaps to be exploited by Soviet/WTO forces, which would on no account reciprocate.[16]

My main concern in this chapter, however, is not to re-fight these Western battles, but to examine the repercussions of these Western policy debates in the East. I will look principally at the Eastern responses to the alternative military modellers, but the anti-bloc radicals' positions are also of great importance for the WTO as a military and political system. For the purposes of the military discussion, I shall use the term 'alternative defence' as interchangeable with the usages 'non-provocative/non-offensive/defensive defence', and will not deal with the fine military detail of different Western alternative proposals.

Eastern responses

In 1984, the late Stephan Tiedtke challenged an assumption which had been implicit in much of the alternative military modellers' discussions:

that Soviet/WTO responses to Western alternative proposals need not be explored until after changes had been made in the West.[17] The alternative defence debate has evolved rapidly, but five years after it was written, Tiedtke's article remains the model for organizing discussions of the Eastern side of that debate. His main points can be summarized as follows:

1 The likely responses and security interests of the WTO countries have not been sufficiently taken into account in formulating alternative defence strategies, but they should be considered if such a strategy is intended to be part of a political scheme of detente.
2 Soviet and Eastern European commentators have difficulty dealing with alternative defence concepts, possibly because they are worried about a widening of debate.
3 Alternative defence strategies in Western Europe would be bound to have *some* effect in the East, so the likely response should be investigated. Military detente should be the goal; 'As regards detente, the aim of alternative defence strategies should . . . be to make it possible for the WTO to forgo its offensive strategy.'
4 A no-first-use of nuclear weapons policy in the West would remove one of the main deterrence-related justifications for Soviet strategy, which is intended to prevent the USA fighting a limited nuclear war in Europe.
5 A conventional defence posture 'should preclude as far as possible the ability to intervene militarily in the domestic conflicts of the opposing system'.
6 Corresponding changes would be needed in Eastern European alliance and also social policy, and there is a sense in which alternative Western conceptions may present a challenge in Eastern Europe, since the repressive use of military integration would become more difficult.

Tiedtke's own conclusion was that the East–West confrontation in Europe could best initially be reduced by altering the alliances rather than by trying to break them up. His critique was a contribution to the German debate, but obviously has much wider application and could, I think, be applied to the British ADC's first Report.[18] The point he made as (6) was of great importance during the years 1980–4 (and beyond) to those Western European peace movements engaged in dialogue with like-minded private citizens in Eastern Europe. The hostility of official Eastern bodies to this dialogue amply demonstrated the threat which the anti-bloc radicals were seen as posing in both halves of Europe.[19]

At the time of Tiedtke's 1984 critique, there had been little indication of Soviet or Eastern European interest in the Western discussions of alternative defence. At this stage, work published in the Soviet Union remained largely within the confines of the Palme Commission's 'common security' advocacy, although on occasions notice was taken of the Western discussions.[20] Tiedtke made the point that although this might be partly explained by a Soviet assessment that there was then little likelihood of such alternatives being implemented, one would still expect more attention to have been paid to them. In 1984 he was certainly correct, and in publications of proceedings of major conferences on alternative security from that time, there was little evidence of substantive East–West discussions either of Soviet strategy or of Western alternatives. Neither a 1983 SIPRI conference, nor a 1985 conference in Toronto, seem to have advanced the discussion very far; indeed, the editor of the latter set of proceedings mentioned the confusion which arose between Eastern and Western participants in a discussion of non-provocative defence.[21]

From 1984 onwards, however, signs emerged of increasing Eastern interest in alternative and non-provocative defence strategies. The number of these discussions was at first small by comparison with the attention paid to trends within Nato such as ALB and FOFA, but from 1986 onwards clear references began to be made to non-offensive concepts in important speeches by Gorbachev himself, and in 1986 and 1987 the WTO's Political Consultative Committee issued statements on defensive military doctrines. The sequence of events suggests that interest spread from foreign policy academics, some of them Eastern Europeans, to the Soviet political leadership itself.

The development of this Eastern interest in alternative concepts can be traced through a variety of Western, Eastern European and Soviet publications. In early 1984, Stephen Shenfield wrote in *ADIU Report* on Viktor Girshfeld, a Soviet academic at the Moscow Institute of World Economy and International Relations (IMEMO) and advocate of 'sufficient defence' (*dostatochnaya oborona*). Girshfeld's concept involved shifting resources from tanks to anti-tank weapons, although without eliminating offensive capabilities altogether.[22] Subsequent interviews with anonymous or pseudonymous Soviet figures in the British journal *Detente* hinted at similar ideas, but did not go into much detail.[23]

Some fuller analyses of alternative defence possibilities came from Eastern European sources, particularly in Hungary and the GDR. A number of papers dealing with alternative defence were written by Professor László Valki, head of the International Law Department at Eötvös Lorand University in Budapest and Secretary-General of the Hungarian Centre for Peace Research Coordination. Valki presented papers at a number of conferences in Western Europe, and published several versions in English.[24] Valki based most of his treatment of alternative defence on German writings, plus discussions in Pugwash circles and Generals for

Peace. He contrasted Nato deep-strike developments with the kind of alternatives advocated by Horst Afheldt and Albrecht von Müller, and was generally positive about the defensive emphasis and stabilizing potential of the concept, but also voiced a number of reservations:

1 the realization of defensive defence was unlikely;
2 defensive defence could be seen as strengthening Nato if Nato could make its European defence impregnable, particularly if any Nato nuclear weapons remained in place while the concept was being implemented;
3 an invulnerable defence might give a perception of superiority even if not an actual superiority;
4 sea-based forces should be involved;
5 conventional war might once again become thinkable in Europe.

Valki tended to be cautious about addressing Soviet strategy directly, but some of the points noted above do merit further examination, in particular his reservations (2) and (3). There was a sense in which these objections rather missed the point of defensive defence, since many of its proponents would not support the retention in Western Europe of offensive nuclear missiles, or would at the very least support a no-first-use policy and a posture which made it credible. However, Valki was also making a point about European developments in a wider strategic context, as in his remark: 'A strategic balance is a global and complex phenomenon.'[25] To put it crudely, he seemed to be saying that the vulnerability of Western Europe to the WTO was at present an important element in a global balance, though he did not say this in so many words. Bjorn Moller has expressed this point slightly differently by saying that: 'Every attempt by NATO to attain conventional parity in the European theatre is perceived by the Soviet Union as an American attempt to attain global superiority.'[26]

One could argue from the WTO point of view that if Western Europe became impregnable even thanks to a non-offensive defence, but this was accompanied by, say, uncontrolled developments in offensive US naval strategies and forward-deployment in other regions, there could still be a net loss to perceived Soviet/WTO security. Much would presumably hinge here on the extent of Western European dealignment from the USA, and this might be evidence to suggest that the USSR would *not* want to see an unpredictable process of US disengagement taking place. If a Soviet/WTO deterrent threat to Western Europe is seen as a way of restraining the US, then a US policy which left Europe to its own non-offensive devices and concentrated US forces elsewhere might create unwanted complications for the USSR.

Some equally sophisticated analyses were produced by writers on alternatives from the GDR. As early as 1983, work was being done within the GDR Federation of Protestant Churches which dealt with the evolution of German–German relations within the existing bloc structure, but in which approval of Palme corridor-type proposals was accompanied by more adventurous comments on the dangers of existing conventional strategies.[27] Writers like Joachim Garstecki and Walter Romberg developed a school of thought which combined a rigorous critique of 'deterrence' (including the argument that deterrence and common security were incompatible) with a search for crisis stability through non-offensive defence strategies.[28] In a paper written for the 1986 IPRA (International Peace Research Association) conference and published in *ADIU Report*, Professor Alfred Bönisch of the GDR Central Social Science Institute quoted Afheldt approvingly on the need to make both sides unable to use their military forces offensively. He went on to say that scientists from socialist countries had been arguing on similar lines, though here he seemed to be referring to flexible response only.[29]

If these contributions from the GDR placed an understandable emphasis on the need for crisis stability in Central Europe, the more global concerns which seemed to underlie Valki's treatment were more noticeable in early Soviet discussions of alternative defence and European security. The global argument seems a comprehensible concern from an orthodox Eastern military standpoint in which 'balance' is important, and something similar was expressed in 1985 by N. Kishilov, writing in *International Affairs* [Moscow] on 'Problems of military detente in Europe'. Kishilov wrote: 'What is the meaning of "the equilibrium of military forces on the European level"? In our view, it is a component element of the global military-strategic parity between the USSR and the USA. The main components of the global military-strategic balance include both offensive and defensive forces of the sides.' Also: 'The equilibrium of military forces on the European level is a complex category comprising many components and at the same time it is a changeable category.'[30] This may not be saying much of substance, but it suggests a military approach likely to be wary of non-offensive defence. After all, whether or not the WTO actually has conventional superiority in Central Europe, this is one of the few areas of the globe where the Soviet Union could have much hope of ever attaining superiority over the USA.

Denis Healey recounted a conversation he had in Moscow with similar implications, and did not seem to appreciate the grounds on which an unnamed Soviet general objected to his (and General Rogers's) alternative suggestion: 'I recently discussed with a Soviet General in Moscow General Rogers' proposal for laying pipes underground on West German territory which could be filled with an explosive slurry to create wide and deep tank traps in case of war. The Soviet General opposed it on the grounds that it would provide NATO forces with "an inviolable sanctuary" – the best recommendation possible, I would have thought!'[31]

Further items in the Soviet press in late 1985 and early 1986 indicated close study of the Western debate and its repercussions in Western European political parties, notably articles in *International Affairs* and *SSHA* by E. Silin and A. A. Kokoshin respectively.[32] These articles were non-committal or cautiously positive about alternative ideas, as was G. Shakhnazarov in a review in mid-1986 of Dietrich Fischer's book *Preventing War in the Nuclear Age*.[33] The Kokoshin article contained an intriguing passage which amounted almost to an acceptance that Nato's nuclear first use policy *was* justified in the 1950s at a time when Nato conventional forces were weak and the USSR still had large ground forces, although it was also critical of alternative writers' treatment of Soviet military thought.[34] The 1986 yearbook from the Moscow Institute of World Economy and International Relations also indicated acquaintance with the Western literature, and made positive comments about a number of the Western concepts.[35]

One comment made repeatedly by these Eastern writers came very close to the first point of Stephan Tiedtke's critique: alternative defence strategies should be regarded as only one element in a broad edifice of European security policy. The point was made implicitly or explicitly by each of Valki, Silin, Kokoshin and Bönisch. Up to a point it may have been an attempt to divert the Western critique of offensive Soviet strategies, but there seemed to be more to it than that. It was clear by early 1986 that there was a discussion going on in a fuller sense than Tiedtke had seen two years before, though there was still a lack of *Western* examination of the Eastern response. The principal Eastern reservations about alternatives could be identified as: (a) a political assessment of the peripherality of alternative concepts, which might nevertheless be declining; (b) a military wariness about the implications of alternatives for a 'global balance'; and (c) a political point about the need for military alternatives to be put forward as part of a broader security concept.

One could also comment that developments in conventional weaponry and electronics might simply be viewed as part of a more general shift towards conventional military strategies, as outlined in chapter 4, and so a possible source of shifts in an East–West military-technological correlation of forces. This was probably one of the aspects of SDI which most worried the USSR, quite apart from its direct impact on nuclear strategy. In this sense one can see why deep strike and alternative strategies might not at first glance look too distinct from a Soviet viewpoint. Conversely, a Soviet interest in developments which look vaguely alternative would not necessarily imply more than an awareness of this area as a key field of competition. If Marshal Ogarkov's celebrated 1984 *Krasnaya Zvezda* interview, calling for increased resources for conventional weaponry, is looked at in this light, it suggests grounds both for Soviet military scepticism about alternative defence on the Nato side, and for a more general scepticism about possible Soviet responses to any Western shifts.[36]

Throughout this period, forums for East–West discussion of alternatives were provided by specialist bodies such as the Pugwash Study Group on Conventional Forces in Europe. This forum began meeting in 1984, and judging by the published reports of its proceedings, it facilitated discussion between civilian and military experts, and also began to look in some detail at WTO strategies.[37] It was also able to make authoritative statements on the problem, such as its Memorandum to the Stockholm Conference in early 1986, 'Force structures specialized for defence as a new approach to European security'.[38]

From 1986 onwards, Mikhail Gorbachev began to make some promising allusions to alternative defence, in contexts which seemed to relate it to the concept of 'reasonable sufficiency' already examined in chapter 5. In making his general secretary's report to the CPSU Congress in February 1986, Gorbachev made a particular effort to address Western fears in his comments that: 'The Soviet military doctrine is also entirely in keeping with the letter and spirit of the initiatives we have put forward. Its orientation is unequivocally defensive. In the military sphere we intend to act in such a way as to give nobody grounds for fears, even imagined, about their security.'[39] Gorbachev's choice of words here seemed to imply a recognition that past Soviet actions had not been sufficiently reassuring, though the reference was not explicit enough to make it clear whether the self-criticism might be directed at nuclear policies or conventional strategies.

More explicit references to non-offensive alternatives began to appear in mid-1986. Speaking in East Berlin in April, Gorbachev followed up his February remarks with a further appeal to Western Europe: 'One more thing. I would like to appeal to all the West Europeans from here, from the capital of the socialist GDR: do not believe allegations about the aggressiveness of the Soviet Union. Our country will never and under no circumstances begin armed operations against Western Europe unless we or our allies become targets of a NATO attack! I repeat, never!'[40] This could perhaps be read both as a political appeal and as a recognition of the interconnections between active and passive defence, though this second interpretation might be reading too much into Gorbachev's words.

The Budapest appeal of the WTO in June 1986 was less ambiguous: 'In the interests of security in Europe and the whole world, the military concepts and doctrines of the military alliances must be based on defensive principles.'[41] New ground was definitely being broken here, since although the statement went on to repeat the traditional position that WTO *doctrine* was defensive in nature, no such claim was made for military *concepts*, and the implied opening-up of a discussion of defensive alternatives seemed to be addressed to both sides. Speaking in Vladivostok in July, Gorbachev mentioned 'reasonable sufficiency' as applicable to conventional forces in Asia, in the course of a speech directed towards China and the Pacific.[42]

In a number of speeches during early 1987, Gorbachev made some even clearer allusions to alternative defence. Speaking to the Moscow Forum for a Nuclear-Weapon-Free-World in February, he said: 'It is important, in our view, while scaling down military confrontation, to carry through such measures as would make it possible to lessen, or better still, altogether exclude the possibility of surprise attack. The most dangerous offensive arms must be removed from the zone of contact. Quite naturally, military doctrines must be purely of a defensive nature.'[43] One of the Western speakers at this forum was Anders Boserup. Boserup's paper 'Road to trust: non-aggressive defence' was published later that year in the Soviet Peace Committee's English-language journal, together with a paper by Professor Hylke Tromp of the Netherlands, voicing some familiar Western criticisms of alternative defence as an attempt to address the symptoms, rather than the causes, of East–West tension.[44] Boserup's contribution to the forum and his principle of 'mutual defensive superiority' were also mentioned positively in an assessment of the event by V. Abakov and V. Baranovskii in *MEMO*.[45]

In a speech to Soviet trade unions shortly afterwards, Gorbachev spoke again of 'sensible, sufficient defence', though without implying that this necessitated defensive conventional postures.[46] Speaking in Czechoslovakia in April, he once again paid more attention to conventional arms. On this occasion, he mentioned 'reasonable sufficiency' alongside the comment on removing the most dangerous armaments from the contact zone, and even acknowledged 'asymmetry' and 'inequality in certain elements' between the opposing forces in Europe.[47] This section of the speech seemed to be a challenge to more extreme Western assertions of Soviet superiority, but together with an admission that changes would be needed in Soviet as well as Western postures, as Gorbachev put it through a process of levelling down, rather than up, any inequalities which might be revealed through an exchange of data. (This formula had originally been used by Gorbachev on the occasion of President Mitterand's visit to the USSR in July 1986.)

At around the same time, Gorbachev also spoke at a dinner for Hafiz al-Assad about the notions 'defensive' and 'offensive' being anachronisms in the nuclear age, and in the course of a critique of nuclear deterrence in his speech during Margaret Thatcher's visit, said again that 'Arms must be reduced to a level of reasonable sufficiency, that is only the level needed to cope with the tasks of defence.'[48] The problem in interpreting Gorbachev's speeches during this period was that they did not go into sufficient detail to provide an entirely clear indication of the relationship between 'reasonable sufficiency' and possible non-provocative conventional strategies. However, Gorbachev's own comments did not come out of the blue, but seemed to have a basis in a number of more detailed commentaries by influential Soviet writers, which provided further evidence of a debate in policy-making and advisory circles.

V. Petrovskii, writing on 'security through disarmament' in early 1987, asked 'What are the characteristics of sufficiency?', and replied that it excluded nuclear weapons, excluded the offensive or aggressive use of force, and was a political rather than a military concept.[49] When he moved on to deal with the details of troop reductions in Europe, however, he shifted back to treating it as a question of purely *numerical* reductions (citing the WTO's Budapest proposal for a 25 per cent cut), rather than of concepts or strategies.

G. A. Trofimenko, of the US–Canada Institute, was more explicit. Shortly after the Budapest WTO meeting, Trofimenko commented that 'the Warsaw Treaty Organization's political and military leaders have in fact treated positively the idea of non-provocative defence.'[50] Later, he wrote that 'The Soviet Union and its partners in the Warsaw Pact are actually planning concrete steps towards the creation on both sides of so-called non-provocative defence, under which conditions the danger of sudden attack would be sharply reduced.'[51]

Anatolii Dobrynin, the former ambassador to Washington appointed as secretary to the CPSU Central Committee's international department, spoke in May 1986 to the All-Union Conference of Scientists on the Problems of Peace and Prevention of Nuclear War of the urgent need for analysis of problems such as the interdependence of the offensive and defensive and the definition of 'reasonable sufficiency'.[52] Dobrynin's remarks carried the clear implication that 'reasonable sufficiency' had been announced as a guiding principle before the Soviet leadership had much of an idea of what it actually meant, and that help was now being requested from a broad community of Soviet scholars. A number of Western journalists and delegations visiting the Soviet Union testified to the existence of the debate, and to the presence on the Soviet agenda of 'reasonable sufficiency' and its application to conventional forces.[53]

In the course of a trip to the Soviet Union in May 1987, I saw a good deal of evidence that Dobrynin's encouragement of discussion had borne some fruit, but equally that the debate appeared to be at a fairly early stage. As far as one could tell, the call had gone out for specialists to give some substance to the concept of 'reasonable sufficiency' after Gorbachev's initial use of the term. Some arms control specialists who had been following Western literature on alternative defence were in a good position to take advantage of this, while others seem to have been more taken by surprise. Presumably the concept itself may have found its way into Gorbachev's congress report and later speeches through the medium of particular advisers and/or speechwriters, perhaps including Dobrynin himself. (Soviet diplomats stationed in Western Europe also seem to have played a role.) In the ensuing debate, some writers and researchers in circles like the Institute of World Economy and International Relations and the US–Canada Institute begun to think about non-provocative concepts as an application of 'reasonable sufficiency' in the conventional sphere. At the same time, however, a number of those who seemed to appreciate the importance of non-provocative defence, as a potential way of convincing Western Europe of the USSR's peaceable intentions, seemed to have few illusions about how unwilling the Soviet military establishment would be to move towards such a concept. Perhaps the most interesting aspect of these developments was the apparent intention to open up areas of discussion which might formerly have been considered the sole preserve of the military, with the possibility that the party could then use more widespread discussion to counterbalance military inputs into decision-making.

Dobrynin alluded to Western European social democrats' discussions of non-offensive defence in a further speech on 4 May 1987, and spoke of the possibility of exchanging opinions on that basis. In the sphere of public proposals, the WTO foreign ministers repeated the idea of diminishing the danger of suprise attack when they met in Moscow in March.[54]

In the weeks preceeding the WTO's PCC meeting in Berlin at the end of May, speculation was again rife that Gorbachev was about to announce another spectacular initiative – a unilateral withdrawal of some Soviet forces from Eastern Europe, or perhaps an initiative on Germany. In the event, the meeting produced only a communiqué and a document on WTO military doctrine, and no speech by Gorbachev was published.[55] The main communiqué dealt with rectifying imbalances and the withdrawal of the most offensive weapons from the contact zone, and backed the Jaruzelski Plan, but left more detailed doctrinal considerations to the second document.

In this second document's treatment, the previous year's advocacy of defensive principles for the 'military concepts and doctrines' of both blocs was taken up again, in the context of a proposal for consultations between the WTO and Nato to compare their respective military doctrines, and study developments which could remove mistrust. There also appeared to be a revision of the traditional definition of military doctrine, the formula used here being: 'The military doctrine of the Warsaw Pact, just like that of each of its member countries, is subordinated to the task of preventing war, both nuclear and conventional.' (The earliest published redefinition of the goals of military doctrine has been identified in the 1986 second edition of the *Military Encyclopaedic Dictionary*.[56]) It was also proposed that conventional armaments should be reduced 'down to the level at which neither side, in ensuring its defence, would have means for a sudden attack on the other side or for starting offensive operations in general' (a blend of numerical and qualitative terminology). There was also a compromise in the application of the term 'sufficiency' in the military doctrine document, since at one point it was claimed that 'they [the Warsaw Treaty states] strictly comply with the limits of sufficiency for defence and for repelling possible aggression', even though familiar terminology about delivering a 'crushing rebuff' to any aggression was also used. Thus, parts of the document accepted fairly explicitly that WTO military concepts had contributed to mistrust and needed changing, while others claimed that present force levels and policies did not exceed the needs of sufficiency. The full term 'reasonable sufficiency' was not, in fact, actually used.

The statements made by the WTO in Budapest and Berlin had some fairly obvious targets in the West: Nato's longstanding policy of envisaging the first use of nuclear weapons, and the emerging concepts of Follow-On Forces Attack, AirLand Battle, and the US Maritime Strategy, would obviously be the subjects of Eastern criticism in any discussion of doctrines. But these doctrinal issues were not raised in such a way as to suggest that the WTO thought it could escape with its own strategic concepts unscrutinized, despite the ambiguities which existed within the Berlin document itself. These WTO approaches went beyond longstanding Eastern proposals for a non-use of force agreement, appeared to reflect the influence of Western alternative discussions, and also suggested that the WTO itself might have an enhanced role in future negotiations – it emerged during 1987 that a WTO Experts' Working Group on Conventional Forces had been formed.[57]

In further statements made after the Berlin meeting, senior Soviet figures offered some clarification, but did not really clear up the ambiguities of the document. At a briefing in late June 1987, Deputy Foreign Minister V. F. Petrovskii and Deputy Chief of General Staff M. A. Gareev dealt in turn with the political and military-technical sides of doctrine. Gareev provided a fairly strong formulation on the implications for military art: 'The basic method of the Soviet Armed Forces in repelling aggression will be defensive operations and combat actions.'[58]

The new Minister of Defence, General D. T. Yazov (who replaced Marshal Sokolov after Mathias Rust's landing in Red Square), was more equivocal in an article for *Pravda* entitled 'The Warsaw Pact's military doctrine – a doctrine for the defence of peace and socialism'. Yazov combined a traditional exposition of the WTO as dedicated to the 'defence of the gains of socialism' with an explanation of 'sufficiency' and of the need for forces which could not carry out offensive operations. However, this capacity was described as something desirable in the future rather than a present reality, and Yazov also appeared concerned to reassure his audience with his comments that: 'The limits of sufficiency are set not by us, but by the actions of the USA and Nato', and 'The Warsaw Pact's defensive military doctrine, geared exclusively to repulsing the external military threat, does not mean that our actions will have a passive character.' Marshal Akhromeev provided a similar exposition in a piece written for an international audience.[59]

These statements, therefore, did not remove the impression of an unresolved policy discussion. Gareev did provide a useful expansion of the new formulation of doctrine at a Novosti press briefing in February 1988, when he contrasted it with the traditional definition:

> The present military doctrine of the Warsaw Treaty states is a system of officially received fundamental views on the prevention of war, military organization, the preparation of [WTO] countries and armed forces for the repulsion of aggression and the means of armed combat for the defence of socialism.
>
> What is new here is that if earlier military doctrine was determined as a system of views on the preparation for war and its conduct, now the basis of its content is the prevention of war. The task of war-prevention is becoming the main goal, the kernel of military doctrine, the basic function of the state and its armed forces. Of course, world war must be prevented mainly by political means, but this must also be reflected in military activity.[60]

Explaining the reassessment

What factors might account for this apparent Soviet/WTO interest in defensive military strategies? More importantly, perhaps, what are its practical implications, and what do the ambiguities noted above tell us about the recent and current state of Soviet civil–military relations? In answer to the first question, I would suggest that in addition to the factors involved in Soviet 'new thinking' at a general foreign policy level, there are four specific influences at work on these developments in the field of conventional forces and strategies.

(1) Western influence The strong circumstantial evidence of interest among civilian analysts and the political leadership in Western alternative defence concepts has been reviewed above. There is, however, a need for caution here, since the circumstantial evidence in itself provides no way of judging the weight or extent of this Western influence. It is not easy to establish the facts of this process without much more evidence than we have available at present, and it is not *a priori* altogether convincing to put the Soviet interest down to Western influence alone. There are also some crucial items of evidence which suggest that it is less a matter of direct Western influence than of the Western writings having been in the right place, at the right time, to be taken notice of.

For example, Gareev's 1985 book identified a 1984 decision to set up a *nomenklatura* of specialists to examine questions of military science: 'It was precisely from these positions that it was determined in 1984 by the State Committee of the Council of Ministers of the USSR for Science and Technology to establish a *nomenklatura* of specialist scholarly workers in the field of military science and other social, natural, and technical sciences.'[61] Thus, although the calls to involve civilian specialists in military analysis became more open later on, some kind of decision to that effect was taken as early as 1984.[62] This is not to say, however, that the civilian specialists would not have been interested anyway, and it does seem clear that once the Soviet debate had been officially opened up to Western influences, they were able to play a substantial role.

(2) Strategic revisions The most elegant hypothesis which would explain the Soviet interest in alternative defence at a more fundamental level has been offered by Michael MccGwire. MccGwire suggests that further major strategic revisions have been made by Soviet military planners during the course of the 1980s, which updated the priorities established after 1966 (see chapter 4). He argues that during the early 1980s, Soviet planners became increasingly aware of a danger of conflict with the USA in the region north of the Persian Gulf. They concluded, however, that such a regional conflict would not inevitably escalate to world war, and from this followed a further conclusion: in those circumstances, there would be no point in escalating the conflict horizontally by launching an offensive into Western Europe, and 'holding' operations in the West would be sufficient.[63]

MccGwire also associates this new strategic shift with the creation of the TVD command structure, but is not entirely convincing here as that particular reorganization seems to have commenced before his postulated strategic revision. The value of his hypothesis lies in the fact that it accounts for Soviet thinking at a satisfactory basic level of national security concerns, and solves the problems involved in attributing the

alternative defence interest to an implausibly high degree of Soviet openness to influence from Western Europe. Since this account is of a pre-
Gorbachev shift in thinking and planning, it also gives more grounds for
seeing the changes as relatively independent of Gorbachev's personal
position and diplomacy.

The relative shift of Soviet military attention away from Central Europe
towards the southern Soviet border can be documented to a certain
extent. There has been considerable attention paid to US and Nato
deployments away from Europe, such as the US Rapid Deployment
Force, obvious concern about the Iran–Iraq War, and of course the
long-running war in Afghanistan.[64] The war in Afghanistan undoubtedly
gave rise to much operational rethinking in an army poorly prepared for
combat against guerrilla opponents in mountainous terrain, and may well
also have caused a reappraisal of the relationship between offence and
defence along the southern border regions, and innovative thinking on
questions like the use of helicopters. In early 1983, a new mountain
warfare training centre was reported to have been set up in the Central
Asian Military District.[65] Service in Afghanistan and the Southern TVD
also led to rapid advances in the careers of a number of senior officers who
gained significant promotions in the mid-1980s. A note of caution should
be introduced here, however. The sheer size of the territory which the
Soviet armed forces have to defend makes a capacity for relatively rapid
redeployment imperative, and central strategic reserves would have to
maintain this capacity whatever the tactical guidelines issued to forces
stationed on the borders. Thoroughgoing non-offensiveness therefore
seems an unlikely option, even if MccGwire's hypothesis is essentially
correct.

A more familiar point made in numerous Western and Soviet analyses
of Gorbachev's foreign policy has been that it is premised on a reduction
in international tension providing a breathing-space for the Soviet economy. One or two qualifications are necessary here, although the point is
no doubt quite correct in general terms. Nuclear arms reductions will not
save the USSR much money in the short term, which provides an
additional impetus for savings on conventional forces, as some Soviet
commentators have stated. Even with savings on conventional forces,
however, it is not clear that the civil economy will benefit greatly, if the
Soviet economy's most basic problems are caused by the inefficiency of
civil investment rather than the relative or absolute level of military
spending.[66] In mid-1988 General Vitalii Shabanov, the First Deputy
Minister of Defence for Armaments, claimed in an interview that the
Soviet military budget had been declining since 1986 and would continue
to do so, though this clashed with other comments which came close to
admitting that before price reforms were carried out, the USSR was

unable to say precisely how much it spent on defence as a proportion of GNP.[67]

(3) The role of Western Europe   The strategic reassessment identified by MccGwire would pre-date Gorbachev and involve a downgrading of the danger of Central Europe providing a *casus belli* between East and West. There is also a further sense in which Gorbachev's diplomacy revises Soviet attitudes towards Western Europe, and which seems more clearly associated with Gorbachev's own leadership: the appreciation of the political disutility of an offensive military strategy towards a neighbouring region.

This problem seems to have been understood, if not clearly stated, by the Eastern European analysts who took up Western alternative ideas at an early stage. It challenges orthodox thinking both in the West, in the form of traditional arguments about a potential Soviet capacity for blackmail and intimidation, and in the USSR, in the sense that the offensive capability was traditionally seen as a simple strategic necessity.

Orthodox Soviet analyses of the history of detente see the process as having deeper roots in Western Europe than in the USA, and on the Western side this gives rise to the familiar but superficial allegations of Soviet 'wedge-driving' within Nato. More soberly, however, a search for improved relations with Western Europe in the post-INF world can be explained in terms of the desirability of increasing economic and techno-logical ties with the region, and of attempting to influence US policy via close US allies like Britain and the FRG. The Soviet Academy of Sciences announced in late 1987 its intention to set up a new institute to study Western Europe. Under Gorbachev there has been a good deal of rather vague talk about Europe as 'our common home', which seems to be partly an expression of a historical Russian/Soviet desire not to be considered an outcast nation. For Gorbachev and a number of academics and advisers, however, there seems also to be a very basic military factor involved: they think offensive military strategies are a bad thing.

In rather more general terms, the policy of seeking improved relations with regional powers relatively independently of US–Soviet relations applies to other regions as well as Europe, though there must be fairly narrow limits beyond which the USA will not be downgraded as the USSR's primary diplomatic interlocutor.[68]

(4) Reactions to Nato   Since the apparent Soviet strategic reassessment may be partly a reaction to Western military priorities to the south of the USSR, it is worth investigating whether this might also be the case in Europe itself. Careful analysis reveals a good deal of evidence that improved US and Nato capabilities have played a significant role in

influencing Soviet revisions. There is evidence that WTO air defence may have undergone reorganization partly in response to the West; that the pattern of Soviet naval deployments has been affected by the need to cope with the US Maritime Strategy; and that increased attention in Soviet writings to strategic defence, over a period of several years, can be attributed to a fear of US nuclear and/or general military-technological superiority. There is a distinction to be drawn here between operational-tactical defence, to be used during a conventional phase of war before a transition to the counteroffensive, and strategic defence, which has more application in a possible nuclear war. In this analysis, increased Soviet attention to the defensive can be related to expressed concerns about FOFA, AirLand Battle, and advanced conventional technologies, at the operational-tactical level (see chapter 4), and about SDI at the nuclear level. Even the non-realization of SDI in any form close to its original conception would not invalidate this hypothesis, since it has always been part of the Soviet concern that shifts in the overall military-technological correlation of forces were a possible outcome of intensive SDI research.

In a development which ties in with the hypothesis of Michael MccGwire, as outlined above, material in *Voenno-Istoricheskii Zhurnal* and elsewhere began to reflect increased attention to strategic defence around 1984/5. This discussion was partly conducted in terms of shortcomings in military planning before 1941 which left Soviet forces well-prepared to go on to the offensive, but insufficiently prepared to conduct strategic defensive operations.

This hypothesis might appear inconsistent with the suggestion that Central Europe has been downgraded as an area of concern, but its main contention is that adequate attention should be paid to Western initiatives in assessing shifts in Soviet priorities, which is quite consonant with the 'southern border regions' framework of analysis. The Pentagon's *Soviet Military Power 1988* contained a number of strikingly explicit comments on Soviet shifts as responses to ALB and FOFA. These comments came as something of a surprise, as Western sources had previously been reluctant to acknowledge the possible influence of offensive US/Nato capabilities.[69]

Post-Berlin Soviet debates

During the year which followed the May 1987 publication of the WTO's Berlin document on military doctrines, a number of Western commentators were given access to the Soviet press to discuss conventional forces and strategies, often in the form of exchanges with Soviet analysts. A number of these Westerners were advocates of alternative defence strategies, though not all; they included Andreas von Bülow, Admiral Sir

James Eberle, Dan Smith, Jonathan Steele, Stephen Shenfield and John Keegan.[70] Some of these exchanges were more interesting than others. Andrei Kokoshin's indirect reply to a point made by Eberle about Operational Manoeuvre Groups was perhaps the most explicit comment: 'The political tenets of WTO military doctrine are obligatory for the military art and structuring of the Soviet Armed Forces and the allied armies. The basic method of the Soviet Armed Forces in repelling aggression will be defensive operations and combat actions.'[71] Gorbachev himself also replied to a letter from a group of Western proponents of alternative strategies (Anders Boserup, Robert Neild, Frank von Hippel, Albrecht von Müller); a mistaken newspaper report that Gorbachev had personally asked one of these writers to submit a position paper on conventional force reductions seems to have been based on a slightly distorted account of this exchange.[72]

Soviet commentators themselves were engaged over this period in an involved process of commentary both on military doctrine in general, and on the conventional applications of 'reasonable sufficiency' in particular. The pattern which emerged was, not unexpectedly, one of civilian writers being relatively adventurous in drawing out the implications of the new terminology, while military writers tended to be either more cautious or, on occasions when they were not called upon to comment on doctrine *per se*, to ignore the changes which were supposed to be in progress. Military writers tended to treat 'reasonable sufficiency' as a purely quantitative force concept, while civilians were more likely to endorse structural non-offensiveness as a goal, though the division was not absolute.[73] The overall effect was to confirm the sense of uncertainty surrounding the Berlin document itself and the explanations given immediately afterwards.

Civilian commentators included some who were reluctant to apply 'reasonable sufficiency' to anything other than nuclear weapons, and others who formulated its application in the conventional field as legitimizing both unilateral troop cuts on the lines of Khrushchev's late 1950s reductions, and defensive tactics as well as operational art.[74] There were also a number of round-table discussions published between civilian and retired military analysts which confirmed the hypothesis that the content of 'reasonable sufficiency' was not finalized, but that non-provocative defence was among the elements it might be taken to include.[75]

Several interesting pieces were published in *MEMO* by A. A. Kokoshin, Deputy Director of the US–Canada Institute. In the first, co-authored with V. Larionov, he picked out the 1943 Battle of Kursk as an event from Soviet military history which showed that prepared positional defence could withstand a powerful attack, and thus had some relevance to non-provocative defence (*neprovotsiruyushchaya oborona*).[76] In a second piece a few months later, Kokoshin was less adventurous, but endorsed Boserup's principle of mutual defensive superiority without specifying its source. In a further joint article in mid-1988, the two authors moved on to discuss much more concrete and explicit alternative military models in terms of the relationship between offence, defence, and the counteroffensive.[77]

A number of military writers struck a rather different note. Lieutenant-General Dmitrii Volkogonov more or less equated 'reasonable sufficiency' with traditional conceptions of parity and called for staunchness in face of the danger of war.[78] A series of articles in *Mezhdunarodnaya Zhizn'* (*International Affairs*) appeared to pay lip-service to defensive principles as a new doctrine while arguing on traditional lines that the aggressiveness of imperialism was growing; that ideological struggle was intensifying (neither of which points matched the co-operative emphasis more normal in Gorbachev's own 'new thinking' speeches); and insisted in particular on the aggressive nature of US military doctrine.[79] Some high-ranking officers came close to contradicting Gorbachev directly. General A. I. Gribkov (WTO Chief of Staff) told an interviewer that counteroffensives would be used in repelling aggression, and also that new developments were taking place in the theory of military art to ensure that this could be done more effectively.[80] General Ivan Tret'yak (C-in-C of Air Defence Forces) spoke of 'reliable defence' as the key to 'reasonable sufficiency', and met the comparison with Khrushchev's troop cuts head-on with a comment that that they had damaged both defence capacity and the morale of officer personnel.[81]

Material published in *Voenno-Istoricheskii Zhurnal* continued to draw offensive lessons from past operations, notably the 1945 assault on Berlin, and acknowledged the debt due to Tukhachevskii.[82] The monthly journal *Voennyi Vestnik* announced that it would be paying particular attention to defensive combat during 1988, though some of the articles then published went no further than treating the defensive as a way of providing conditions to return to the offensive.[83] At around the same time a Pentagon estimate was reported as calculating that the figure for defensive exercises as a percentage of total recent Soviet military exercises was up from 10–20 per cent to about 30 per cent, and reports surfaced about new Soviet Defence Ministry directives which were claimed to have reached the West.[84]

The very confusion of these varied contributions seemed to confirm that something was indeed afoot. Some senior military officers followed in Yazov's footsteps with articles which veered between offensive and defensive terminology.[85] Probably the most important material published during this period was Yazov's short book *Na strazhe sotsializma i mira* (*In defence of socialism and peace*), which was signed to press on 9 October 1987.[86]

This text incorporated both a degree of caution about 'sufficiency' and some genuinely new formulations. Yazov did not avoid the term 'sufficiency' and used a mixture of quantitative and qualitative terminology to explain it, as had the Berlin document on doctrine. On the other hand, he seemed to favour the term 'reliable defence' as the basic criterion, and did not use the full term 'reasonable sufficiency'. Most notably, however, Yazov reversed the traditional formulation which had in the past prioritized the offensive as the main form of military actions (see chapter 4). His key passage read as follows:

> Soviet military doctrine regards the *defence* as the main form of military actions in repulsing aggression. The defence must be reliable and stable, firm and active, and must be calculated to halt the opponent's attack, exhaust him, prevent any loss of territory, and achieve the defeat of the enemy groups' incursion.
>
> However, the defence cannot defeat an aggressor on its own. Therefore, after repulsing the attack, troops and naval forces must be capable of carrying out a *decisive offensive*. The transition to the offensive will take the form of a counteroffensive, which must be carried out in a complex and tense situation of combat with a well-armed opponent.[87] (Emphases in original)

There was clearly an inconsistency in Yazov's position here, as this passage followed shortly after a specification that neither side should have the capacity to start offensive operations (a phrase taken from the Berlin document). Nevertheless, this passage about the relationship between defence and counteroffensive was still a revision of the more traditional formula. One cannot, of course, tell from the text alone whether Yazov's reformulation was substantive or merely verbal. Yazov also provided a similar, but less adventurous, formulation in an article written as a commentary on the INF Treaty. Here, he defined sufficiency in both its nuclear and conventional sense:

> Guided by its defensive doctrine, the USSR implements the structuring of its armed forces on the basis of the principle of sufficiency for defence. For strategic nuclear forces, sufficiency today is determined by the capability not to permit a nuclear attack to go unpunished, even in the most unfavourable circumstances. For conventional arms, sufficiency provides for the *minimum* necessary number and a high quality of armed forces and armaments, which are capable of reliably ensuring the defence of the country. [. . .]
>
> Starting from the principle of sufficiency, the USSR is making

every effort to lower decisively the level of confrontation, to reduce
military potentials so that both East and West retain only those
forces and means which are necessary for defence. But this must
apply to everyone.[88]

This was less than a ringing endorsement of non-offensiveness, since it
gave no guidance on what exactly was considered 'necessary for defence',
and the formulation was again quantitative rather than structural. Similar
uncertainties emerged from Yazov's meeting with US Defense Secretary
Frank Carlucci in March 1983 in Berne. Reports of the meeting attributed
three rather different views to Yazov: that no changes were needed since
Soviet doctrine had always been defensive; that any changes would have
to be mutually agreed rather than unilaterally implemented; that changes
would soon be visible in Soviet training and manoeuvres. Yazov's own
press conference statement contained hints of all three positions, though
with more stress on the second.[89]

The terminological uncertainties were compounded in documents and
speeches from the 19th Party Conference in June–July 1988, by which
time Gorbachev himself seemed to have settled for 'defence sufficiency',
and the only person to stick to 'reasonable sufficiency' seems to have been
Evgenii Primakov. The WTO defence ministers, meeting shortly afterwards, came up with 'necessary sufficiency of armaments and troops'.[90]

Perhaps the most explicit academic admission of the inconsistency
between a defensive doctrine and offensive military-technical concepts
came in Alexei Arbatov's chapter on 'Military doctrines' in the 1987
IMEMO Yearbook *Disarmament and Security*, which appeared in mid-1988.
Arbatov provided a critique of earlier Soviet writings on the possibility of
victory, and also quoted comments from Akhromeev and Gribkov on the
importance of the counteroffensive, in such a way as to suggest a preference for tighter constraints on counteroffensive capacities than the military might like.[91]

These uncertainties raise a set of further questions about civil–military
relations under Gorbachev, and about the processes by which military
reforms are instigated and carried through. Reforms of conventional
military strategy would appear to contain even more potential for civil–
military conflict than revised requirements for nuclear forces, and examples have already been given which suggest the existence of a spectrum of
views in both fields.

The potential for civil–military conflict in a shift towards greater
emphasis on defensive conventional defence depends partly on one's
estimation of the recent processes at work, and partly on one's general
model of Soviet civil–military relations. If a reassessment has been made

by the political leadership relatively independently of military advice, then the party leadership will need to rely on its traditional ultimate responsibility for determining defence policy in order to push the desired reforms through (even if it is not yet sure what they are). A shift towards the defensive in military art and the technical side of doctrine represents a more obvious intrusion on military privileges than political initiatives on questions like the level of military spending, arms control and the utility of nuclear weapons; this makes the task look a daunting one.

The problem may not be quite so acute if the reassessment has been a more complicated product of a variety of military and political concerns, as seems possible. If that is the case, the reassessment might amount to a revision of the offence–defence relationship along all Soviet borders, perhaps involving a different balance in different regions, but within an agreed overall framework of downgrading the role of military capabilities in foreign policy. It would follow from this that the resolution of the debates thrown up would be less a matter of a straight civil–military argument, but the fact remains that a shift towards the defensive would be a very radical reform indeed for Soviet military policy, and the likelihood of its being seen by some of the military as a political intrusion remains.

Different models of Soviet civil–military relations have some bearing here. Are these relations characterized principally by incipient political–military conflict, such that the military has to be kept under control by the Main Political Administration (MPA)? Or is the MPA really a joint administrator of a military system in which there is a general congruence between political and military priorities? Are Soviet military politics better described in terms of competing institutional interests, in which case the military institutions most obviously under threat under Gorbachev would appear to be the traditionally-dominant Strategic Rocket Forces and Ground Forces?[92]

Whichever of these models is judged most accurate, the potential radicalism of Gorbachev's military reforms is greater than anything proposed since Khrushchev's day, and their effect on the system would be considerable. Gorbachev's own relations with the military leadership during his first three years as general secretary seemed smoother than had been the case before Ogarkov's removal as chief of staff in 1984. There were substantial changes in the high command, including Sokolov's replacement by Yazov. The apparently increasing role of civilian advisers during this period has already been noted, though their weight did not necessarily increase sufficiently for them to be able to challenge the general staff on technical matters.[93] During 1988, some Western journalists reported extremely frank comments from civilians and academics about their differences with the military and the difficulty of convincing them about non-offensiveness.[94]

Jack Snyder has argued that projected reforms in military doctrine and strategy can be related to Gorbachev's broader reform programme in the sense that his political, economic and military reforms are all challenging entrenched institutions whose dominance dates back to the Stalin period. In military policy, these institutions traditionally operated on expansionist assumptions and zero–sum approaches to security. The success of Gorbachev's security reforms, Snyder argues, is thus closely tied to his political and economic programmes.[95]

On the basis of the evidence offered above, I would suggest that the different influences which can be identified as possible contributors to the reassessment only came together at the highest level of policy-making. Lower down, the academics and advisers were reading Western literature, and the military planners were making their own reassessments, but independently of each other. Gorbachev's personal openness to Western influences was an important factor, but Yazov approached these questions from a more orthodox military perspective. The subsequent confluence of different influences left a substantial degree of uncertainty and fluidity in the situation, at least up until mid-1988. One must therefore conclude that some of the existing models of Soviet civil–military rela tions may have to be reconsidered in the light of the potential radicalism of some of Gorbachev's reforms.

The connections between security policy and broader reform programmes can also be looked at via an examination of the meaning of military *perestroika*. In the most general terms, the meaning of *perestroika*, in the sense of the demands it makes of Soviet society as a whole, involves efficiency as well as reform. In the military sphere, this might imply not only the reform of doctrine and strategy in the directions that have been speculated on, but also efficiency in the simple sense of doing the job better, both politically and technically. This requirement is not likely to be in conflict with reforms favoured by the political leadership, since Gorbachev himself certainly does not want an *inefficient* military system. It can be argued that shifts towards a more defensive emphasis would serve the security of the Soviet Union more effectively, and perhaps enable resources to be conserved. General Yazov's first year in his post showed him to be particularly insistent on seeing the military system working effectively, and in this sense his views did not diverge from traditional concerns that an apparently more conciliatory posture abroad should not detract from vigilance and military preparedness at home.[96]

Increased efficiency *per se* does not entail greater defensiveness, though, and there is a sense in which the goal of military *perestroika* might be presented as a slimmed-down but more effective 'conventional' fighting force on the kind of lines favoured by Ogarkov, even if this was not Gorbachev's own vision of the future.[97] One could certainly see Yazov's influence in a formulation used by Gorbachev himself at the 19th Party Conference, specifying the importance of 'qualitative parameters' for technology, military science and the composition of the armed forces.[98] The possibility that offensive capabilities in the Soviet armed forces have their own technological momentum is something else that should be taken into consideration. Even with political determination on the part of the leadership and serious negotiations with the West in progress, the development and deployment of further offensive capabilities could still outstrip attempts to control them.[99] Calls for maintained or increased ideological vigilance, however, have to rely on formulations which distort Gorbachev's own expressed views, such as a claim about sharpening ideological confrontation.[100]

Alternatives and the WTO

A re-examination in mid-1988 of the questions posed in 1984 by Stephan Tiedtke prompts one to say that alternative defence possibilities had been taken up to an impressive extent by Soviet commentators and politicians during the intervening period. Whatever combination of Western influence and internal discussion led to their emergence, they were certainly present on the Soviet/WTO agenda to some degree by 1987–8. However, there are some interesting paradoxes in the possible implications for the WTO itself, and these relate back to the different approaches in the Western alternative debate which were identified at the beginning of this chapter.

These paradoxes can be illustrated by looking at the kinds of alternatives which came under increased discussion after the INF Treaty was signed in December 1987. Simply put, they are that non-offensive defence strategies might not by themselves entail changes in the WTO's functions in Eastern Europe, and that force cuts by themselves would not necessarily entail changes in the WTO posture towards Western Europe, unless they were cuts of a certain type.

In connection with the first point, it has sometimes been argued within the Western alternative debate that the USSR would be unwilling to forgo its offensive capacity against Western Europe because of the internally coercive function of its forces in the Eastern part of the continent. I would argue, however, that this is not quite the problem, and that unless one accepts a very straightforward version of Christopher Jones's argument about the WTO (see chapters 2 and 3) the real issue about these forces as far as Eastern Europe is concerned is not their traditionally offensive configuration, but their very presence. Although it may not be easy to specify exactly what it would look like, there seems to be no *a priori* reason why a Soviet posture could not be devised which looked less provocative to Western Europe, but which safeguarded traditional concerns for political-military hegemony within WTO borders.

Even a greater stress on territorial defence by Eastern European forces would not seem incompatible with this goal, particularly if we look once again at the pattern of military intervention in the region from 1953 to 1981. The ,Soviet interventions in Hungary and Czechoslovakia did depend on the availability of tank-dominated Soviet divisions to cow and, if necessary, to crush resistance. In Poland in 1981, however, it was a domestic military establishment which acted, using elite security forces rather than the army's rank-and-file, though tanks were certainly used. If other domestic military institutions could be relied on to do the same if necessary, Soviet capabilities become less important, and neither non-offensive capabilities nor quantitative cuts in front-line forces need place constraints on the use or expansion of paramilitary forces for domestic control purposes.

One might argue against this by saying that if the Soviet disposition towards military intervention in the region has in any event declined from its 1968 'high point', then perhaps the connection does still exist and this is why offensive requirements can be relaxed. There might be some truth in this, but it would not re-establish an organic connection between offensive strategy and internal intervention. Declining willingness to use Soviet forces in Eastern Europe seems a political calculation as much as a military one, and the hesitations over intervention in Poland in 1980–1 occurred before any signs of increased attention to defensive strategies, and indeed at a time when OMG-type manoeuvres were first being observed in Soviet military exercises (some of which, admittedly, were designed to intimidate Poland).

On the second point, Nato strategists have argued that even quite sharply asymmetrical cuts in conventional force levels in Central Europe could benefit the WTO because the vital factor for offensive success is relative force density rather than numerical levels. Nor would numerical cuts in themselves threaten internal functions, since balanced cuts could be made in Soviet and Eastern European forces to avoid disadvantaging Soviet forces, and it is hard to argue that 380,000 Soviet troops have ever been needed in the GDR for internal purposes alone. Troop withdrawals might still be much more significant as a symbol of a degree of Soviet political disengagement from Eastern Europe, if there were, say, a complete withdrawal from Hungary or a large cut in GSFG at the same time as a political initiative on German–German relations. An initiative on Germany and troop withdrawals were among the steps rumoured to be planned by Gorbachev before the Berlin WTO meeting in May 1987, and again in the summer of 1988, though in neither case were any unilateral steps taken. It is also worth noting that in the event of significant cuts in Soviet forces, the weight of Eastern European military establishments might be enhanced, in particular that of the GDR.[101]

The existence of these paradoxes does not necessarily imply insincerity in Soviet/WTO diplomacy, and the possibility of their resolution in negotiations would depend on Western positions as well as on Soviet policy priorities. It is worth mentioning some ways in which their existence has not always been adequately reflected in the Western discussions of alternative defence, taking as an example the British Alternative Defence Commission (ADC)'s work.

The ADC's central line of argument was to treat the decoupling of Western Europe from the USA as a positive goal, and to say that while Soviet/WTO reciprocation should be sought, it should not be seen as a condition. Up to a point, denuclearization and a reduction in the US military presence in Europe would clearly also be in Soviet security interests, and could be welcomed by the Soviet Union in the context of the kind of threat perceptions lying behind Soviet strategy as described by MccGwire. However, it is not entirely clear that the Soviet Union would see complete decoupling of the USA from Europe as being in its own security interests, and we have seen that Eastern responses to alternative defence suggestions for Europe reflect the fact that Soviet strategy is not simply constructed on the basis of *European* 'balance' calculations. A further problem is that the ADC focused on changing Nato strategy while admitting the possibility that the USA might ultimately not follow Western European advice or pressure, and this tended to obscure the fact that the USSR might remain more concerned with developments in US policy, such as the relative shift of focus away from Europe.

Perhaps the real problem here is one of which the ADC was well aware – that it was proposing a non-provocative *defence* concept, but a *foreign* policy concept ('unfreezing the blocs') which was potentially very provocative to the USSR in so far as it challenged Soviet hegemony and the existing political structures in Eastern Europe. From the Soviet point of view, it may be that US *military* disengagement from Europe would be unproblematic and desirable – and this would imply an increased threat to Western Europe only if one accepts uncritically Donnelly's, rather than MccGwire's, account of Soviet policy. US *political* disengagement, however, might be seen as threatening instability in both Western and Eastern Europe, and raising the spectre of a stronger Germany and/or unpredictable developments in Western Europe military integration. The ADC did recognize the tension between a short-term goal of detente and disengagement, and a longer-term goal of bloc dissolution and superpower withdrawal, and posed the question of what social models might eventually be acceptable to the Soviet Union in Eastern Europe. The point can also be made that there may be a sense in which even a totally disarmed Western Europe could still be seen as a threat to Soviet security, so difficult is it to untangle security from ideological motivations in Soviet policy, and, conversely, that a friendlier Soviet Union makes it much more difficult to maintain Nato's own political cohesion.[102]

The discontinuity between short-term detente or disengagement and more radical long-term objectives is also relevant to non-provocative defence possibilities, and does not rest only on making the distinction between an anti-bloc position and the more neutral 'alternative military modelling' approach. I have already suggested that it might be possible for a more defensive WTO strategy to evolve which was consistent with the maintenance of Soviet hegemony, and some capacity for intervention, in Eastern Europe, in which case the possibility of bloc dissolution would become an even more explicit challenge to the Soviet position. However, the central respect in which the alternative defence debate shifted ground between the early 1980s and 1987–8 lay in the fact that the alternative writers had never expected their ideas to receive more governmental recognition in the East than in the West, at least as far as alternative military models were concerned.

What of the anti-bloc approach? It will be remembered that many Eastern writers stressed the broader political context of alternative defence strategies. Unfortunately, not all Western alternative writing has addressed the different facets of these problems in sufficient detail. *Protest and Survive*, for example, dealt in some detail with Soviet military policy, but its successor, *Prospectus for a Habitable Planet*, refocused its attention almost entirely on to Eastern Europe, in spite of some generally positive comments about Gorbachev's initiatives. Even the anti-bloc proponents, therefore, have not been able to contribute much to an assessment of how far Eastern European aspirations to greater autonomy might be accommodated within evolving Soviet policy. It is hard to avoid this question, whether one regards it either as a question of political justice for Eastern Europeans, or as a central factor in the Cold War which will need to be addressed at some point if Western European public opinion is to be fully convinced of benevolent Soviet intentions. In short, the question is: what will happen to the existing socialist system in Eastern Europe under conditions of a new detente?

In a sense, therefore, the argument of this study has come full circle, to resolve itself once more into the question of whether Soviet policy in Eastern Europe can best be understood in classical security terms or in terms of political security, legitimation and bloc politics. Although I have argued that a posture which appears less of a threat to Western Europe could coexist with some Soviet capacity to intervene in the East, it also seems to be the case that the 'Brezhnev doctrine' in its original form is too crude a model for understanding present-day Soviet–East European relations. The limits of Soviet toleration may not be clearly defined but, if anything, Gorbachev may have brought intra-bloc relations back to a situation in which Soviet reformist tendencies might move too fast for some Eastern European leaderships.

There are still a number of contradictory developments to be observed. In the military sphere, Gorbachev's disarmament diplomacy must be a great relief to the Eastern European leaderships after his predecessors' lack of energy, and the early adventurousness of Hungarian and East German writing on alternative defence suggested that there was a significant Central European constituency which would support further moves in this direction from the WTO. In 1987 there were exchanges between Eastern and Western researchers at conferences on alternative defence in Bulgaria and the GDR, and a Hungarian writer suggested that Hungary might be a good location for initial steps in a non-offensive direction. It seems possible that even though the early Eastern European interest tended to be eclipsed by the Soviet leadership's embracing of non-offensiveness, this constituency could keep the idea alive in the event of slow progress or breakdown at higher levels. It may, indeed, already have become involved in collective discussions on non-offensive alternatives, though not necessarily in the established WTO forums.[103]

Gorbachev himself was generally cautious in commenting on the Eastern European aspects of alternative policies, at least up until the signing of the Soviet–Yugoslav declaration in March 1988. Prior to this he had made hints about troop withdrawal, but without making it appear a central concern.[104] Despite some changes in command of the Groups of Soviet Forces, the top of the WTO command structure itself (Kulikov and Gribkov) remained stable throughout the sweeping changes made in the main echelons of the Soviet high command. At times during this period, important Soviet spokespersons like Gennadii Gerasimov stated when pressed that the era of Soviet intervention in Eastern Europe was over, and this seemed to be endorsed by the Soviet–Yugoslav declaration issued in Belgrade on 18 March 1988.[105]

The declaration was widely reported, and glossed by Yugoslavian officials, as ruling out in principle any future Soviet intervention in Eastern Europe. It disavowed any claims to a 'monopoly of truth' or to the imposition of notions of social development. Each party was said to be responsible only before the working class and people of its own country, and there was an endorsement of the prohibitions of the UN Charter and the Helsinki Final Act against 'all forms of threat and the use of force, or interference in the internal affairs of other countries, regardless of pretext'. In addition, the specification given of 'peaceful coexistence' seemed to apply the concept to relations between all states, not just between those with different social systems.

This certainly amounted to a clear disavowal of intervention, but the declaration was, after all, made in Yugoslavia rather than in a WTO state. It would have been embarrassing for Gorbachev to have said anything so clear during his trip the previous year to Czechoslovakia, where the beneficiaries of a previous Soviet intervention were still in power. The perennial concern for bloc consolidation had been indicated a few days earlier, in a comment Gorbachev made to a group of US senators and scientists visiting Moscow, concerning what he saw as Nato's desire to demonstrate unity in preference to making progress on disarmament: 'It must also be said at the same time that we are against loosening alliances. This would only breed suspicion, and would slow down disarmament.' A similarly cautious comment about bloc affairs was made by Gorbachev just before the Moscow summit, when in an interview with the *Washington Post* and *Newsweek* he spoke of interference from any side as being impermissible, but said that it had first come from the West in Hungary and Czechoslovakia.[106] Thus, in 1988 just as in 1955, the consolidation of one's own bloc was seen as a vital concern at a time of detente with the opposing system, and a basic continuity of the bloc system remained in place in spite of all the changes that had occurred in the meantime. The continuity, however, was not total. Although the reactivation under Gorbachev of the WTO itself (and also of Comecon) as a collective interlocutor of the West served in some respects to reduce the salience of independent Eastern European initiatives, Eastern European freedom of manoeuvre was not sharply reduced as it might have been in previous periods. The GDR leadership, for example, was able to go ahead with the joint SED-SPD document on ideology, published in August 1987, and with Erich Honecker's visit to the FRG in September of that year.[107]

The temptation to overstate the importance of purely military aspects of bloc policy should be avoided, and the Conclusion of this study will look at some of the broader political and economic issues involved.

The discussion in this chapter on military alternatives has tried to pick out some of the paradoxes and uncertainties within the alternative defence debate as it developed between East and West in the 1980s. Eastern commentators, originally much less keen than Western peace researchers to explore concepts of alternative and non-provocative defence, began to do so from around 1985, and these ideas rapidly acquired considerable currency with the Soviet political leadership, and on the post-INF arms control agenda. This Eastern interest contrasted with relative governmental indifference in the West, where the interest in alternative ideas was largely confined to socialist and social democratic parties in opposition. At the same time there was a view shared by a number of participants in the debate that alternative defence concepts should fit into a political fabric of detente politics, and here there is an underlying conflict between concepts of detente which understand it as stabilizing the European bloc structure, and those which understand it as an erosion of that structure.

Within the Western argument, it appears that the less we think there is a 'Soviet threat', and/or the more we think the WTO exists for internal purposes (though these points are not synonymous), the more problematic is the possibility of the 'dissolution of the blocs'. If Western alternative concepts become more radical and imply a challenge to the 'stability' of the Eastern bloc, then the possibility of co-operation with the East in a Palme-type 'common security' regime will not disappear, but may be viewed by the Soviet Union as a Trojan horse for the more radical approach. If, on the other hand, it really is military security in a conventional, territorial sense which matters most for the USSR, then perhaps non-provocative defence alternatives and a disengagement regime are not in conflict with something more far-reaching.

Given the evidence that a state of flux existed in Soviet military doctrine and strategy by late 1988, any overall assessment of the significance of these developments must necessarily be an interim one. Eastern interest in non-provocative alternatives has been indicated, though it has been argued here that there are more complex processes at work than a straightforward acceptance of Western alternative ideas by the East. I have also argued that Soviet military resistance can be expected and is already visible, and also that non-provocative defence *per se* would not resolve some key questions about Soviet–East European relations and the internal functioning of the WTO. It is still possible that a weaker 'Western threat', which delegitimized the Soviet presence in Eastern Europe, might be seen as a mixed blessing by Soviet conservatives, just as a weakening 'Soviet threat' creates problems for Nato. The new fluidity and adventurousness of Soviet and WTO foreign policy has left the future uncertain, and the welcome signature of the INF Treaty seemed to inject into European security politics an element of long-term and potentially creative unpredictability.

Conclusion

This study has sought to relate the internal and external functions of the Warsaw Treaty Organization to the central concerns of Soviet security policy, and at all stages of the argument has tried to illuminate these questions by looking at them through the prism of different theories of the Cold War, seen as either an inter-systemic or an intra-bloc phenomenon. It began with a consideration of the circumstances of the WTO's foundation, at a time of emerging detente and attempted bloc consolidation through liberalization. The institutions of the WTO have been seen to have evolved into structures of some complexity for managing diplomatic activity and intra-alliance bargaining, although they were largely irrelevant to the solutions imposed via a variety of military-political methods in a series of Eastern European crises in 1956, 1968 and 1980–1.

The USSR has been shown to be the alliance's dominant military power both quantitatively and qualitatively. The military command structures of the WTO appear to be thoroughly subordinated to the Soviet Union. Although the WTO itself has a commander-in-chief with a headquarters and staff, the available evidence suggests that most Eastern European forces except the GDR army and some other elite units fall under national command in peacetime, but would pass under the command of the Soviet HQ and general staff if war broke out. The WTO command itself appears to fulfil little more than peacetime training and co-ordination roles, although some of these functions have an evident political utility and a high ideological content. Since Soviet intermediate command structures have themselves undergone recent reorganization, there may have been some corresponding adjustments in Eastern European involvement, but in general Eastern European forces are closely integrated into and subordinated to Soviet structures, and this is likely to continue.

This subordination is symptomatic of the WTO's reliance on Soviet military doctrine and strategy. All WTO forces are trained and equipped to fight according to a strategy which is essentially Soviet in origin, although some Eastern European military establishments may make inputs to its development. (It also seems possible that the most recent revisions have involved some inputs from outside the military establishments.) Soviet forces appear to be the only WTO units with access to nuclear weapons, and so the non-Soviet armies are trained for a possible war in which their own leaderships would have little or no influence over whether and when the conflict would become a nuclear exchange. This uncertainty has contributed to tensions within the WTO which have spilled over into the political arena, since Eastern European leaderships have not always been convinced that their military and security interests coincide entirely with the Soviet Union's interests.

These doubts and tensions have been reflected at various times in periods of unrest inside the WTO. Around 1968, Czechoslovakia and Romania were both unhappy about various aspects of the alliance in the run-up to and aftermath of the intervention in Czechoslovakia. Military spending, strategy and insufficient consultation were among the grievances aired. 1978 saw a further airing of Romanian unhappiness with the alliance, and the 1983–5 period saw evidence of unease about Soviet nuclear policy in the GDR and Czechoslovakia.

The Soviet Union's problems with its alliance partners are not limited to these periodic policy differences, since the problems of domestic legitimacy experienced by Eastern European leaderships have been in large measure a consequence of their relationship with the USSR. The available evidence suggests that in the years since 1968, the USSR has sought to placate possible Eastern European dissatisfaction by creating additional forums in which the allied leaderships can air their views on military and foreign policy issues, even if their influence on the substance of military strategy has not significantly increased. The creation after 1968 of bodies like the Committee of Defence Ministers and Committee of Foreign Ministers has been interpreted by some as a tightening of Soviet control, but it is more plausible that it represented a degree of loosening. Even if the practical influence of the Eastern European leaderships has increased only to a limited extent, these structures might well act to defuse unhappiness, and be used by leaderships to reassure their own populations that national interests are being safeguarded as far as possible within the alliance.

A certain amount of leeway has been the price the Soviet Union has paid for continued support for the bloc in broad terms; in this sense, leeway and cohesion have been complementary rather than conflicting phenomena. It can certainly be argued that the dissolution of the WTO's military structure would affect the East less seriously than the West would be affected by the dissolution of the Nato. On the other hand, the Eastern bloc would still need to find a substitute mechanism for the politically integrative functions of the WTO.

However, there should be no temptation to overestimate the amount of leeway which the WTO structures have given to the Eastern European leaderships. Events in Hungary, Czechoslovakia and Poland have demonstrated clearly that the ideological cohesion of the alliance has been a high priority in Soviet eyes, as well its military unity. Which is the more important consideration? This question may not be a helpful one if it is posed in stark either/or terms. The Cold War is such an over-determined complex of concerns that attempts to disentangle them are rarely satisfactory, and the attempt to distinguish 'military efficiency' from 'political cohesion' in the historical functioning of the WTO may not be a realistic one.

In the chapters on Soviet military strategy and disarmament diplomacy, it was argued that Soviet military strategy has shifted over recent years towards a preference for conventional variants, and that this development served to sustain the traditional importance of Eastern European territory in Soviet military thinking. However, it was also argued that Soviet security thinking and disarmament diplomacy showed substantial innovativeness in the 1985–8 period, and that Mikhail Gorbachev's attempts to downgrade military factors in East–West relations were complemented by potentially far-reaching reassessments of Soviet priorities for conventional forces. The likely effects of these reassessments and the possibility of moves towards more defensive military structures in Europe were examined, but it was suggested that longstanding paradoxes arising from the dual, internal and external, functioning of the WTO would not necessarily be resolved by defensive military structures alone.

There is a perennial temptation among writers on international relations to elect the period in which they have been writing as a 'critical juncture' (or something similar) in world affairs. With the benefits of hindsight, some junctures inevitably turn out to have been less critical than others, but the temptation does not disappear. In making such a claim for early 1988, the period immediately following the December 1987 signing of the INF Treaty, and leading up to the May–June 1988 Moscow Summit and the June–July 19th All-Union Party Conference, I would rely on three specific circumstances:

1 The general outlines of Gorbachev's reform programme in the USSR had become visible, though not its degree of likely success or its full implications for Eastern Europe;
2 The INF Treaty was a measure of significant disarmament which, however Nato tried to explain it away, did undermine the declared Nato military doctrine of flexible response;
3 The West's difficulties in dealing with a reforming Soviet leadership were apparent.

The remainder of this concluding chapter therefore looks at each of these aspects in turn: first East–East relations, then more briefly East–West and West–West relations; and offers some further speculation on the role of the WTO in the 1990s.

Gorbachev's initial prioritization of Soviet–East European relations within his overall foreign policy was not easy to determine. He made an early statement of intention to attend closely to intra-bloc relations, but was in fact inexperienced in Eastern European affairs, and appeared to devote more energy to relations with the West. Nevertheless, he started a round of visits to the WTO countries which was completed with a visit to Romania in May 1987.

Major statements of policy made during this period were ambiguous. Gorbachev's 27th Congress Speech in February 1986 made no mention of 'socialist internationalism', which would have amounted to a re-statement of the 'Brezhnev doctrine', but the phrase did appear in a speech on the occasion of the treaty renewal, in the 1986 CPSU Programme, and in Gorbachev's speech on the seventieth anniversary of the Bolshevik revolution.[1] There were indications of reassessments by some Soviet theorists of vexed questions in Soviet–East European relations such as national interests and the concept of partnership, suggesting that 'new thinking' was legitimizing the study of problems which had not previously been recognized so openly.[2] The reassessment of historical issues seemed to be promised by the setting up of a Polish–Soviet historians' commission, with the wartime Katyn massacre as part of its brief, and other hints about new historical work on Eastern European societies.[3] There was no guarantee, however, that this work would improve Soviet–East European relations, as opposed to worsening them, and a number of Western visitors to Moscow remarked that otherwise reformist Soviet journalists tended to revert suddenly to orthodoxy when discussing the Soviet intervention in Czechoslovakia.[4]

Gorbachev himself stressed mutual tolerance and dialogue within the communist movement, partly in the context of encouraging a broader ideological dialogue, and spoke of the 'absolute independence' of socialist countries when discussing Eastern Europe in his book *Perestroika*.[5] The March 1988 Soviet–Yugoslav Declaration (see previous chapter) then encapsulated a substantial retreat from the terminology of 'socialist internationalism'. However, this declaration shared with the earlier formulations of 'socialist internationalism' and the 'Brezhnev doctrine' a lack of any detailed predictive power. Certainly, Gorbachev would not want to use military force in any future Eastern European crisis, and must have known that any future intervention would be disastrous both for his foreign policy and for his domestic programme. The new formulation itself confirmed that the Eastern Europeans had much more room for manoeuvre than twenty years before, but equally it provided no guidance (to Gorbachev or anyone else) on the likely Soviet response *if* there were to be another serious political crisis in, say, Poland or Romania. Moreover, General Yazov's own formulation of WTO doctrine in June 1987, as noted in chapter 6, continued to use the traditional terminology of 'defence of the gains of socialism'. (The Romanian case might indeed furnish an instance in which the outside world would see more justification for a degree of Soviet political involvement, if not for military action.)

As mentioned in chapter 6, the Soviet-Yugoslav declaration specified that 'peaceful coexistence' should apply to relations within the world socialist system. The first hint of this was given by Gorbachev in November 1987, when he advocated: 'A strict observance of the principles of peaceful coexistence by all. This is what the practice of socialist internationalism rests on.' This contradictory reformulation was explored by Bovin's mid-1988 article, which moved cautiously from Sino-Soviet and Sino-Vietnamese relations to discuss Eastern Europe in a subtle manner, but without resolving the basic ambiguity.[6]

What of the Eastern European leaderships? As I argued in the previous chapter, there is a limited sense in which they may be constrained by the revival of the WTO as a diplomatic actor, but in general they must have been quite satisfied with the reinvigoration of Soviet foreign policy. It enabled the GDR and Czechoslovakia to see the back of at least some of the unwanted 'counterdeployment' missiles; it promised greater stability and even some demilitarization in Central Europe, and did not prevent them from pursuing their own diplomatic initiatives (German–German diplomacy for Honecker, the Jaruzelski Plan for Poland, Hungary's concern for the role of small states in diplomacy); and they were kept in the picture at regular WTO meetings.

The link with domestic policies was more problematic. In the first place, Gorbachev's diplomacy had contradictory consequences for civil rights, anti-bloc and anti-militarist activists in Eastern Europe, who have unfortunately remained almost invisible through most of this study's concentration on military and diplomatic activity. In the circumstances of Gorbachev's disarmament diplomacy it became much more difficult to legitimize repression of these activists, which is not to say that the repression was discontinued.[7] The scepticism of Eastern European activists towards their own leaderships was well illustrated by Adam Michnik's comments on the Jaruzelski Plan: 'General Jaruzelski could make a genuine peace initiative by seeking a peaceful rapprochement with his own nation. But so far he hasn't done so.'[8]

This problem does not relate simply to security policy as a domestic question, but applies in a more general sense to the Eastern European relationship to Soviet political and economic reforms. One can see the Gorbachev reform period as a successor to the Khrushchev period in the sense that reforms licenced by Soviet practice may have much more unpredictable consequences in Eastern Europe than in the USSR itself.

No historical parallel like this is ever exact, and thirty years after Khrushchev the USSR was in effect applying Eastern European-type reforms to its own economy rather than exporting its own (though this is not to say that 'marketizing' reforms had *worked* in Eastern Europe). However, the possibility of popular Eastern European aspirations outstripping conservative tolerance was still there, just as it was under Khrushchev.

For example, when Gorbachev made his trip to Czechoslovakia in April 1987 he appeared to be more popular with the Prague public than were the Czech leaders, and shortly after this a May Day Solidarity demonstration in Warsaw used some of Gorbachev's own words on the need for democracy as a challenge to the Polish authorities.[9] In Czechoslovakia, Gustav Husak was forced to step down in favour of Milos Jakes at the end of the year, but this did not seriously affect the composition of the leadership. Some incidents in GDR also suggested that in certain circumstances Gorbachev could serve as a symbol of reform for Eastern Europeans dissatisfied with their own leaderships.[10] On the other hand, Gorbachev's July 1988 trip to Poland seems to have been a fairly uninspiring occasion.[11]

Gorbachev is a much more intelligent politician than Khrushchev, and in spite of his demonstrated boldness in foreign policy he must have been aware of the potential of events in Eastern Europe to disrupt his own reform project. If that project could be crudely characterized as short-term economic austerity, in return for political and cultural liberalization/democratization and control of bureaucratic privileges, in the interests of longer-term economic 'efficiency' and prosperity, then some of the Eastern European leaderships, perhaps those of Hungary and Poland, seemed prepared to follow somewhat similar strategies. Such a strategy represented an interesting reversal of the 1960s–70s Eastern European 'social contract', whereby rising material expectations were traded off against the denial of political rights, and was shown by the November 1987 Polish referendum to be unacceptable to the Polish population – at least, in the form offered by the Jaruzelski government, where the balance was heavily tipped towards economic austerity.[12] Equally noticeably, it did not seem an attractive trade-off to some of the other leaderships, which were either prepared for economic reform but wary of its political implications (Bulgaria), or lukewarm about both (Czechoslovakia, and the GDR on the basis of an argument that its economy was already efficient).

In all probability, Gorbachev would have liked to see Eastern European economies functioning as more efficient contributors to Soviet economic restructuring, without being averse to a greater bloc participation in the international division of labour. Eastern European reform economists appeared particularly concerned about the increasing marginalization of their own region within the world economy, and so may be less enthusiastic about contributing via increased Comecon integration, but there may in fact be more room for them to manoeuvre within Comecon than within the WTO.

An extended process of generational leadership change was getting under way by mid-1988 with Janos Kadar's replacement by Karoly Grosz in Hungary, which seemed to signal an improvement in the prospects for a Gorbachev-type reform strategy. One can speculate that in the longer term Gorbachev might feel able to initiate a more actively adventurous political strategy towards Eastern Europe, but he would have to be sure not only that he had judged the Eastern European situation correctly, but also that he was sufficiently secure at home to be invulnerable to criticism from domestic conservatives. For Eastern European societies themselves, however, the apparent easing of the threat of Soviet intervention may have meant that, as Timothy Garton Ash has suggested, the immediate obstacles to reform were by 1988 more internal than external, and related primarily to the relationship between the ruling parties and their own populations.[13]

In the sphere of East–West relations, the most curious feature of the US debate during 1987–8 was its contradictory combination of near-panic and triumphalism. Despair at the apparently irreversible decline of US economic and political hegemony was a particularly powerful theme in the attention paid to Paul Kennedy's book *The Rise and Fall of the Great Powers*.[14] In many respects, however, these concerns merely repeated the fear of US decline which had assisted Reagan's election in 1980, and illustrated how little his policies over two administrations had done to resolve the perceived problems.

On the triumphalist wing, other writers were painting a heady picture of a US Cold War victory. Here is William G. Hyland, editor of *Foreign Affairs*, writing in intoxicated vein in mid-1987: 'We have won the ideological war; we are close to winning the geopolitical contest in the Third World, except for the Middle East. We long ago won the economic competition. As James Reston remarked in his final regular column for *The New York Times*: "I think we've won the cold war and don't know it."'[15] Or Zbigniew Brzezinski, reprinted in a British newspaper the following February: '[The Soviet Union's] capacity to project and develop military power remains enormous. Beyond that, it has already lost the ideological and economic competition which provide the underpinning for world domination.'[16] I outlined earlier (see chapter 5) some of the arguments which might suggest that the USSR's reforms in security policy had come about partly as a result of a reappraisal of its weakness as a superpower, and which might in part support Hyland and Brzezinski's case. However, this line of argument, if pursued exclusively, ignores the genuinely co-operative elements of Gorbachev's 'new thinking' and distorts some key features of late 1980s geopolitics.

One can reconcile the two tendencies by arguing that of the two superpowers, the USA's relative decline during the 1970s–80s had been less steep than the USSR's, but the USA as a state had been losing an economic competition with the Far East and Europe while it fought its partly imaginary (but highly functional) war with the USSR. The continuing greater strength of capitalism as a system remained undeniable, and would probably have been conceded by Gorbachev and his advisers. Hyland and Brzezinski's argument might thus be decoded as a plea for the USA to arrest the decline of its *national* hegemony by turning its attention to the other competition within the capitalist world system; some other US authors did indeed say this more explicitly, and in more moderate tones than Hyland and Brzezinski.[17]

These diverse assessments of East–West relations inevitably had their repercussions within Nato. However much Nato spokespersons tried to pretend otherwise, and in spite of the fact that the treaty was numerically very much in the West's favour, the INF 'double-zero' agreement did disrupt flexible response. The strategy had previously been articulated as requiring a capacity for nuclear retaliation on the USSR from Western Europe whether or not there were SS-20s targeted on the West from the USSR, and so the removal of cruise and Pershing II was indeed in theory a disruption to the 'ladder of escalation'. The conclusion of the deal could be put down to a combination of the Reagan administration's need for a foreign policy success, long-term pressure by peace movements and new flexibility on the USSR's part. The signature of the treaty prompted the re-emergence of differences among Western European elites on policy towards the East, even though conservative governments had been firmly established in the main Western European countries for much of the 1980s. Margaret Thatcher voiced the temporary uncertainty of Nato governments with her comment that a friendly Soviet leadership caused problems for Western cohesion, in response to views such as those expressed by the veteran Bavarian conservative Franz Josef Strauss during a trip to Moscow shortly before his death: 'After the proposals made by the General Secretary, it is impossible to ascribe offensive military intentions to the Soviet side, or an intention to fight with the West. These fears, whether they were objectively justified or imagined, are today a thing of the past.'[18]

    These alliance problems for Nato did not, of course, seriously challenge the Western leaderships' short-term ability to coordinate their military and political response to Gorbachev, including nuclear 'modernization', but they served to take some of the edge off Hyland and Brzezinski's triumphalism. Many US and European liberal and left-wing writers were taking Gorbachev seriously as a reformer and co-operative leader rather than simply the head of a defeated superpower, and counter-arguments were offered about the limitations placed on US actions by the USA's own economic plight and indebtedness, in terms which supported Kennedy's arguments. Significantly, there were sharper disagreements within the Western left over the desirability of Gorbachev's domestic reforms than there were on the centre-left. On the left, the main concerns expressed were about the disciplinary role of marketizing economic reforms and the possibly instrumental nature of political liberalization, as measured against genuine radicalism.[19]

During the 1988 US Presidential election, Jesse Jackson's effective campaign gave some grounds for optimism about the medium-term prospects for US foreign policy. However, for all the talk of 'ending the Cold War' which surrounded the May–June 1988 Moscow summit, the most optimistic assessment of the possibilities for East–West relations in the immediate post-Reagan period should more realistically have been made in terms of two superpowers sharing a rather more sober awareness of their own relative decline, and of the damage done to their economies and security by over-reliance on military strength. A degree of retreat from the erratic Third World activism of the Reagan administrations seemed possible, though by no means inevitable, and there was little indication that George Bush, elected in November, would approach issues of East–West relations with much imagination. Even if Michael Dukakis had won it seems unlikely that policy towards the USSR would have been very different.

The Moscow summit itself achieved little of substance beyond the exchange of ratification documents for the INF Treaty, and the USA showed little or no interest in a Soviet attempt to offer a new proposal on force and troop reductions in Europe. Nevertheless, the symbolic importance of Reagan's Red Square walkabout and apparent endorsement of Gorbachev's reform policies should not be neglected, both for their positive potential and for the negative reactions they may have caused among conservatives on both sides. For the most part, however, the US leadership appeared blithely unconcerned about the political struggle going on within the USSR, the existence of which was testified to before and during the summit by the controversy over *Sovetskaya Rossiya*'s anti-*perestroika* manifesto and by Boris Yel'tsin's public intervention on Western television.[20]

The 19th All-Union Party Conference, running from 28 June to 1 July, seemed to bring the debates to a head and to give Gorbachev's reform programme further impetus by largely endorsing his proposals for constitutional reform. Gorbachev's own speech amplified some of the remarks in the pre-conference Theses concerning foreign policy (see chapter 5), but probably the most remarkable feature of the conference was the scope it provided for policy differences within the party to be semi-publicly aired and debated before both Soviet and Western audiences.[21]

Looking beneath the surface of the Moscow summit and of domestic developments affecting the two major powers, one could see the outlines of one possible configuration for East–West geopolitics in the 1990s. With Gorbachev's words about ensuring the security of the Soviet state (see chapter 5), Soviet reluctance to take on further Third World security obligations was made even clearer than previously. Conversely, the USA could claim with some justification that the 'Reagan doctrine' had achieved some significant successes in the Third World: raising the cost of the Soviet intervention in Afghanistan through the supply of sophisticated weaponry; pressurizing the Sandinista government in Nicaragua through a variety of military and economic devices. The Soviet policy offer to the USA therefore boiled down to what Richard Falk has outlined as a kind of 'new geopolitical bargain': in return for relaxation on the East–West axis, and denuclearization and even perhaps some demilitarization in Europe, a Soviet retreat from the Third World would remove some impediments to US and/or Western policy there.[22]

To an orthodox or liberal analyst this bargain may seem unproblematic, given its effect of reducing the danger of superpower confrontation arising from Third World crises. It is, however, far more problematic for anyone with a more principled and critical analysis of US/Western policy; whatever may have been the benefits or costs of earlier Soviet engagement in the Third World, it is hard to see how the granting of a freer hand to US policy in Third World states would benefit the majority of their citizens.[23]

If there is any validity in this projection for the 1990s, it seems to suggest that the WTO itself might decline in importance as an actor in East–West relations. If the USSR is offering and seeking a major relaxation in the Cold War confrontation in Europe, this conclusion would seem to follow. However, as this study has shown, the WTO has not simply co-ordinated the Eastern bloc in periods of East–West tension, but has been of major importance in managing East–West and East–East relations in periods of relaxation and detente: indeed, this was shown to have been an important part of its original function.

Therefore, the WTO and the issues examined in this study are unlikely to be pushed to the periphery of international politics in the 1990s. Although talk of bloc dissolution continues from the Eastern side, this seems traditional and rather routine, and all the more unlikely in circumstances in which increased partnership and collaboration with Western Europe is a far more realistic option for the USSR than similar relations with the USA, which seems uninterested in anything very far-reaching. The WTO and Comecon will remain of considerable importance for managing relations with Western Europe in any new detente.

In addition, the forces which may emerge from within Eastern European societies in the forthcoming period will, as outlined earlier in this chapter, be likely to put pressure on the internal mechanisms of the

Eastern bloc, for all that those mechanisms have been shown to have evolved significantly since 1955.

Finally, and perhaps most importantly in the light of the main military concerns of this study, the future of conventional arms control is likely to be a major factor both in East–West relations and in Soviet domestic politics and civil–military relations. Thus, the role of the WTO in East–West and East–East relations will remain a central issue in European security politics, whatever forum and mandate are decided upon for the post-MBFR negotiations. As has been noted, the WTO's diplomatic activity in this area increased during Gorbachev's first three years in office.

It was clear by mid-1988 that the future of the post-MBFR negotiations had been turned into something of a Western litmus test for the sincerity of Soviet political and strategic reforms. I would conclude by arguing that this development was at best exaggerated and at worst misleading, notwithstanding the high degree of political and intellectual importance attaching to the Soviet reforms, which I have tried to capture in the final chapters of this study. The degree of attention focused on these prospective negotiations was unfortunate for two reasons. Firstly, because the negotiations were likely to be immensely complex and difficult, and perhaps unproductive for many years, however genuine Soviet and WTO intentions might be. Furthermore, if they were seen by the USA as an opportunity to follow up the INF Treaty by demanding further concessions without any serious degree of Western reciprocation, especially in nuclear forces, it was questionable whether Eastern flexibility would be sustained. The indications of the 1985–8 period were that whatever was on offer from the Eastern side would not necessarily remain available whatever the Western response. Secondly, because an exclusive focus on the conventional force negotiations would serve to obscure the more fundamental processes which were already at work or might develop within the European bloc systems, in particular the development of US–Western European relations, the evolution of East–East relations and Eastern European politics, and the political-military processes which seemed to be beginning within Soviet society.

The Warsaw Treaty Organization's traditional structures may find it hard to react and adapt to these emerging policy issues, though they are unlikely to be the only institutions in East and West to encounter such difficulties. Even so, they will be around for some time yet, and will be bound to play a role in any new detente which can be constructed in the 1990s by the leaders, and equally importantly by the citizens, of the states concerned.

Appendix I: Treaty of Friendship, Co-operation and Mutual Assistance

Between the People's Republic of Albania, the People's Republic of Bulgaria, the Hungarian People's Republic, the German Democratic Republic, the Polish People's Republic, the Romanian People's Republic, the Union of Soviet Socialist Republics, and the Czechoslovak Republic.
14 May 1955

The Contracting parties,

Reaffirming their desire for the organization of a system of collective security in Europe, with the participation of all the European states, irrespective of their social and state system, which would make it possible to combine their efforts in the interests of securing peace in Europe,

Taking into consideration at the same time the situation obtaining in Europe as the result of ratification of the Paris agreements, which provide for the formation of a new military grouping in the shape of the 'Western European Union' together with a remilitarized Western Germany and for the integration of Western Germany in the North Atlantic bloc, which increases the danger of another war and creates a threat to the national security of the peace-loving states,

Convinced that, under these circumstances, the peace-loving states of Europe should take the necessary measures for safe-guarding their security, and in the interests of maintaining peace in Europe,

Guided by the purposes and principles of the United Nations Charter,

In the interests of further strengthening and promoting friendship, co-operation and mutual assistance, in accordance with the principles of respect for the independence and sovereignty of states, and also with the principle of non-interference in their internal affairs,

Have resolved to conclude this Treaty of friendship, co-operation and mutual assistance and have appointed as their authorized representatives:

[The Presidium of the People's Assembly of the People's Republic of Albania – Mehmet Shehu, Chairman of the Council of Ministers of the People's Republic of Albania,

The Presidium of the People's Assembly of the People's Republic of Bulgaria- –Vulko Chervenkov, Chairman of the Council of Ministers of the People's Republic of Bulgaria,

The Presidium of the Hungarian People's Republic – Andras Hegedus, Chairman of the Council of Ministers of the Hungarian People's Republic,

The Presidium of the German Democratic Republic – Otto Grotewohl, Prime Minister of the German Democratic Republic,

The State Council of the Polish People's Republic – Jozef Cyrankiewicz, Chairman of the Council of Ministers of the Polish People's Republic,

The Presidium of the Grand National Assembly of the Romanian People's

Republic – Gheorghe Gheorghiu-Dej, Chairman of the Council of Ministers of the Romanian People's Republic,

The Presidium of the Supreme Soviet of the Union of Soviet Socialist Republics – Nikolai Alexandrovich Bulganin, Chairman of the Council of Ministers of the USSR,

The President of the Czechoslovak Republic – Viliam Siroky, Prime Minister of the Czechoslovak Republic,]

Who, having presented their credentials, found to be executed in due form and in complete order, have agreed on the following:

ARTICLE 1

The contracting parties undertake, in accordance with the Charter of the United Nations Organization, to refrain in their international relations from the threat or use of force, and to settle their international disputes by peaceful means so as not to endanger international peace and security.

ARTICLE 2

The contracting parties declare their readiness to take part, in the spirit of sincere co-operation, in all international undertakings intended to safeguard international peace and security, and they shall use all their energies for the realization of these aims.

Moreover, the contracting parties shall work for the adoption, in agreement with other states desiring to co-operate in this matter, of effective measures towards a general reduction of armaments and the prohibition of atomic, hydrogen and other weapons of mass destruction.

ARTICLE 3

The contracting parties shall take council among themselves on all important international questions relating to their common interests, guided by the interests of strengthening international peace and security.

They shall take council among themselves immediately whenever, in the opinion of any of them, there arises the threat of an armed attack on one or several states that are signatories of the treaty, in the interests of ensuring their joint defence and of upholding peace and security.

ARTICLE 4

In the event of an armed attack in Europe on one or several states that are signatories of the treaty by any state or group of states, each state that is a party to this treaty shall in the exercise of the right to individual or collective self-defence in accordance with Article 51 of the Charter of the United Nations Organization, render the state or states so attacked immediate assistance, individually and in agreement with other states that are parties to this treaty, by all the means it may consider necessary, including the use of armed force. The states that are parties to this treaty shall immediately take council among themselves concerning the necessary joint measures to be adopted for the purpose of restoring and upholding international peace and security.

In accordance with the principles of the Charter of the United Nations Organization, the Security Council shall be advised of the measures taken on the basis of the present article. These measures shall be discontinued as soon as the Security Council has taken the necessary measures for restoring and upholding international peace and security.

ARTICLE 5

The contracting parties have agreed on the establishment of a joint command for their armed forces, which shall be placed, by agreement among these parties, under this command, which shall function on the basis of jointly defined principles. They shall also take other concerted measures necessary for strengthening their defence capacity, in order to safeguard the peaceful labour of their peoples, to guarantee the inviolability of their frontiers and territories and to provide defence against possible aggression.

ARTICLE 6

For the purpose of holding the consultations provided for in the present treaty among the states that are parties to the treaty, and for the purpose of considering problems arising in connection with the implementation of this treaty, a Political consultative committee shall be formed in which each state that is a party to this treaty shall be represented by a member of the government, or any other specially appointed representative.

The committee may form the auxiliary organs for which the need may arise.

ARTICLE 7

The contracting parties undertake not to participate in any coalitions and alliances and not to conclude any agreements the purposes of which would be at variance with those of the present treaty.

The contracting parties declare that their obligations under existing international treaties are not at variance with the provisions of this treaty.

ARTICLE 8

The contracting parties declare that they will act in the spirit of friendship and co-operation with the object of the further development and strengthening of the economic and cultural relations between them, adhering to the principles of mutual respect for their independence and sovereignty, and of non-interference in their internal affairs.

ARTICLE 9

The present Treaty is open to the accession of other states – irrespective of their social and state system – which may express their readiness to assist, through participation in the present treaty, in combining the efforts of the peace-loving states for safeguarding the peace and security of the peoples. This act of acceding to the Treaty shall become effective with the consent of the states which are party to the Treaty, after the instrument of accession has been deposited with the Government of the Polish People's Republic.

ARTICLE 10

The present treaty is subject to ratification, and the instruments of ratification shall be deposited with the Government of the Polish People's Republic.

The treaty shall take effect on the date on which the last ratification instrument is deposited. The Government of the Polish People's Republic shall advise the other states party to the treaty of each ratification instrument deposited with it.

ARTICLE 11

The present Treaty shall remain in force for twenty years. For the contracting parties which will not have submitted to the Government of the Polish People's Republic a statement denouncing the Treaty a year before the expiration of its term, it shall remain in force throughout the following ten years.

In the event of the organization of a system of collective security in Europe, and the conclusion of a general European Treaty of collective security to that end, which the contracting parties shall unceasingly seek to bring about, the present Treaty shall cease to be effective on the date the general European Treaty comes into force.

Drawn up in Warsaw on the 14 May 1955, with one copy in each of the Russian, Polish, Czech and German languages, each of which has the same force. Certified copies of the present treaty shall be sent by the government of the Polish People's Republic to all the other signatories.

The authorized representatives have certified this by signing the present treaty and affixing their seal to it.

Sources: *Pravda* 15 May 1955; author's translation from V. F. Mal'tsev (ed.), *Organizatsiya Varshavskogo Dogovora 1955–1985, dokumenty i materialy*, Izdatel'stvo Politicheskoi Literatury, 1986.

1985 Protocol of Renewal

PROTOCOL

On prolonging the period of validity of the Treaty of Friendship, Co-operation and Mutual Assistance, signed in Warsaw on May 14, 1955.
26 April 1985

The member states of the Treaty of Friendship, Co-operation and Mutual Assistance – the People's Republic of Bulgaria, the Hungarian People's Republic, the German Democratic Republic, the Polish People's Republic, the Socialist Republic of Romania, the Union of Soviet Socialist Republics and the Czechoslovak Socialist Republic – have decided to sign the present protocol and agreed on the following:

ARTICLE 1

The Treaty of Friendship, Co-operation and Mutual Assistance, signed in Warsaw on 14 May 1955, shall remain in force for the next twenty years. For the contracting parties, which a year before the expiry of this period of time shall not present to the Government of the Polish People's Republic statements of denunciation of the treaty, it shall remain in force for another ten years.

ARTICLE 2

The present protocol is subject to ratification. The instruments of ratification shall be deposited with the Government of the Polish People's Republic.

The protocol shall enter into force on the day of the presentation for deposition of the last instrument of ratification. The Government of the Polish People's Republic shall inform the other states party to the treaty of the presentation for deposition of each instrument of ratification.

Done in Warsaw on 26 April 1985 in one copy in each of the Bulgarian, Hungarian, German, Polish, Romanian, Russian and Czech languages, each of which has the same force. Certified copies of the present protocol shall be sent by the Government of the Polish People's Republic to all the other parties to the protocol.

For the People's Republic of Bulgaria: Todor Zhivkov, General Secretary of the Central Committee of the Bulgarian Communist Party, President of the State Council of the People's Republic of Bulgaria.

For the Hungarian People's Republic: Janos Kadar, General Secretary of the Hungarian Socialist Workers' Party.

For the German Democratic Republic: Erich Honecker, General Secretary of the Central Committee of the Socialist Unity Party of Germany, President of the State Council of the German Democratic Republic.

For the Polish People's Republic: Wojciech Jaruzelski, First Secretary of the Central Committee of the Polish United Workers' Party, Chairman of the Council of Ministers of the Polish People's Republic.

For the Socialist Republic of Romania: Nicolae Ceausescu, General Secretary of the Romanian·Communist Party, President of the Socialist Republic of Romania.

For the Union of Soviet Socialist Republics: M. S. Gorbachev, General Secretary of the Central Committee of the Communist Party of the Soviet Union.

For the Czechoslovak Socialist Republic: Gustav Husak, General Secretary of the Central Committee of the Communist Party of Czechoslovakia, President of the Czechoslovak Socialist Republic.

Sources: *Pravda* 27 April 1985; author's translation from V. F. Mal'tsev (ed.), *Organizatsiya Varshavskogo Dogovora 1955–1985, dokumenty i materialy*, Izdatel'stvo Politicheskoi Literatury, 1986.

Appendix II: Forces in Eastern Europe

Table 1 Forces in Eastern Europe – personnel

	Ground	Air	Navy	Total regular forces	+ Paramilitary forces	+ Soviet forces
Bulgaria	110,000	34,000	8,800	152,800	172,500	–
Czechoslovakia	145,000	56,000	–	201,000	131,000	80,000
German Democratic Republic (GDR)	120,000	40,000	16,000	176,000	84,000	380,000
Hungary	84,000	22,000	–	106,000	76,000	65,000
Poland	230,000	80,000	19,000	394,000	52,000	40,000
Romania	140,000	32,000	7,500	179,000	35,000	–

Source: *The Military Balance 1987–88* (International Institute for Strategic Studies, London 1987).

Table 2 Soviet forces in Eastern Europe

	Ground forces	Divisions	Other units
Group of Soviet Forces, Germany (GSFG)	380,000 Group HQ: 5 Army HQ: Zossen-Wünsdorf Furstenberg Magdeburg Dresden Weimar Ebersvald	10 tank 9 motorized rifle	1 artillery division 1 air assault brigade 5 artillery brigades + combat aircraft and helicopters
Northern Group of Forces (NGF) (Poland)	40,000 Group HQ } Army HQ } Legnica	2 tank	Combat aircraft and helicopters
Central Group of Forces (CGF) (Czechoslavakia)	80,000 Group HQ 2 Army HQ: Milovice Boleslav Olomouc	2 tank 3 motorized rifle	1 air assault battalion 1 artillery brigade + combat aircraft and helicopters
Southern Group of Forces (SGF) (Hungary)	65,000 Group HQ } Army HQ } Budapest-Matyasfold	2 tank 2 motorized rifle	1 air assault brigade + combat aircraft and helicopters

Source: Figures from *The Military Balance 1987–88*, with additional HQ information from David C. Isby, *Weapons and Tactics of the Soviet Army*, Jane's, 1981

Table 3 Ground forces in Eastern Europe (non-Soviet)

	Ground forces: total	Number of Divisions	Readiness (where known)	Additional specialized units
Bulgaria	110,000	8 motorized rifle divisions 5 tank brigades	3 MR divs at cat.III	4 SSM brigades with SCUD 3 artillery regiments 1 SAM brigade (air defence) 1 parachute regiment Special commando companies
Czechoslovakia	145,000	5 armoured divisions 5 motorized rifle divisions	1 cat.I, 2 cat.II, 2 cat.III 3 cat.I, 1 cat.II, 1 cat.III	1 artillery division incl. 3 SCUD and SS-21 SSM brigades 1 airborne regiment 6 engineer brigades 5 civil defence troops regiments
GDR	120,000	2 tank divisions 4 motorized rifle divisions	2 category I All category I	2 SCUD and SS-21 SSM brigades 2 artillery, 1 anti-aircraft artillery regiment 8 SAM air defence regiments 1 signals brigade 3 engineer regiments 1 railway construction regiment 2 anti-tank battalions 1 amphibious regiment 1 special forces brigade

Hungary	84,000	1 tank division	Category II	1 artillery brigade
		5 motorized rifle divisions	3 category II, 2 category III	1 SCUD SSM brigade
				1 anti-aircraft artillery regiment
				4 SAM air defence regiments
				1 airborne battalion
Poland	230,000	5 tank divisions	All category I	1 airborne brigade (cat. I)
				1 amphibious assault brigade (cat. I)
		8 motor rifle divisions	3 category I, 5 category III	5 artillery brigades
				3 anti-tank regiments
				4 SCUD SSM brigades
				1 SAM air defence brigade
Romania	140,000	2 tank divisions	1 category I, 1 category II	3 mountain brigades/regiments
				2 artillery brigades
		8 motorized rifle divisions	1 category I, 3 category II, 4 category III	2 anti-aircraft brigades
				1 anti-tank brigade
				2 SCUD SSM brigades
				2 airborne regiments

Source: Information from *The Military Balance 1987–88*

Table 4 Comparison between WTO 'northern and southern tiers'

NORTHERN TIER

	Czechoslovakia	GDR	Poland	Total Northern Tier
Total population	15,700,000	16,610,000	37,780,000	70,090,000
Total regular forces	201,000	176,000	394,000	771,000
Ground	145,000	120,000	230,000	495,000
Air	56,000	40,000	80,000	176,000
Navy	–	16,000	19,000	35,000
Tanks	3,500	3,000 (incl. 1000 in storage)	3,400	9,900
Combat aircraft	465 + helicopters	334 + helicopters	665 + helicopters	1,464 + helicopters
Military spending (billion $)	5.42 (1987)	11.54 (1987)	5.90 (1987)	22.86

SOUTHERN TIER

	Bulgaria	Hungary	Romania	Total Southern Tier
Total population	9,060,000	10,622,000	23,670,000	43,352,000
Total regular forces	152,800	106,000	179,500	438,300
Ground	110,000	84,000	140,000	334,000
Air	34,000	22,000	32,000	88,000
Navy	8,800	–	7,500	16,300
Tanks	2,100	1,200	1,430	4,730
Combat aircraft	270 + helicopters	160 + helicopters	368	798 + helicopters
Military spending (billion $)	1.656 (1985)	2.425 (1986)	1.171 (1987)	5.252

Notes

Introduction

1 The UNU programme's initial contribution to this process in Mary Kaldor and Richard Falk (eds), *Dealignment: A New Foreign Policy Perspective* (Basil Blackwell, 1987). See also the important work which has emerged out of the British debate on peace issues, as a complement to the public activity of the British peace movement: *Defence Without The Bomb: The Report of The Alternative Defence Commission* (Taylor and Francis, 1983); and *The Politics of Alternative Defence: A Role For A Non-Nuclear Britain* (Paladin, 1987).

2 Useful recent discussions include the following: Barry Buzan, *People, States and Fear: The National Security Problem in International Relations* (Wheatsheaf Books, 1983); Allen Lynch, *The Soviet Study of International Relations* (Cambridge University Press, 1987); Klaus von Beyme, *The Soviet Union in World Politics* (Gower, 1987); Pál Dunay, *Hungary's Security Policy* (Hamburg Institut für Friedensforschung und Sicherheitspolitik, 1987); Egbert Jahn, Pierre Lemaitre, Ole Waever, *European Security: Problems of Research on Non-military Aspects* (Copenhagen Papers 1, August 1987); Margot Light, *The Soviet Theory of International Relations* (Wheatsheaf, 1988).

3 For the wider context, see the discussions in Mary Kaldor, Gerard Holden and Richard Falk (eds), *The New Detente: Rethinking East–West Relations* (Verso/ United Nations University, 1989).

4 For example: William J. Lewis, The Warsaw Pact: Arms, Doctrine, and Strategy (McGraw-Hill, 1982); Friedrich Wiener, *The Armies of the Warsaw Pact Nations* (Carl Ueberreuter, 1981); and (though principally an assesment of Soviet forces) John Erickson, Lynn Hansen and William Schneider, *Soviet Ground Forces: An Operational Assesment* (Westview/Croom Helm, 1986).

5 Christopher D. Jones, *Soviet Influence in Eastern Europe: Political Autonomy and the Warsaw Pact* (Praeger, 1981). Jones has also contributed to several other collections on the WTO, and to a major study published in several parts by the Canadian Deparment of National Defence between 1981 and 1986.

6 Examples include: Ivan Volgyes, *The Political Reliability of the Warsaw Pact Armies: The Southern Tier* (Duke University Press, 1982), in particular chapters 6 and 7; Edward B. Atkeson, 'The "fault line" in the Warsaw Pact: implications for NATO strategy' *Orbis* 30 (1) spring 1986, pp. 111–31; and Jeffrey Simon and Trond Gilberg (eds), *Security Implications of Nationalism in Eastern Europe* (Westview, 1986), chapter 14. More nuanced discussions can be found in Richard D. Vine (ed.), *Soviet–East European Relations As A Problem for the West* (Croom Helm, 1987.

7 Robin Alison Remington, *The Warsaw Pact: Case Studies in Communist Conflict Resolution* (MIT Press, 1971); David Holloway and Jane M. O. Sharp (eds), *The Warsaw Pact: Alliance in Transition?* (Macmillan, 1984). See also Remington's useful review essay, 'Western images of the Warsaw Pact', *Problems of Communism* XXXVI (2) March–April 1987, pp. 69–80.

8 See: Isaac Deutscher, *The Great Contest: Russia and the West* (Oxford University

Press, 1960); Fred Halliday, *The Making of the Second Cold War* (Verso, 2nd edn
1986); Noam Chomsky, 'Strategic arms, the cold war and the Third World',
in Edward Thompson et al., *Exterminism and Cold War* (Verso, 1982); Mary
Kaldor, *The Imaginary War* (Basil Blackwell, forthcoming); Edward Thompson, 'Notes on exterminism, the last stage of civilization', in *Exterminism and
Cold War*.

9 J. F. Brown, 'The future of political relations within the Warsaw Pact', in
Holloway and Sharp, *The Warsaw Pact*, p. 197.

Chapter 1   Origins of the WTO

1 For the Russian text, see V. F. Mal'tsev (ed.), *Organizatsiya Varshavskogo
Dogovora 1955–1985, dokumenty i materialy* (Izdatel'stvo Politicheskoi Literatury,
1986), document 1, p. 9. An English translation is reproduced in appendix I to
this study.

2 On the origins of COMECON, see Michael Kaser, *COMECON: Integration
Problems of the Planned Economies* (Oxford University Press for the Royal Insti-
tute of International Affairs, 1967), chapter II. On the events of 1953 in the
GDR, see: Jonathan Steele, *Socialism With a German Face: The state that came in
from the cold* (Cape, 1977), chapter 5; David Childs, *The GDR: Moscow's German
Ally* (Allen and Unwin, 1983), chapter 1; Chris Harman, *Class Struggles in
Eastern Europe, 1945–83* (Pluto, 1983), chapter 4; and Ann L. Phillips, *Soviet
Policy Toward East Germany Reconsidered: The Postwar Decade* (Greenwood, 1986),
chapter 4.

3 For Soviet accounts see: K. I. Savinov, *Varshavskii Dogovor – faktor mira, shchit
sotsializma* (Mezhdunarodnye Otnosheniya, 1986), chapter 1; and D. A. Volkogonov (ed.), *Armii stran Varshavskogo Dogovora – spravochnik* (Biblioteka Ofitsera,
Voennoe Izdatel'stvo, 1985), pp. 3–10. On the 'moment of hope', see Philip
Noel-Baker, *The Arms Race: A Programme for World Disarmament* (Atlantic Books,
1958), chapter 2, and Lincoln P. Bloomfield, Walter C. Clemens Jr and
Franklyn C. Griffiths, *Khrushchev and the Arms Race: Soviet Interests in Arms Control
and Disarmament, 1954–1964* (MIT Press, 1966), chapter 1.

4 See Volkogonov, *Armii Stran Varshavskogo Dogovora*, p. 7, and Valentin Alexandrov, *The Warsaw Treaty and Peace in Europe* (Novosti, 1980). p. 11.

5 Useful accounts of the different influences at work include: Malcolm Mackin-
tosh, *The Evolution of the Warsaw Pact* (Adelphi Paper no. 58, June 1969); and
'The Warsaw Treaty Organization: a history', in David Holloway and Jane
M. O. Sharp (eds), *The Warsaw Pact: Alliance in Transition?* (Macmillan, 1984);
Robin Alison Remington, *The Warsaw Pact: Case Studies in Communist Conflict
Resolution* (MIT Press, 1971); Francois Fejtö, *A History of the People's Democracies:
Eastern Europe Since Stalin* (Penguin, 1977), chapter 2; Vojtech Mastny,
'Kremlin politics and the Austrian settlement', *Problems of Communism* XXXI
(4) July–August 1982, pp. 37–51.

6 For the bilateral treaties, see Zbigniew K. Brzezinski, *The Soviet Bloc: Unity and
Conflict* (Praeger, 1962), chapter 6, especially p. 109, which gives a chart of
them.

7 *Khrushchev Remembers, Volume 2 – The Last Testament*, translated and edited by
Strobe Talbott (Penguin, 1977): chapter 9, 'East Europe: the making of an
alliance'.

8 See *Khrushchev Remembers, Volume 1*, translated by Strobe Talbott (Sphere,
1971), chapter 13.

9 See appendix I.

10 *NATO Handbook* (NATO Information Service, April 1986), p. 13.
11 *Ibid.*, p. 14. See Ben Lowe, 'NATO and domestic politics: Britain, Italy and West Germany during cold war and detente', in Mary Kaldor and Richard Falk (eds), *Dealignment: A New Foreign Policy Perspective* (Basil Blackwell, 1987).
12 Mal'tsev, *Organizatsiya Varshavskogo Dogovora*, document 2, p. 14. English text in Remington, *The Warsaw Pact*, p. 205.
13 See: Remington, *The Warsaw Pact*, chapter 3; Brzezinski, *The Soviet Bloc*, chapter 10; Harman, *Class Struggles in Eastern Europe*, chapter 7; Bill Lomax, *Hungary 1956* (St Martin's Press, 1976); F. Stephen Larrabee, 'Soviet crisis management in Eastern Europe', in Holloway and Sharp, *The Warsaw Pact*. The best short account covering both 1956 and 1968 is probably Michel Tatu, 'Intervention in Eastern Europe', in Stephen S. Kaplan, *Diplomacy of Power: Soviet Armed Forces as a Political Instrument* (The Brookings Institution, 1981).
14 See: Philip Windsor and Adam Roberts, *Czechoslovakia 1968. Reform, Repression and Resistance*, (Chatto and Windus, for the Institute of Strategic Studies, 1969); Jiri Valenta, *Soviet Intervention in Czechoslovakia, 1968: Anatomy of a Decision* (Johns Hopkins University Press, 1979); Zdenek Mlynar, *Night Frost in Prague: The End of Humane Socialism* (Hurst, 1980); Karen Dawisha, *The Kremlin and the Prague Spring* (University of California Press, 1984); F. Stephen Larrabee, 'Soviet crisis management in Eastern Europe', in Holloway and Sharp, *The Warsaw Pact*; Harman, *Class Struggles in Eastern Europe*, chapter 8.
15 Basic histories of the period include: Neal Ascherson, *The Polish August* (Penguin, 1981); Timothy Garton Ash, *The Polish Revolution: Solidarity* (Coronet, 1985); Harman, *Class Struggles in Eastern Europe*, chapter 9. See also chapter 2 below.
16 Savinov, *Varshavskii Dogovor*, p. 20; also Alexandrov, *The Warsaw Treaty*, p. 11.
17 See Fejtö, *A History of the Peoples' Democracies*, chapter 7, and Remington, *The Warsaw Pact*, chapter 3.
18 The most painstaking Western account of this entire period is contained in Raymond L. Garthoff, *Detente and Confrontation: American–Soviet Relations from Nixon to Reagan* (The Brookings Institution, 1985), but see also Robin Edmonds, *Soviet Foreign Policy: The Brezhnev Years* (Oxford University Press, 1983). For Soviet accounts, see Savinov, *Varshavskii Dogovor*, chapter 2 and further discussion in chapter 2 below.
19 Mal'tsev, *Organizatsiya Varshavskogo Dogovora*, document 105, p. 378. See appendix I to this study.
20 The possibility of a smaller alliance is mentioned in: Jörg K. Hoensch, 'The Warsaw Pact and the northern member states', in Robert W. Clawson and Lawrence S. Kaplan (eds), *The Warsaw Pact: Political Purpose and Military Means* (Scholarly Resources Inc., 1982).

Chapter 2 WTO Political Structures and History

1 See appendix I; Russian text in V.F. Mal'tsev (ed.), *Organizatsiya Varshavkogo Dogora 1955–1985, dokumenty i materialy* (Izdatel'stvo Politicheskoi Literatury, 1986), document 1, p. 9.
2 Ibid.
3 *Sovetskaya Voennaya Entsiklopediya (SVE)*, vol. 2, 1976, p. 21.
4 See K. I. Savinov *Varshavskii Dogovor – faktor mira, shchit sotsializma* (Mezhdunarodnye Otnosheniya, 1986), p. 23; also 'Varshavskii Dogovor: politicheskii i rabochii mekhanizm vzaimodeistiviya ego uchastnikov', *Vestnik Ministerstva Inostrannykh Del SSSR* 15, 15 August 1988, pp. 21–2.

5 *Pravda* 29 May and 30 May 1987; *Krasnaya Zvezda* 17 July 1988.
6 Mal'tsev, *Organizatsiya Varshavskogo Dogovora*, document 5, p. 23, is the 1956 document. The later date is given by Savinov, in *Varshavskii Dogovor*, p. 24, and Valentin Alexandrov, *The Warsaw Treaty and Peace in Europe* (Novosti, 1980), p. 22.
7 For example the *SVE* description cited in note 3 above.
8 The 1969 expansion is dealt with in chapter 3. For meetings, see: Malcolm Mackintosh, *The Evolution of the Warsaw Pact* (Adelphi Paper no. 58, 1969); A. Ross Johnson, Robert W. Dean and Alexander Alexiev, *East European Military Establishments: The Warsaw Pact Northern Tier* (Crane Russak, 1982); and Jeffrey Simon, *Warsaw Pact Forces: Problems of Command and Control* (Westview, 1985), p. 29.
9 Savinov, *Varshavskii Dogovor*, p. 24.
10 See *The Military Balance 1982–83* (IISS, 1982), p. 18.
11 Savinov, *Varshavskii Dogovor*, p. 23.
12 Mal'tsev, *Organizatsiya Varshavskogo Dogovora*, document 65, p. 199, and document 67, p. 200. The November 1976 document is the one which again refers to the setting up of the Joint Secretariat.
13 In April 1959 the foreign ministers met the Chinese Foreign Minister in Warsaw – see Mal'tsev, *Organizatsiya Varshavskogo Dogovora*, document 9, p. 46.
14 Mal'tsev, *Organizatsiya Varshavskogo Dogovora*, p. 199.
15 *Vestnik Ministerstva Inostrannykh Del SSSR* 15, p. 22.
16 *Sovetskaya Voennaya Entsiklopediya*, vol. 2, 1976, p. 21.
17 Savinov, *Varshavskii Dogovor*, pp. 4–5.
18 V. Kulikov, 'Nadezhnyi shchit mira', *Kommunist* 8, 1985, pp. 67–76, at p. 69.
19 General A. Gribkov, 'Brat'ya po klassu, brat'ya po oruzhiyu', *Voennyi Vestnik* 5, 1985, pp. 11–14, at p. 11.
20 A. Yakovlev, 'Mezhdunarodnoe znachenie Varshavskogo Dogovora', *MEMO* 7, 1985, pp. 14–25, at p. 14.
21 See particularly Christopher D. Jones, *Soviet Influence in Eastern Europe: Political Autonomy and the Warsaw Pact* (Praeger, 1981), chapter 6 and pp. 274–8. For a complete chart of bilateral treaties between the WTO states for the whole period 1943–80, see Robert L. Hutchings, *Soviet–East European Relations: Consolidation and Conflict 1968–1980* (University of Wisconsin Press, 1983), table 5.8, p. 161; table 5.9 p. 166, is also useful as a summary of their contents.
22 Quoted in David Childs, *The GDR: Moscow's German Ally* (Allen and Unwin, 1983).
23 Alexandrov, *The Warsaw Treaty and Peace in Europe*, p. 26. For contrast see Savinov, *Varshavskii Dogovor*, p. 35, where the bilateral treaties are described in terms of the inviolability of state boundaries only.
24 See Jones, *Soviet Influence in Eastern Europe*, pp. 274–8. The USSR–Romania Treaty text can be found in Robin Alison Remington, *The Warsaw Pact: Case Studies in Communist Conflict Resolution* (MIT Press, 1971), document 14, pp. 245–5.
25 Jones, *Soviet Influence in Eastern Europe*; more recent material by Jones includes his contributions to David Holloway and Jane M. O. Sharp, *The Warsaw Pact: Alliance in Transition?* (Macmillan, 1984); to a series of Canadian Department of Defence studies; and to Jeffrey Simon and Trond Gilberg (eds), *Security Implications of Nationalism in Eastern Europe* (Westview, 1986), entitled 'Agencies of the alliance; multinational in form, bilateral in content'. Jones's status as probably the most regular and prolific contributor to English-language studies of the WTO means that his work requires careful examination.

26 See the accounts in Jones, *Soviet Influence in Eastern Europe*, chapter 3; in Ross Johnson et al., *Eastern European Military Establishments*, chapter V; and Condoleezza Rice, *The Soviet Union and the Czechoslovak Army, 1948–1983: Uncertain Allegiance* (Princeton University Press, 1984), chapter 5.

27 See Margot Light, *The Soviet Theory of International Relations* (Wheatsheaf Books, 1988), chapter 7.

28 See: Karen Dawisha, *The Kremlin and the Prague Spring* (University of California Press, 1984); Zdenek Mlynar, *Night Frost in Prague: The End of Humane Socialism* (Hurst, 1980); Jiri Valenta, *Soviet Intervention in Czechoslovakia, 1968: Anatomy of a Decision* (Johns Hopkins University Press, 1979); David W. Paul, 'Soviet foreign policy and the invasion of Czechoslovakia: a theory and a case study', *International Studies Quarterly* 15 (2), June 1971, pp. 159–202.

29 These statements can be found as follows: Warsaw Letter in appendix II of Philip Windsor and Adam Roberts, *Czechoslovakia 1968: Reform, Repression and Resistance* (Chatto and Windus, 1969); Bratislave Declaration in *Current Digest of the Soviet Press*, 21 August 1968; 'Brezhnev doctrine' statements in *Pravda* 26 September 1968, and *Current Digest of the Soviet Press* 16 October 1968 (S. Kovalev, 'Sovereignty and the international obligations of socialist countries'–'every Communist Party is responsible not only to its own people but also to all the socialist countries and to the entire Communist movement'); also Brezhnev's speech in Poland on 12 November 1968, *Pravda* 13 November 1968.

30 There is an eye-witness account of Ceausescu addressing a rally in Bucharest in August 1968 in Julian Hale, *Ceausescu's Romania* (Harrap, 1971). On the 1969 manoeuvres, see Simon, *Warsaw Pact Forces*, chapter 5.

31 Francois Fejtö, *A History of the People's Democracies: Eastern Europe Since Stalin* (Penguin, 1977), chapter 7.

32 N. Edwina Moreton, *East Germany and the Warsaw Alliance: The Politics of Detente* (Westview, 1978).

33 A useful survey is Fritz Ermarth, *Internationalism, Security, and Legitimacy: The Challenge to Soviet Interests in East Europe, 1964–1968* (RAND Memorandum RM–5909 PR, March 1969).

34 See 'Special report: Poland in crisis, 1980–81', *Orbis* 32 (1), winter 1988, pp. 3–48; Timothy Garton Ash, *The Polish Revolution: Solidarity* (Coronet, 1985); Sidney I. Ploss, *Moscow and the Polish crisis: an interpretation of Soviet policies and intentions* (Westview Press, 1986); Richard D. Anderson, Jr, 'Soviet decision-making and Poland' *Problems of Communism* XXXI (2), March–April 1982, pp. 22–36.

35 See George Sanford, *Military Rule in Poland: The Rebuilding of Communist Power, 1981–1983* (Croom Helm, 1986); George C. Malcher, *Poland's Politicized Army: Communists in Uniform* (Praeger, 1984). For the March 1981 WTO meeting, see *Pravda* 4 March 1981, and Ploss, *Moscow and the Polish Crisis*, p. 67.

36 See A. A. Timorin, 'Sotsial'no-politicheskaya priroda i naznacheniya sotsialisticheskikh armii', chapter XIX in D. A. Volkogonov, A. S. Milovidov and S. A. Tiushkevich (eds), *Voina i armiya – Filosofsko-sotsiologicheskii ocherk* (Voennoe Izdatel'stvo, 1977), and the 1986 CPSU Programme in *Soviet News* 19 March 1986 (*Pravda* 7 March 1986), which includes the sentence, 'From the standpoint of internal conditions our society does not need an army.'

37 Two exceptions are: S. P. Voitenko, K. F. Pavlikov, 'Velikaya sila Varshavskogo Dogovora i bessilie ego kritikov', *Voenno-Istoricheskii Zhurnal* 4, 1987, pp. 71–8, and a 1987 Main Political Administration pamphlet, S. A. Tiushkevich, *Kritika burzhuaznykh kontseptsii po voprosam sovetskogo voennogo stroitel'stva* (Voennoe

Izdatel'stvo, 1987), which engages with some Jones-type arguments without identifying him.

38 See Dawisha, *The Kremlin and the Prague Spring*, Mlynar, *Night Frost in Prague* and Rice, *The Soviet Union and the Czechoslovak Army*.

39 See Jiri Valenta, *Soviet Intervention in Czechoslovakia*, chapter 1.

40 See Michel Tatu, *Power in the Kremlin* (Collins, 1969), part 4, and Michael Shafir, 'Eastern Europe', in Martin McCauley (ed.), *Khrushchev and Khrushchevism* (Macmillan/SSEES, 1987).

41 For a useful survey documenting the apparent expansion of the bounds of Soviet tolerance, see Richard Löwenthal, 'The limits of intra-bloc pluralism: the changing threshold of Soviet intervention', *International Journal* XXXVII (2), spring 1982, pp. 263–84. These points are taken up again in my conclusion.

42 See Moreton, *East Germany and the Warsaw Alliance*, especially chapter 1.

43 May 1958 PCC meeting in Moscow; documents 6–8 in Mal'tsev, *Organizatsiya Varshavskogo Dogovora*, pp. 24–46. For a summary of PCC proceedings in this period, see Simon, *Warsaw Pact Forces*, chapter 2.

44 On the Rapacki and disengagement questions, see: Jonathan Steele, 'A nuclear free zone in Central Europe: reviving the Rapacki plan', *END Journal* no. 1, December 1982–January 1983; M. Saeter, 'Nuclear disengagement efforts 1955–80: politics of status quo or political change?', in Sverre Lodgaard and Marek Thee (eds), *Nuclear Disengagement in Europe* (SIPRI/Pugwash, Taylor and Francis, 1983); Jane Sharp, 'Security through detente and arms control', in Holloway and Sharp, *The Warsaw Pact*; and Alternative Defence Commission, *The Politics of Alternative Defence* (Paladin, 1987), chapter 3. A contemporary survey of proposals made up to 1958 is Michael Howard, *Disengagement in Europe* (Penguin, 1958).

45 See Sharp, 'Security through detente and arms control', in Holloway and Sharp, p. 165, and John Erickson, 'The Soviet Union and European detente', in Kenneth Dyson (ed.) *European detente: Case studies of the politics of East–West relations* (Frances Pinter, 1986).

46 Savinov, *Varshavskii Dogovor*, p. 78; Vadim Nekrasov, *The Roots of European Security* (Novosti, 1984), 73.

47 1966 document in Mal'tsev, *Organizatsiya Varshavskogo Dogovora*, document 21, p. 81; 1969 document is document 27, p. 110. The 1969 document is still addressed only to European countries, but without the anti-US polemics of three years earlier.

48 See the memorandum of a meeting of WTO foreign ministers, 22 June 1970, in Mal'tsev, *Organizatsiya Varshavskogo Dogovora*, document 37, p. 124, and Remington, *The Warsaw Pact*, document 13, p. 240 (English version).

49 Most of this account is drawn from Moreton, *East Germany and the Warsaw Alliance*, chapters 3–4, and 'The German factor', in Edwina Moreton and Gerald Segal (eds), *Soviet Strategy Towards Western Europe* (Allen and Unwin, 1984); see also A. James McAdams, *East Germany and Detente: Building Authority After the Wall* (Cambridge University Press, 1985), chapter 4.

50 Mal'tsev, *Organizatsiya Varshavskogo Dogovora*, document 39, p. 128.

51 Henry Kissinger, *The White House Years* (Weidenfeld and Nicolson and Michael Joseph, 1979), p. 529.

52 For Brandt's own outline of his intentions, written before he became Chancellor, see Willy Brandt, *A Peace Policy for Europe* (Holt, Rinehart and Winston, 1969). For insightful surveys of US–European relations, see Mary Kaldor and Richard Falk (eds), *Dealignment: A New Foreign Policy Perspective* (Basil Black-

well, 1987), especially Richard Falk, 'Superseding Yalta: a plea for regional self-determination in Europe', Alan Wolfe, 'American domestic politics and the Atlantic alliance: crisis and controversy' and Hanne-Margret Birckenbach, Christiane Rix, Albert Statz and Christian Wellmann, 'Transatlantic crisis – a framework for an alternative West European peace policy?'.

53 See Lawrence Freedman, 'The United States factor', in Moreton and Segal, *Soviet Strategy Towards Western Europe*.

54 See Jane Sharp, 'Security through arms control and detente', in Holloway and Sharp, *The Warsaw Pact*.

55 Mal'tsev, *Organizatsiya Varshavskogo Dogovora*, document 63, p. 181.

56 See Raymond L. Garthoff, *Detente and Confrontation: American–Soviet Relations from Nixon to Reagan* (The Brookings Institution, 1985), chapter 17.

57 Garthoff (ibid.) presents an interesting example of an American analysis which attempts an even-handed overview while making the USA's greater fundamental hostility to detente quite plain in his detailed treatment of the 1970s. For a range of widely diverging analyses, see: Edward Thompson et al., *Exterminism and Cold War* (Verso, 1982); Fred Halliday, *The Making of the Second Cold War* (Verso, 2nd edn, 1986); John Erickson, 'The Soviet Union and European detente', in Dyson, *European detente*; Mike Bowker and Phil Williams, 'Helsinki and West European security', *International Affairs* [London] 61 (4), autumn 1985, pp. 607–18 – Bowker and Williams make the point about the very precise meaning of 'inviolability'; Mick Cox, 'The Cold War as a system', *Critique* 17, 1986, pp. 17–82; Mary Kaldor, 'The imaginary war', in Dan Smith and E. P. Thompson (eds), *Prospectus for a Habitable Planet* (Penguin, 1987).

For examples of Soviet assessments of detente and Helsinki, see: Georgi Arbatov, *Cold War or Detente? The Soviet Viewpoint* (Zed Press, 1983); *Ten Years After Helsinki: The Results and Prospects of the Process of European Security and Co-operation*, report of the Soviet Committee for European Security and Co-operation (Progress, 1985); A. Yakovlev, 'Mezhdunarodnoe znachenie Varshavskogo Dogovora', *MEMO* 7, 1985, pp. 14–25; 'Exchange of opinion: for peace and security in Europe', *International Affairs* [Moscow] 9, 1985, pp. 70–115; A. A. Gromyko and B. N. Ponomarev (eds), *Soviet Foreign Policy, Volume II, 1945–1980* (Progress, 1981), chapter XXXI. A Polish view can be found in Adam Daniel Rotfeld, 'The CSCE process and European security,' in Kari Möttölä (ed.), *Ten Years After Helsinki: The Making of the European Security Regime* (Westview, 1986).

58 Reported by Sharp in Holloway and Sharp, *The Warsaw Pact*.

59 The literature on Afghanistan is now voluminous. Among the most careful accounts are Garthoff, *Detente and Confrontation*, chapter 26; Jonathan Steele, *The Limits of Soviet Power: The Kremlin's Foreign Policy – Brezhnev to Chernenko* (Penguin, 1985), chapter 7. On the Eastern European response, see Simon, *Warsaw Pact Forces*, chapter 8.

60 Thomas W. Wolfe, *Soviet Power and Europe 1945–70* (Johns Hopkins Press, 1970), p. 151. Parts of this sub-section are drawn from an earlier version, published as 'Warsaw Treaty Organization', chapter 7 of Scilla McLean (ed.), *How Nuclear Weapons Decisions are Made* (Macmillan/Oxford Research Group, 1986).

61 Declaration text published in English by Panorama DDR, with the GDR statement contained in the same pamphlet. Russian text in Mal'tsev, *Organizatsiya Varshavskogo Dogovora*, document 89, p. 305.

62 Reports included: *Guardian* 29 June 1983, *Times* 30 June 1983, *International Herald Tribune* 30 June 1983. The English text of the statement is in *International*

Affairs [Moscow] September 1983; Russian text in Mal'tsev, *Organizatsiya Varshavskogo Dogovora*, document 93, p. 334.

63 *Soviet News* 26 October 1983; Mal'tsev, *Organizatsiya Varshavskogo Dogovora*, document 94, p. 341.

64 *Guardian* 14 October 1983.

65 Press reports of Chervov's interview and the Romanian statements: GND/ DPA/UPI/Reuter report, Bonn, 17 October 1983; *The Guardian* 19 October 1983; *Financial Times* 26 October 1983; CDM and Comecon texts both in *Soviet News* 26 October 1983; CDM also in Mal'tsev, *Organizatsiya Varshavskogo Dogovora*, document 95, p. 349.

66 Reports and texts in: US Foreign Broadcasts Information Service (FBIS) Report 25 October 1983; BBC Monitoring Service Summary of World Broadcasts (SWB) 26 October 1983.

67 Statement by Yuri Andropov, General Secretary of the CPSU Central Committee and President of the Presidium of the Supreme Soviet of the USSR, *Soviet News* 30 November 1983.

68 Mal'tsev, *Organizatsiya Varshavskogo Dogovora*, document 101, p. 362.

69 *Soviet News* 18 January 1984.

70 On rumours about Poland, see D. Warszawski, 'The Soviet "nyet"', *Across Frontiers* winter–spring 1985, pp. 23–4.

71 Robert English, 'Eastern Europe's doves', *Foreign Policy* no. 56, fall 1984, pp. 44–60.

72 See J. Goldblat, S. Lodgaard and F. Blackaby (eds), *No First Use* (SIPRI, Taylor and Francis, 1984), p. 20.

73 Martin McCauley, 'Soviet–GDR relations and European detente', in Dyson, *European detente*; Ronald D. Asmus, 'The dialectics of detente and discord: the Moscow–East Berlin–Bonn triangle', *Orbis* 28 (4), winter 1985, pp. 743–74; Jonathan Dean, 'Directions in inner-German Relations', *Orbis* 29 (3), fall 1985, pp. 609–32; A. James McAdams, 'Inter-German détente: a new balance', *Foreign Affairs* 65 (1), fall 1986, pp. 136–53, and *East Germany and Detente*, chapter 6 and Conclusion.

74 Mal'tsev, *Organizatsiya Varshavskogo Dogovora*, document 105, p. 378; English text of renewal protocol in *Soviet News* 1 May 1985 (see appendix I).

75 Ulrich Albrecht, 'The political background of the Rapacki plan of 1957 and its current significance', in Rudolf Steinke and Michael Vale (eds), *Germany Debates Defence: The NATO Alliance at the Crossroads* (M. E. Sharpe, 1983), pp. 129 and 131. For a fuller examination of the problems of political legitimacy, see the essays in T. H. Rigby and Ferenc Feher (eds), *Political Legitimacy in Communist States* (Macmillan/St Antony's College, 1982).

76 Jiri Dienstbier, 'Pax Europeana: a view from the East', in Smith and Thompson, *Prospectus for a Habitable Planet*, p. 185. Miklos Haraszti interview, 'Ending the cold civil war', in *END Journal* 34/35, summer 1988, quotation from p. 11.

77 Chris Harman, *Class Struggles in Eastern Europe, 1945–83* (Pluto, 1983).

78 'The imaginary war', in Smith and Thompson, *Prospectus for a Habitable Planet*, p. 77.

Chapter 3 The Military Command Structures

1 Their predecessors were, as C-in-C: I. S. Konev (1955–60), A. A. Grechko (1960–7), I. I. Yakubovskii (1967–76); as Chief of Staff: A. I. Antonov (1955–62), P. I. Batov (1962–5), M. I. Kazakov (1965–8), S. M. Shtemenko

(1968–76). See D. A. Volkogonov (ed.), *Armii stran Varshavskogo Dogovora* (Biblioteka Ofitsera, Voenizdat, 1985), pp. 28–9.

2 The communiqué refers only to the creation of the CDM plus other unspecified measures for strengthening the WTO's defence organization, but one of these measures seems to have been the creation of the MC. See V.F. Mal'tsev (ed.), *Organizatsiya Varshavskogo Dogovora 1955–1985, dokumenty i materialy* (Izdatel'stvo Politicheskoi Literatury, 1986), document 28, p. 113. More detailed information has recently emerged via Polish sources; see Michael Checinski, 'Warsaw Pact/CEMA military-economic trends', *Problems of Communism* XXXVI (2), March–April 1987, pp. 15–28.

3 John Erickson 'The Warsaw Pact: past, present, and future', in Milorad M. Drachkovitch (ed.), *East Central Europe: Yesterday, Today, Tomorrow* (Hoover Institution Press, 1982). Jeffrey Simon also favours this interpretation, using a Romanian source – see page 65 of *Warsaw Pact Forces: Problems of Command and Control* (Westview, 1985).

4 Details from Volkogonov, *Armii stran Varshavskogo Dogovora*, pp. 20–31; K. I. Savinov, *Varshavskii Dogovor: faktor mira, shchit sotsializma* (Mezhdunarodnye Otnosheniya, 1986), pp. 22–6; *Sovetskaya Voennaya Entsiklopediya*, vol. 2, 1976, pp. 20–2; Malcolm Mackintosh, 'The Warsaw Treaty Organization: a history', in David Holloway and Jane M. O. Sharp (eds), *The Warsaw Pact: Alliance in Transition?* (Macmillan, 1984).

5 Mal'tsev, *Organizatsiya Varshavskogo Dogovora*, document 51, p. 154.

6 Robin Alison Remington (ed.), *Winter in Prague: Documents on Czechoslovak Communism in Crisis* (MIT Press, 1969), documents 32 and 33, pp. 213–23. See also Thomas O. Cason, 'The Warsaw Pact today: the East European military forces', in Robert W. Clawson and Lawrence S. Kaplan (eds), *The Warsaw Pact: Political Purpose and Military Means* (Scholarly Resources Inc., 1982), and Condoleezza Rice, *The Soviet Union and the Czechoslovak Army, 1948–1983: Uncertain Allegiance* (Princeton University Press, 1984), chapter 5.

7 See Christopher D. Jones, *Soviet Influence in Eastern Europe: Political Autonomy and the Warsaw Pact* (Praeger, 1981), chapter 5; R. A. Remington, *The Warsaw Pact: Case Studies in Communist Conflict Resolution* (MIT Press, 1971), chapters 4 and 5; also Thomas W. Wolfe, *Soviet Power and Europe 1945–70* (Johns Hopkins Press, 1970), chapter XII. The most detailed account is in Robert L. Hutchings, *Soviet–East European Relations: Consolidation and Conflict 1968–1980* (University of Wisconsin Press, 1983), especially chapters 1 and 3.

8 See John Erickson, Lynn Hansen and William Schneider, *Soviet Ground Forces: An Operational Assessment* (Westview/Croom Helm, 1986), chapter 2, and Ann L. Phillips, *Soviet Policy Toward East Germany Reconsidered: The Postwar Decade* (Greenwood, 1986).

9 See Malcolm Mackintosh, *The Evolution of the Warsaw Pact* (Adelphi Paper no. 58, 1969), p. 4; Remington, *The Warsaw Pact*, chapter 3, and Francois Fejtö, *A History of the People's Democracies: Eastern Europe Since Stalin* (Penguin, 1977), chapter 5.

10 *Khrushchev Remembers, Volume 1* (Sphere Books, 1971), chapter 21 (quotations from pp. 468 and 470), and *Volume 2* (Penguin, 1977), chapter 10.

11 The withdrawals were announced by the May 1958 PCC meeting in Moscow, which also announced general WTO force reductions and proposed a non-aggression treaty to Nato. See Mal'tsev, *Organizatsiya Varshavskogo Dogovora*, documents 6, 7 and 8, pp. 24–46.

12 See Lincoln P. Bloomfield, Walter C. Clemens Jr and Franklyn Griffiths,

Khrushchev and the Arms Race: Soviet Interests in Arms Control and Disarmament 1954–1964 (MIT Press, 1966), pp. 100–1. For a recent survey of GSFG and details of deployment, see Günter Lippert, 'GSFG: spearhead of the Red Army', *International Defense Review* 20 (5), 1987, pp. 553–63.

13 See: David Holloway, *The Soviet Union and the Arms Race* (Yale University Press, 1983), chapters 3 and 5; Wolfe, *Soviet Power and Europe*, chapters VI, VII, VIII. Although opinions differ, the military do not seem to have played any major role in Khrushchev's actual fall from power in 1964. See Roy Medvedev, *Khrushchev* (Basil Blackwell, 1982), chapter 21; John McDonnell, 'The Soviet defense industry as a pressure group', in Michael MccGwire, Ken Booth and John McDonnell (eds), *Soviet Naval Policy: Objectives and Constraints* (Praeger, 1975); Michel Tatu, *Power in the Kremlin: From Khrushchev's Decline to Collective Leadership* (Collins, 1969), part 4 chapter 3.

14 For text see Philip Windsor and Adam Roberts, *Czechoslovakia 1968: Reform, Repression and Resistance* (Chatto and Windus, 1969), appendix 10.

15 *The Military Balance 1980–1981*, p. 5.

16 *The Warsaw Treaty Organization: Alliance for Peace* (Novosti, 1984), p. 42. Here a figure is given of 2,140,000 Soviet troops cut in the same period.

17 Mackintosh in Holloway and Sharp, *The Warsaw Pact*, pp. 42–3.

18 See Mackintosh, *The Evolution of the Warsaw Pact*, p. 4. A series of studies by the Canadian Department of National Defence represents a thorough survey of the interplay between nationalist and internationalist policies within the WTO. On the late 1950s 'renationalization' period, see in particular: ORAE Extra-Mural Paper no. 33, November 1984, *Warsaw Pact: The Question of Cohesion. Phase II. Volume 2: Poland, German Democratic Republic and Romania*, by Teresa Rakowska-Harmstone, Christopher D. Jones and Ivan Sylvain, chapter 1 on Poland; and ORAE Extra-Mural Paper no. 39, March 1986, *Warsaw Pact: The Question of Cohesion. Phase II. Volume 3: Union of Soviet Socialist Republics; Bulgaria, Czechoslovakia and Hungary*, by Teresa Rakowska-Harmstone, Christopher D. Jones, John Jaworsky, Ivan Sylvain and Zoltan Barany, chapter 3 on Czechoslovakia. (Both papers Department of National Defence, Canada, Operational Research and Analysis Establishment, Ottawa.) Also Rice, *The Soviet Union and the Czechoslovak Army*, chapter 4.

19 *Khrushchev Remembers, Volume 1*, chapter 21. See also Holloway, *The Soviet Union and the Arms Race*, chapter 3; Stephen M. Meyer, *Soviet Theatre Nuclear Forces, Part 1: Development of Doctrine and Objectives* (Adelphi Paper no. 187, 1983/4); Lawrence Freedman, *The Evolution of Nuclear Strategy* (Macmillan, 1981), chapter 17; Matthew A. Evangelista, *Innovation and the Arms Race: How the United States and the Soviet Union Develop New Military Technologies* (Cornell University Press, 1988), chapter 5.

20 See Jones, *Soviet Influence in Eastern Europe*, chapter 4; and Simon, *Warsaw Pact Forces*, chapter 2.

21 See Jutta and Stephan Tiedtke, 'The Soviet Union's internal problems and the development of the Warsaw Treaty Organization', in Egbert Jahn (ed.), *Soviet Foreign Policy: Its Social and Economic Conditions* (Allison and Busby, 1978).

22 For Soviet accounts, see: P. A. Zhilin (ed.), *Stroitel'stvo armii evropeiskikh stran sotsialisticheskogo sodruzhestva 1949–1980* (Izdatel'stvo Nauka, 1984), chapter 2, and pp. 38–57 of D. A. Volkogonov (ed.), *Armii stran Varshavskogo Dogovora* (Voennoe Izdatel'stvo, 1985).

23 See A. Alexiev, 'The Czechoslovak military', in A. Ross Johnson, Robert W. Dean and Alexander Alexiev, *East European Military Establishments: The Warsaw*

Pact Northern Tier (Crane Russak, 1982), and Rice, *The Soviet Union and the Czechoslovak Army*, chapter 6.

24 On the pre-1968 pressure, see Condoleezza Rice, 'Nuclear weapons and the Warsaw Pact', in Jeffrey D. Boutwell, Paul Doty and Gregory Treverton (eds), *The Nuclear Confrontation in Europe* (Croom Helm for the Center for Science and International Affairs, Harvard University, 1985); Jörg K. Hoensch, 'The Warsaw Pact and the Northern Member States', in Clawson and Kaplan, *The Warsaw Pact*; and Jiri Valenta, *Soviet Intervention in Czechoslovakia, 1968: Anatomy of a Decision* (Johns Hopkins University Press, 1979), chapter IV.

25 Thomas M. Forster, *The East German Army: The Second Power in the Warsaw Pact* (George Allen and Unwin, 1980). Recent articles include: Major Jeff McCausland, 'The East German army – spear point or weakness?', *Defense Analysis* 2 (2), 1986, pp. 137–53, and 'The East German army – an integral part of the conventional threat to NATO', *International Defense Review* 20 (4), 1987, pp. 401–3.

26 Mal'tsev, *Organizatsiya Varshavskogo Dogovora*, document 5, p. 23. Reportedly, Czechoslovakia and Poland had originally objected to the immediate integration of the GDR.

27 Mackintosh, *The Evolution of the Warsaw Pact*, p. 3; the figures for the Hungarian armed forces are the IISS's for the relevant years. See also P. Topolev, 'Vengerskaya narodnaya armiya', *Krasnaya Zvezda* 30 November 1985, and Ferenc-Antal Vajda, 'Hungary's air force: from rebirth to reliability', *Air International*, June 1988, pp. 290–307.

28 See A. Ross Johnson 'The Polish military', in Johnson et al., *East European Military Establishments*; Christopher Donnelly, 'The military significance of the Polish crisis', in *RUSI and Brassey's Defence Yearbook 1983* (Brassey's, 1983); and George Sanford, *Military Rule in Poland: The Rebuilding of Communist Military Power, 1981–1983* (Croom Helm, 1986).

29 *Financial Times* 18 October 1986, and 'Referendum on military cuts: Ceausescu speech at rally', *BBC Summary of World Broadcasts* 25 November 1986, Eastern Europe 8425/B/1.

30 Figure given in Johnson et al., *East European Military Establishments*, p. 14.

31 *The Military Balance 1987–8*, p. 39.

32 See, for example: William P. Mako, *US Ground Forces and the Defense of Central Europe* (The Brookings Institution, 1983); John J. Mearsheimer, 'Why the Soviets can't win quickly in Central Europe', *International Security* 7 (1), summer 1982, pp. 3–39, and *Conventional Deterrence* (Cornell University Press, 1983); E. Dinter and P. Griffith, *Not over by Christmas: NATO's Central Front in World War III* (Anthony Brett, 1983); B. R. Posen, 'Measuring the European conventional balance: coping with complexity in threat assessment', *International Security* 9 (3), winter 1984–5, pp. 47–88; Andrew Kelly, *The Myth of Soviet Superiority: A Critical Analysis of the Current Balance of Conventional Forces on the Central Front in Europe and of Possible Defence Alternatives for NATO* (University of Bradford School of Peace Studies Peace Research Report no. 14, March 1987); 'Policy focus: the European conventional balance', *International Security* 12 (4), spring 1988, pp. 152–202.

33 *The Military Balance 1987–8*. For details of the location of units in Eastern Europe and the western USSR, based on a West German survey, see the three-part article: 'Warsaw Pact forces in Europe: a new survey', in *Jane's Defence Weekly* 28 March, 4 April and 11 April 1987.

34 This NATO ratio includes French and Spanish forces; if they are excluded, the

ratio of US to allied forces is closer to parity (2.1 million to 2.3 million). All these calculations, however, exclude allies on both sides who are not members of NATO or the WTO.

35 *Sovetskaya Voennaya Entsiklopediya*, vol. 2, 1976, p. 21.
36 For example: *The Warsaw Treaty Organization: Alliance for Peace* (Novosti, 1984), p. 91; Volkogonov, *Armii stran Varshavskogo Dogovora*, p. 25; Savinov, *Varshavskii Dogovor*, p. 42.
37 David Isby, *Weapons and Tactics of the Soviet Army* (Jane's, 1981); Friedrich Wiener, *The Armies of the Warsaw Pact Nations* (Carl Ueberreuter, 1981); John Erickson, 'The Warsaw Pact – the shape of things to come?', in K. Dawisha and P. Hanson (eds), *Soviet–East European Dilemmas* (Heinemann for RIIA, 1981). For the 1964 USSR–GDR Treaty, see: UN Treaty Series v. 553, no. 8093, p. 249 (258).
38 Harriet Fast Scott and William F. Scott, *The Armed Forces of the USSR* (Westview, 1979), p. 206. See also Günter Lippert, 'GSFG: spearhead of the Red Army', *International Defense Review* 20 (5), 1987, pp. 553–63.
39 *The Military Balance 1982–83*, p. 18.
40 Viktor Suvorov, *Inside the Soviet Army* (Hamish Hamilton, 1982), part I, and Malcolm Mackintosh in Holloway and Sharp, *The Warsaw Pact*; Ryszard Kuklinski, 'The Crushing of Solidarity', *Orbis* 32 (1), winter 1988, pp. 7–31.
41 Mackintosh in Holloway and Sharp, *The Warsaw Pact*.
42 These arguments are most clearly expressed in Jones's 1981 book, *Soviet Influence in Eastern Europe*, and in two almost identically titled essays: 'Agencies of the alliance: multinational in form, bilateral in content', in Jeffrey Simon and Trond Gilberg (eds), *Security Implications of Nationalism in Eastern Europe* (Westview, 1986) and 'Agencies of the alliance: multilateral in form, bilateral in content', in *ORAE 29* (Canadian Department of National Defence, 1984).
43 See Daniel N. Nelson, *Alliance Behavior in the Warsaw Pact* (Westview, 1986), chapter 3, and Jeffrey Simon, 'Evaluation and integration of non-Soviet Warsaw Pact forces into the Combined Armed Forces', in Simon and Gilberg, *Security Implications of Nationalism in Eastern Europe*. Simon provides a useful chart of major Soviet and WTO exercises for the 1961–82 period at appendix A of *Warsaw Pact Forces: Problems of Command and Control*.
44 See J. Simon, 'Evaluation and integration', ibid., and in *Warsaw Pact Forces*, chapter 9.
45 Pointed out in *Keesing's Treaties and Alliances of the World* (Longman, 1981), p. 210. Romania, as noted earlier, is an exception. See also the chart of treaty contents provided by Hutchings, in *Soviet–East European Relations*, chapter 5.
46 The evidence for this is rather sketchy; see Simon, *Warsaw Pact Forces*, chapter 5, and Raymond L. Garthoff, *Detente and Confrontation: American–Soviet Relations from Nixon to Reagan* (The Brookings Institution, 1985), chapter 6.
47 See chapter 2, and *The Middle East*, December 1985.
48 See Jonathan Steele, *Socialism With a German Face: The state that came in from the cold* (Cape, 1977), chapter 5.
49 Accounts of 1956 can be found in: Neal Ascherson, *The Polish August* (Penguin, 1981), chapter 2; A. Ross Johnson, 'The Polish military', in Johnson et al., *East European Military Establishments*; Bill Lomax, *Hungary 1956* (Allison and Busby, 1976).
50 There is a chronology of the events of 1968 in Robert Rhodes James (ed.), *The Czechoslovak Crisis 1968* (Weidenfeld and Nicolson, 1969).
51 See, for example, Viktor Suvorov, *The Liberators* (Hamish Hamilton, 1981);

Gene Sharp, *Making Europe Unconquerable: The Potential of Civilian-based Deterrence and Defence* (Taylor and Francis, 1985).
52 Andrew Cockburn, in *The Threat* (Hutchinson, 1983), cites a *Washington Post* report from February 1981 about a chaotic attempted mobilization in the USSR's Carpathian Military District. Cockburn suggests that Brezhnev used this event as an argument against intervention at a time when others in the Soviet leadership were pressing for firm measures.
53 Mentioned by A. Ross Johnson in his chapter, 'Soviet military policy in Eastern Europe', in Sarah Meiklejohn Terry (ed.), *Soviet Policy in Eastern Europe* (Yale University Press, 1984).
54 There is a substantial body of English-language literature on Romanian doctrine, partly because the policy has been made so clear in Romanian speeches and documents. I have drawn on: Ivan Volgyes, 'Romania, a dubious partner', in *The Political Reliability of the Warsaw Pact Armies: The Southern Tier* (Duke Press Policy Studies, 1982); Christopher D. Jones, 'Romania', in *ORAE 33* (Canadian Department of National Defence, Ottawa, November 1984); Walter M. Bacon Jr, 'Romania', in Daniel N. Nelson (ed.), *Soviet Allies: The Warsaw Pact and the Issue of Reliability* (Westview, 1984); Edgar O'Ballance, 'The three southern members of the Warsaw Pact', in Clawson and Kaplan, *The Warsaw Pact*; William Zimmerman, 'Soviet relations with Yugoslavia and Romania', in Terry, *Soviet Policy in Eastern Europe*; David P. Burke, 'Defense and mass mobilization in Romania', *Armed Forces and Society* 7 (1), fall 1980, pp. 31–49; Alex Alexiev, 'Romania and the Warsaw Pact: the defense policy of a reluctant ally', *The Journal of Strategic Studies* 4 (1), March 1981, pp. 5–15; Mark L. Urban, 'Romanian land forces today', *Jane's Defence Review* 4 (5), 1983, pp. 475–8. For Romanian accounts, see: *National Defence: The Romanian View* (Military Publishing House, Bucharest 1976); *Pages From the History of the Romanian Army* (Centre for Military History and Theory Studies and Research, Bucharest 1975); Colonel-General Dr Constantin Olteanu, *The Romanian Armed Power Concept: A historical approach* (Military Publishing House, Bucharest 1982); *The Army and Romanian Society* (Military Publishing House, Bucharest 1980); Sigeo Mututshika, 'Fundamental directions of Romanian foreign policy for the strengthening of its national sovereignty', *Revue Roumaine d'Etudes Internationales* XX (5), Sept–Oct 1986, pp. 427–43.
55 See Volgyes, *The Political Reliability of the Warsaw Pact Armies*.
56 Agerpress release cited by Volgyes, *The Political Reliability of the Warsaw Pact Armies*, p. 57.
57 On the 1978 episode see O'Ballance, in Clawson and Kaplan, *The Warsaw Pact*; on the pre-1968 issues, see Wolfe, *Soviet Power and Europe*, and Hutchings, *Soviet–East European Relations*.
58 See Volkogonov, *Armii stran Varshavskogo Dogovora*, pp. 124–41, and Zhilin, *Stroitel'stvo armii evropeiskikh stran sotsialisticheskogo sodruzhestva*, chapter 6. The former account says that only Romanian staff representatives participate in WTO manoeuvres; the latter speaks of Romanian participation in exercises in 1970 and 1972 (a naval exercise); staff map exercises in Romania in 1973, 1974 and 1978; and of 'representatives' participating in the 'Shield-82' exercise. For further treatment of Romanian participation in particular exercises, see Simon, *Warsaw Pact Forces*.
59 See Volgyes, *The Political Reliability of the Warsaw Pact Armies*, p. 55; Bacon in Nelson, *Soviet Allies*.
60 Michael Kaser, *COMECON: Integration Problems of the Planned Economies* (Ox-

ford University Press, 1967), chapter VI.

61 See the analysis in Aurel Braun, *Romanian Foreign Policy Since 1965: The Political and Military Limits of Autonomy* (Praeger, 1978).

62 For example: *Financial Times* 25 March and 8 April 1986; *International Herald Tribune* 6 January 1987; Mark Jackson, 'Romania: recent trends', *Labour Focus on Eastern Europe* 8 (2), May 1986, pp. 37–8; Alan H. Smith, 'Romania: internal economic development and foreign economic relations', in Philip Joseph (ed.), *The Economies of Eastern Europe and their Foreign Economic Relations* (Nato Colloquium, Brussels 1986); *New Statesman* 30 October 1987; *The Independent* 28 November 1987; Gus Fagan, 'Misery under the "conducator"', *Labour Focus on Eastern Europe* 10 (1), April 1988, pp. 30–3.

63 Inevitably, the sources available do not agree on every point of interpretation concerning these bodies. See: Julian Cooper, 'The Soviet Union', in Scilla McLean (ed.), *How Nuclear Weapons Decisions Are Made* (Macmillan/Oxford Research Group, 1969); *Soviet Military Power:An Assessment of the Threat 1988* (US Department of Defense), chapter 1; Scott and Scott, *The Armed Forces of the USSR*, chapter 4; David Holloway, *The Soviet Union and the Arms Race* (Yale University Press, 1983), chapter 6; Vernon V. Aspaturian, 'Continuity and change in Soviet party–military relations', in Simon and Gilberg, *Security Implications of Nationalism in Eastern Europe*; Ulrich-Joachim Schulz-Torge, 'The Soviet military high command (part I)' *Military Technology* IX (8), 1985, pp. 111–21.

64 Andrew Cockburn, *The Threat: Inside the Soviet Military Machine* (Hutchinson, 1983), chapter 4.

65 See David Isby, 'Ogarkov's demise may reveal new command in Eastern Europe', *Defense Week* 3 December 1984; and *Jane's Defence Weekly*, 22 September and 27 October 1984.

66 See the account in Scott and Scott, *The Armed Forces of the USSR*. This account is useful as it was published in 1979, and so gives a clear view of the pre-reorganization system.

67 On the importance of air defence from an early stage in the 1940s, see John Erickson in Drachkovitch, *East Central Europe*; Matthew A. Evangelista, 'Stalin's postwar army reappraised', *International Security* 7 (3), winter 1982/1983, pp. 110–38; David R. Jones, 'Air defence forces', in *Soviet Armed Forces Review Annual* 6, 1982 (Academic International Press, 1982).

68 This account draws on: *The Military Balance 1984–85*, pp. 13–14; 'Soviet military aviation forces', in *International Air Forces and Military Aircraft Directory* (Aviation Advisory Services, updated to October 1985); 'Organization of the Soviet armed forces', *Air Force*, March 1985; Mark L. Urban, 'Major reorganization of Soviet air forces', *International Defense Review* 16 (6), 1983, p. 756; Matthew A. Evangelista, 'The evolution of the Soviet tactical air forces', in *Soviet Armed Forces Review Annual* 7, 1982; Alfred L. Marks, 'Air Forces', in *Soviet Armed Forces Review Annual* 8, 1983–84; William P. Baxter, *Soviet Airland Battle Tactics* (Presidio, 1986).

69 Ogarkov mentioned 'strategic nuclear forces' (as opposed to strategic *rocket* forces) in his 1981 article, 'Na strazhe mirnogo truda', *Kommunist* no. 10, pp. 80–91, at p. 87. General Yazov also used the term in 1987; see D. T. Yazov, *Na strazhe sotsializma i mira* (Voennoe Izdatel'stvo, 1987), p. 34.

70 Accounts drawn on here include: Michael J. Deane, Ilana Kass and Andrew G. Porth, 'The Soviet command structure in transformation', *Strategic Review* XII (2), 1984, pp. 55–70; John Erickson, 'The implications of Soviet military

power', *Catalyst* 1 (2), summer 1985, pp. 11–18, contribution to *The World Tonight* (BBC Radio 4), 6 September 1984, on the occasion of Ogarkov's apparent dismissal; *Jane's Defence Weekly* 21 and 28 December 1985. On the lecture materials, see 'Lectures from the Voroshilov General Staff Academy', *The Journal of Soviet Military Studies* 1 (1), April 1988, pp. 29–53.

71 See Deane, Kass and Porth, 'The Soviet command structure in transformation'; also Yossef Bodansky, 'Reorganizing the Soviet high command for war', *Defense and Foreign Affairs*, August 1985, pp. 27–32; Kenneth Currie, 'Soviet General Staff's new role', *Problems of Communism* XXXIII (2), March–April 1984, pp. 32–40. This last article, however, was written at a time when Ustinov and Ogarkov were still in their respective posts as Minister and Chief of Staff.

72 Sources here include the articles already cited by Deane, Kass and Porth, Erickson, and Bodansky. In addition: *The Military Balance 1984–85*, pp. 13–14; *Soviet Military Power*, various years; Suvorov, *Inside the Soviet Army*, parts I and III, and 'Strategic command and control: the Soviet approach' *International Defense Review* 17 (12), 1984, pp. 1813–20; John G. Hines and Phillip A. Petersen, 'Changing the Soviet system of control: focus on theater warfare' *International Defense Review* 19 (3), 1986, pp. 281–9, and 'Is NATO thinking too small? a comparison of command structures', *International Defense Review* 19 (5), 1986, pp. 563–72; Ulrich-Joachim Schulz-Torge, 'The Soviet military high command (part II)', *Military Technology* IX (9), 1985, pp. 102–11; Brigadier John Hemsley, 'The Influence of technology upon Soviet operational doctrine', *RUSI Journal* 131 (2), June 1986, pp. 21–8.

73 *Sovetskaya Voennaya Entsiklopediya* vol. 8 (Voennoe Izdatel'stvo, 1980), pp. 8–9.

74 See, for example: Charles O. Cutshaw, 'Who's in Charge', *Proceedings of US Naval Institute*, April 1986, pp. 79–83; George C. Weickhardt, 'Ustinov versus Ogarkov' *Problems of Communism* XXXIV (1), Jan–Feb. 1985, pp. 77–82; Tsuyoshi Hasegawa, 'Soviets on nuclear-war-fighting', *Problems of Communism* XXXV (4), July–August 1986, pp. 68–79; Mary C. Fitzgerald, 'Marshal Ogarkov on the modern theater operation', *Naval War College Review* XXXIX (4), autumn 1986, pp. 6–25. A more detailed treatment follows in chapter 4.

75 For example in *Armed Forces* October 1985; *International Defense Review* 10, 1985; *Jane's Defence Weekly* 26 October 1985.

76 See D. L. Smith and A. L. Meier, 'Ogarkov's revolution: Soviet military doctrine for the 1990s', *International Defense Review* 20 (7), 1987, pp. 869–73; Phillip A. Petersen, 'Soviet offensive operations in Central Europe', *NATO's Sixteen Nations* 32 (5), August 1987, pp. 26–32; John Erickson, 'The Soviet Union in the Warsaw Pact: military thinking and influence', lecture at Royal United Services Institute, London, 21 October 1987; Dr Milan Vego, 'Command and control of the Warsaw Pact navies', *Proceedings of the US Naval Institute*, Sept. 1987, pp. 115–18; *Soviet Military Power 1988*, p. 113.

77 Robin Alison Remington, 'The Warsaw Treaty Organization's third decade: systemic transformations', in Nelson, *Soviet Allies*.

Chapter 4   Strategy and Politics

1 See Matthew A. Evangelista, 'Stalin's postwar army reappraised', *International Security* 7 (3), winter 1982/3, pp. 110–38.

2 See John Lewis Gaddis, 'The emerging post-revisionist synthesis on the origins of the cold war', *Diplomatic History* summer 1983, pp. 171–204.

3 Recent work includes: Mary Kaldor and Richard Falk (eds), *Dealignment: A New Foreign Policy Perspective* (Basil Blackwell, 1987), especially the editors' introduction and Alan Wolfe's chapter, 'American domestic politics and the Atlantic alliance: crisis and controversy'; Henry Butterfield Ryan, *The Vision of Anglo-America: The US–UK Alliance and the Emerging Cold War, 1943–1946* (Cambridge University Press, 1987); Fraser J. Harbutt, *The Iron Curtain: Churchill, America and the Origins of the Cold War* (Oxford University Press, 1986). Gian Giacomo Migone, 'A second look at the history of the cold war', in Mary Kaldor, Gerard Holden and Richard Falk (eds), *The New Detente: Rethinking East–West Relations* (Verso/United Nations University, 1989).

4 For a range of views, see: Adam B. Ulam, *Expansion and Coexistence: Soviet Foreign Policy, 1917–73* (Holt, Rinehart and Winston, 1974); Alexander Werth, *Russia: The Post-War Years* (Robert Hale, 1971); William O. McCagg, Jr, *Stalin Embattled 1943–1948* (Wayne State University Press, 1978); Vojtech Mastny, *Russia's Road to the Cold War: Diplomacy, Warfare, and the Politics of Communism, 1941–1945* (Columbia University Press, 1979); Werner G. Hahn, *Postwar Soviet Politics: The Fall of Zhdanov and the Defeat of Moderation, 1946–53* (Cornell University Press, 1982); Chris Harman, *Class Struggles in Eastern Europe, 1945–83* (Pluto, 1983).

5 Contrast the accounts of Werth and Hahn with those of Hugh Thomas, *Armed Truce: The Beginnings of the Cold War 1945–46* (Hamish Hamilton, 1986), chapters 1–2, and Mick Cox, 'The cold war as a system', *Critique* 17, 1986, pp. 17–82.

6 Mary Kaldor, *The Imaginary War* (Basil Blackwell, forthcoming), chapters 2–3.

7 See Stephen M. Meyer, *Soviet Theatre Nuclear Forces, Part II: Capabilities and Implications* (Adelphi Paper no. 188, 1983/4), p. 4; and Matthew A. Evangelista, *Innovation and the Arms Race: How the United States and the Soviet Union Develop New Military Technologies* (Cornell University Press, 1988), chapter 5.

8 See Duncan Campbell, *The Unsinkable Aircraft Carrier: American Military Power in Britain* (Paladin, 1986), chapter 1, and Andy Thomas and Ben Lowe, *How Britain Was Sold – Why the US bases came to Britain* (Peace News/Housmans, 1984).

9 Alternative Defence Commission, *The Politics of Alternative Defence: A Role for a Non-Nuclear Britain* (Paladin, 1987), pp. 100–1.

10 On the history and influence of 'deep operations' thinking, see Kurt S. Schultz, 'Vladimir K. Triandafillov and the development of Soviet "deep operations"', in David R. Jones (ed.), *Soviet Armed Forces Review Annual, Volume 9, 1984–1985* (Academic International Press, 1986); Richard Simpkin in association with John Erickson, *Deep Battle: The Brainchild of Marshal Tukhachevskii* (Brasseys, 1987); Bruce W. Menning, 'The deep strike in Russian and Soviet military history', *The Journal of Soviet Military Studies* 1 (1), April 1988, pp. 9–28.

11 Among the Western sources drawn on here are the following. Thomas W. Wolfe, *Soviet Power and Europe 1945–1970* (Johns Hopkins Press, 1970). John Erickson, 'The ground forces in Soviet military policy', *Strategic Review* winter 1978, pp. 64–79, and, with Lynn Hansen and William Schneider, *Soviet Ground Forces: An Operational Assessment* (Westview/Croom Helm, 1986). C. N. Donnelly, 'Tactical problems facing the Soviet army – recent debates in the Soviet military press', *International Defense Review* 11 (9), 1978, pp. 1405–12; 'The development of Soviet military doctrine', *International Defense Review* 14 (12), 1981, pp. 1589–96; 'Soviet operational concepts in the 1980s', supporting paper for the Report of the European Security Study, ESECS, in *Strengthening*

Conventional Deterrence in Europe: Proposals for the 1980s (Macmillan, 1983). Harriet Fast Scott and William F. Scott, *The Armed Forces of the USSR* (Westview, 1979). Derek Leebaert (ed.), *Soviet Military Thinking* (Allen and Unwin, 1981). Lawrence Freedman, *The Evolution of Nuclear Strategy* (Macmillan, 1981). John Baylis and Gerald Segal (eds), *Soviet Strategy* (Croom Helm, 1981). Robert P. Berman and John C. Baker, *Soviet Strategic Forces: Requirements and Responses* (The Brookings Institution, 1982). P. H. Vigor, *Soviet Blitzkrieg Theory* (Macmillan, 1983). David Holloway, *The Soviet Union and the Arms Race* (Yale University Press, 1983). Stephen M. Meyer, *Soviet Theatre Nuclear Forces* (Adelphi Papers nos 187 and 188, 1983/4). Phillip A. Petersen, 'The Soviet conceptual framework for the development and application of military power', in Hylke Tromp (ed.), *Non-Nuclear War in Europe* (Groningen University Press, 1986).

12 Quotations in this paragraph from: *Sovetskaya Voennaya Entsiklopediya* (Soviet Military Encyclopaedia, identified below as *SVE*), volume 3 (Voennoe Izdatel'stvo, 1976), p. 225; *Voennyi Entsiklopedicheskii Slovar'* (Military Encyclopaedic Dictionary, *VES*) (Voennoe Izdatel'stvo, 1983), p. 240; *SVE* vol. 3, p. 229.

13 Quotations in this paragraph from *SVE* vol. 2, p. 183, *SVE* vol. 2, p. 211, *SVE* vol. 2, pp. 214–17, *VES*, pp. 477 and 497. For further discussion see Holloway, *The Soviet Union and the Arms Race*, chapter 3.

14 *Soviet Military Review* 1, 1987, p. 21.

15 V. Sokolovsky, (Soviet) *Military Strategy*, 3rd edn, ed. with analysis and commentary by H. F. Scott (Crane Russak, 1975). See also the commentary by Holloway in *The Soviet Union and the Arms Race*, chapter 3.

16 A. A. Sidorenko, *The Offensive* (Moscow 1970); another relevant publication from a couple of years later is V Ye. Savkin, *The Basic Principles of Operational Art and Tactics* (A Soviet View) (Moscow 1972). Both were translated and published under the auspices of the United States Air Force, Soviet Military Thought series, Washington DC, 1970[?] and 1972[?].

17 A particularly useful source for tracing these developments through military exercises is Jeffrey Simon, *Warsaw Pact Forces: Problems of Command and Control* (Westview, 1985).

18 'Na strazhe mirnogo truda', *Kommunist* 10, 1981, pp. 80–91; quotations from pp. 86 and 85.

19 N. V. Ogarkov, *Istoriya uchit bditel'nosti* (Voennoe Izdatel'stvo, 1985), pp. 72–4.

20 S. Akhromeev, 'Prevoskhodstvo sovetskoi voennoi nauki i sovetskogo voennogo iskusstva – odin iz vazhneishikh faktorov pobedy v velikoi otechestvennoi voine', *Kommunist* 3, 1985, pp. 49–63.

21 M. A. Gareev, 'Tvorcheskii kharakter sovetskoi voennoi nauki v Velikoi Otechestvennoi Voine', *Voenno-Istoricheskii Zhurnal* 7, 1985, pp. 22–30; this has been translated in *Soviet Press Selected Translations*, March–April 1986 (Directorate of Soviet Affairs, US Air Force Intelligence Service), as 'The creative nature of Soviet military science in the Great Patriotic War'. I have made some small changes in the translation of this particular passage.

22 M. A. Gareev, *M. V. Frunze – voennyi teoretik* (Voennoe Izdatel'stvo, 1985), p. 441.

23 The texts on which I am basing this argument are the following. C. N. Donnelly: 'The Soviet Operational Manoeuvre Group – a new challenge for NATO', *International Defense Review* 15 (9), 1982, pp. 1177–86; 'Soviet operational concepts in the 1980s', in ESECS Report (see note 11 above); *Heirs of*

Clausewitz: Change and Continuity in the Soviet War Machine (Institute for European Defence and Strategic Studies Occasional Paper no. 16, 1985). Michael MccGwire: 'Dilemmas and delusions of deterrence', *World Policy Journal* I (4), summer 1984, pp. 745–67; 'Deterrence: the problem – not the solution', *International Affairs* [London] 62 (1), winter 1985–6, pp. 55–70; 'Soviet military objectives', *World Policy Journal* III (4), fall 1986, pp. 667–95; *Military Objectives in Soviet Foreign Policy* (The Brookings Institution, 1987).

24 MccGwire 1987, chapter 4.

25 Donnelly 1983, p. 107.

26 Donnelly 1985, p. 21.

27 P. H. Vigor, *Soviet Blitzkrieg Theory* (Macmillan, 1983).

28 Vigor may not intend this, but I can see no other way of reading his argument on pages 190–1.

29 For example, General Bernard W. Rogers, 'Follow-on Forces Attack (FOFA): Myths and Realities', *NATO Review* December 1984, pp. 1–9.

30 MccGwire 1984 and 1985–6.

31 MccGwire 1984, p. 755.

32 Ibid., p. 756.

33 MccGwire 1986, p. 685.

34 Ibid., p. 668.

35 MccGwire 1987, chapter 3.

36 MccGwire 1987, chapters 3 and 11.

37 Soviet views have been presented to the West in publications such as *Whence the Threat to Peace* (several editions), as well as in the consistently-held position that NATO's Euromissiles were war-fighting and/or first-strike weapons. For Western discussions, see: William V. Garner, *Soviet Threat Perceptions of NATO's Eurostrategic Missiles* (Atlantic Papers nos 52–3, The Atlantic Institute for International Affairs, 1983). Raymond L. Garthoff, *Detente and Confrontation: American–Soviet Relations from Nixon to Reagan* (The Brookings Institution, 1985), especially chapters 22 and 25. Stephen Shenfield, 'Assertive and reactive threats', in Stan Windass (ed.), *Avoiding Nuclear War* (Brassey's, 1985).

38 Compare Michael Howard, 'The future of deterrence', *RUSI Journal* 131 (2), June 1986, pp. 3–10, with chapter 2, 'What threats should a defence policy meet?', in *Defence Without the Bomb: The Report of the Alternative Defence Commission* (Taylor and Francis, 1983).

39 'The ground forces in Soviet military policy', *Strategic Review* winter 1978, pp. 64–79, at p. 78.

40 'The Soviet view of deterrence: a general survey', *Survival* XXIV (26), Nov.–Dec. 1982, pp. 242–50.

41 'The implications of Soviet military power', *Catalyst* 1 (2), summer 1985, pp. 11–18.

42 Erickson et al., *Soviet Ground Forces*.

43 MccGwire 1987, appendix A, details his identification of the December 1966 Central Committee plenum which, he argues, formally adopted the new doctrinal assumptions.

44 MccGwire's work on Soviet naval policy includes contributions to three major books published during the 1970s: Michael MccGwire (ed.), *Soviet Naval Developments: Capability and Context* (Praeger, 1973); Michael MccGwire, Ken Booth and John McDonnell (eds), *Soviet Naval Policy: Objectives and Constraints* (Praeger, 1975); Michael MccGwire and John McDonnell (eds), *Soviet Naval Influence: Domestic and Foreign Dimensions* (Praeger, 1975).

45 See two pieces in *International Security* 12 (3), winter 1987/88, pp. 93–131, 203–14: Jack Snyder, 'The Gorbachev revolution: a waning of Soviet expansionism?' and Matthew Partan, 'Soviet military objectives' (book review). Partan is right to say that MccGwire overlooks Soviet counterforce developments, but seems to overstate his case by himself overlooking the fact that MccGwire says the pre-1966 Soviet targeting hierarchy remains in reserve. His main argument about MccGwire's weakness on institutional analysis, however, is surely correct. Another useful review essay is Christoph Bluth, 'The evolution of Soviet military doctrine', *Survival* XXX (2), March/April 1988, pp. 149–61.

46 Notably: Desmond Ball, *Can Nuclear War Be Controlled?* (Adelphi Paper no. 169, autumn 1981); Paul Bracken, *The Command and Control of Nuclear Forces* (Yale University Press, 1983); William M. Arkin and Richard W. Fieldhouse, *Nuclear Battlefields: Global Links in the Arms Race* (Institute for Policy Studies, Ballinger, 1985); Daniel Ford, *The Button: The Nuclear Trigger – Does it Work?* (Unwin, 1986).

47 Among the literature on the maritime strategy which Soviet planners have doubtless read are: Admiral James D. Watkins, 'The maritime strategy', supplement to *Proceedings of US Naval Institute*, January 1986; Commander S. V. Mackay, 'The maritime strategy: an allied reaction', *Proceedings of US Naval Institute*, April 1987, pp. 82–9; Colin S. Gray, 'Maritime strategy and the Pacific: the implications for NATO', *Naval War College Review* XXXX (1), winter 1987, pp. 8–19. For Western critiques and a view of Soviet naval policies, see: John J. Mearsheimer, 'A strategic misstep: the maritime strategy and deterrence in Europe', *International Security* 11 (2), fall 1986, pp. 3–57; Jack Beatty, 'In harm's way', *The Atlantic*, May 1987, pp. 37–53; C. G. Jacobsen, 'Soviet strategy – the naval dimension', *Naval War College Review* XXXX (2), spring 1987, pp. 17–27. MccGwire's own views are given in 'The changing role of the Soviet navy', *Bulletin of the Atomic Scientists*, September 1987, pp. 34–9.

48 MccGwire 1984, p. 765.

49 MccGwire 1985–6, p. 65.

50 Several arguments to this effect have already been cited. For an 'establishment' version, see Michael Howard, 'Reassurance and deterrence', *Foreign Affairs* (2), winter 1982–3, pp. 309–24.

51 MccGwire 1987, p. 376.

52 *The Political Reliability of the Warsaw Pact Armies: The Southern Tier* (Duke University Press, 1982), p. 16.

53 Valentin Alexandrov, *The Warsaw Treaty and Peace in Europe* (Novosti, 1980), p. 24.

54 Alexander Alexiev, 'The Czechoslovak military', in A. Ross Johnson, Robert W. Dean and Alexander Alexiev (eds), *East European Military Establishments: The Warsaw Pact Northern Tier* (Crane Russak, 1982); Christopher D. Jones, *Soviet Influence in Eastern Europe: Political Autonomy and the Warsaw Pact* (Praeger, 1981), chapters III and VII, and chapter 3 on Czechoslovakia in *ORAE 39* (Canadian Department of National Defence, Ottawa, March 1986); Condoleezza Rice, *The Soviet Union and the Czechoslovak Army, 1948–1983: Uncertain Allegiance* (Princeton University Press, 1984), chapters 4 and 5; John Erickson, 'International and strategic implications of the Czechoslovak reform movement', in V. V. Kusin (ed.), *The Czechoslovak Reform Movement 1968* (International Research Documents, 1973). Lt-General Prchlik's press conference, as reported on

Prague Radio, can be found in Robin Alison Remington (ed.), *Winter in Prague: Documents on Czechoslovak Communism in Crisis* (MIT Press, 1969), document 32, pp. 214–20.

55 Alexiev, 'The Czechoslovak military', p. 116.
56 Jozef Hodic, cited by Jones and Rice.
57 See Johnson in Johnson, Dean and Alexiev, and also chapter 1 on Poland (Teresa Rakowska-Harmstone), in *ORAE 33* (Canadian Department of National Defence, Ottawa, November 1984).
58 See George Sanford, *Military Rule in Poland: The Rebuilding of Communist Power, 1981–1983* (Croom Helm, 1986), *passim*.
59 For recent comments see Jonathan Eyal, 'Ceausescu's armed forces', *Armed Forces* March 1987, pp. 114–7, and Robert van Tol and Jonathan Eyal, 'The new Romanian navy: a weapon without a target', *RUSI Journal* 132 (1), March 1987, pp. 37–46.
60 Jeffrey Simon, 'Evaluation and integration of non-Soviet Warsaw Pact forces into the Combined Armed Forces', in Jeffrey Simon and Trond Gilberg (eds), *Security Implications of Nationalism in Eastern Europe* (Westview, 1985); and chapter 9 in *Warsaw Pact Forces: Problems of Command and Control* (Westview, 1985).
61 Most of the features of this debate were encapsulated in *Strategic Review* fall 1982, pp. 36–58 – a Garthoff–Pipes debate on Soviet strategic doctrine, comprising: Raymond L. Garthoff, 'Mutual deterrence and strategic arms limitation in Soviet policy'; Richard Pipes, 'Soviet strategic doctrine: another view'; 'A rebuttal by Ambassador Garthoff'.
62 Arguments broadly supportive of Garthoff's side of the debate have included John Erickson, 'The Soviet view of deterrence: a general survey', *Survival* XXIV (6), Nov.–Dec. 1982, pp. 242–50; David Holloway, *The Soviet Union and the Arms Race*. Garthoff updated his account in 'Strategic balance and military detente, 1977–80', in *Detente and Confrontation*.
63 *Soviet Military Power: An Assessment of the Threat 1988* (US Department of Defense, April 1988), p. 12.
64 The references to victory occur in pages 563–5 of *SVE* vol. 7 (1979). The debates over subsequent developments can be followed through: George C. Weickhardt, 'Ustinov versus Ogarkov'. *Problems of Communism* XXXIV (1), Jan.–Feb. 1985, pp. 77–82; Tsuyoshi Hasegawa, 'Soviets on nuclear war-fighting'. *Problems of Communism* XXXV (4), July–August 1986, pp. 68–87; Mary C. Fitzgerald, 'Marshal Ogarkov on the Modern Theater Operation', *Naval War College Review* XXXIX (4), autumn 1986, pp. 6–25, and 'Marshal Ogarkov and the new revolution in Soviet military affairs', *Defense Analysis* 3 (1), March 1987, pp. 3–19; James M. McConnell, 'Shifts in Soviet views on the proper focus of military development', *World Politics* XXXVII (3), April 1985, pp. 317–43.
65 *Istoriya uchit bditel'nosti*, pp. 77, 78 and 90.
66 On the 1972 statement, see Garthoff, *Detente and Confrontation*, chapter 9.
67 Gareev, *M. V. Frunze*. For interpretations see: James M. McConnell, 'The irrelevance today of Sokolovskiy's book *Military Strategy*', *Defense Analysis* 1 (4), December 1985, pp. 243–54 (curiously, McConnell's argument here does not seem consistent with the one he puts forward in the article cited in note 64 above), and 'SDI, the Soviet investment debate and Soviet military policy', *Strategic Review* XVI (1), winter 1988, pp. 47–62; Stephen Shenfield, 'Nuclear winter and the USSR', *Millenium, Journal of International Studies* 15 (2), summer

1986, pp. 197–208, and *The Nuclear Predicament: Explorations in Soviet Ideology* (Chatham House Papers 37, Royal Institute of International Affairs/Routledge and Kegan Paul, 1987). The passages in Gareev which seem most clearly to refer to the continued possibility of nuclear 'victory' are at pages 240 and 241. In his preface to Pergamon's English translation of the book, Joseph D. Douglass Jr misleadingly cites some passages which are making rather different points (opposing nuclear pacifism); see Col. Gen. Makhmut Akhmetovich Gareev, *M. V. Frunze: Military Theorist* (Pergamon-Brassey's, 1988), Introductory Note.

68 *XX Century and Peace* 7, 1986.

69 G. A. Trofimenko, 'Novye real' nosti i novoe myshlenie', *SSHA* 2, 1987, pp. 3–15; and the exchange between N. Grachev and D. Proektor in *Mezhdunarodnaya Zhizn'* 1 and 4, 1988.

70 See Stephen Shenfield, 'The Soviet undertaking not to use nuclear weapons first and its significance', *Detente* 1, 1984, pp. 10–11; D. Ustinov in *Pravda* 12 July 1982; Mikhail A. Mil'shtein, 'On the question of non-resort to the first use of nuclear weapons', in Frank Blackaby, Jozef Goldblat and Sverre Lodgaard (eds), *No-First-Use* (Taylor and Francis for SIPRI, 1984). Similar comments were later made by O. Bykov in *Creating a Climate of Confidence*, at p. 63 and V. Petrovsky, *Soviet Security Concept*, at p. 25 (both Nauka Publishers for Scientific Research Council on Peace and Disarmament, 1986).

71 This point is made in Blackaby et al., *No-First-Use*, p. 20.

72 In Adelphi Paper 188.

73 On the shorter-range systems, see Paul Rogers, *Guide to Nuclear Weapons* (Berg, 1988), pp. 58–61; on the possible integration of nuclear systems into battlefield planning, see Ilana Kass and Michael J. Deane, 'The role of nuclear weapons in the modern theater battlefield: the current Soviet view', *Comparative Strategy* 4 (3), 1984.

74 Stephen M. Meyer, Adelphi Papers 187 and 188, and 'The Soviet theatre nuclear force posture: doctrine, strategy and capabilities', in Jeffrey D. Boutwell, Paul Doty and Gregory F. Treverton (eds), *The Nuclear Confrontation in Europe* (Croom Helm for the Center for Science and International Affairs, Harvard University, 1985); Raymond L. Garthoff, 'The Soviet SS-20 decision', *Survival* XXV (3), May/June 1983, pp. 110–19, and chapter 25 of *Detente and Confrontation*; Björn Hagelin, 'Swords into daggers: a study of Soviet missile R& D with special reference to the SS-20', *Bulletin of Peace Proposals* 15 (4), 1984, pp. 341–53 (a rather different perspective, arguing that the SS-20 was not a planned system, but resulted from a failed attempt to build a solid-fuelled ICBM, the SS-16); Don Clark, 'Why the SS-20?', *Defense Analysis* 1 (3), September 1985, pp. 211–13); Patrick Litherland, *Current Soviet Thinking on the Use of Intermediate-Range Nuclear Forces* (Peace Studies Briefing, University of Bradford, August 1984).

75 Some key references from Christopher Donnelly have already been cited in note 23 above. Others include: C. J. Dick, 'Soviet Operational Manoeuvre Groups – a closer look', *International Defense Review* [IDR] 16 (6), 1983, pp. 769–76; P. A. Petersen and J. G. Hines, 'The conventional offensive in Soviet theater strategy', *Orbis* 27 (3), fall 1983, pp. 695–739; John G. Hines and Phillip A. Petersen, 'The Warsaw Pact strategic offensive – the OMG in context', *IDR* 16 (10), 1983, pp. 1391–5; Chris Bellamy, 'Antecedents of the modern Soviet OMG', *RUSI Journal* 129 (3), Sept. 1984, pp. 50–8; C. N. Donnelly, 'The development of the Soviet concept of echeloning', *NATO Review*

32 (6), Dec. 1984, pp. 9–17; Charles J. Dick, 'Soviet operational concepts, parts I and II', *Military Review* LXV (9 and 10), September and October 1985; Dennis M. Gormley, 'A new dimension to Soviet theater strategy', *Orbis* 29 (3), fall 1985, pp. 537–69; C. J. Dick 'Catching NATO unawares – Soviet Army surprise and deception techniques', *IDR* 19 (1), 1986, pp. 21–6; D. L. Smith and A. L. Meier, 'Ogarkov's revolution: Soviet military doctrine for the 1990s', *IDR* 20 (7), 1987, pp. 869–73; Phillip A. Petersen, 'Soviet offensive operations in Central Europe', *NATO's Sixteen Nations* 32 (5), August 1987, pp. 26–32.

76 For example Fitzgerald 1987, cited in note 64 above, especially pp. 15–16.

77 For Soviet commentaries see Ogarkov, *Istoriya uchit bditel'nosti*, pp. 68–72; Gen.-Major M. Belov and Lt-Colonel V. Shchukin, 'Razvedyvatel'noporazhayushchie kompleksy armii SSHA', *Voennyi Vestnik* 1, 1985, pp. 86–9; Major-General Ivan Vorobyob, 'Tactics today', *Soviet Military Review* 3, 1985, pp. 10–12, and 'New weapons require sound tactics', *Soviet Military Review* 1 and 2, 1987, pp. 16–18, 16–18; G. Vorontsov, 'SSHA, NATO i gonka obychnikh vooruzhenii', *MEMO* 5, 1985, pp. 49–60; M. Proskurin, 'Chto kroetsya za "Planom Rodgersa"', *Krasnaya Zvezda* 3 December 1985; Aleksandr Shevchenko, 'What lies behind the "Rogers Plan"', *Soviet Military Review* 3, 1986, pp. 46–7; Yu. Molostov, 'Zashchita ot vysokotochnogo oruzhiya', *Voennyi Vestnik* 2, 1987, pp. 83–5; Col. V. Alekseyev, '"Conventional" wars and ways of waging them', from *Soviet Press Selected Translations*, reprinted in *Current News* Special Edition 21 April 1987; N. Nikitin, 'Nastavlenie dlya voisk NATO', *Voennyi Vestnik* 8, 1987, pp. 86–9; Col. Yu. Molostov and Major An. Novikov, 'High-precision weapons against tanks', *Soviet Military Review* 1, 1988, pp. 12–13; Oleg Amirov, Nikolai Kishilov, Vadim Makarevsky, Yuri Usachev, '"Conventional War": Strategic Concepts', chapter 18 in *Disarmament and Security 1987*, Yearbook of the Institute of World Economy and International Relations, USSR Academy of Sciences (Novosti,) 1988.

On the ALB/FOFA/OMG debate, see 'New Directions in Conventional Defence?' in *Survival* XXVI (2), March–April 1984, pp. 50–78, comprising two pieces, 'Deep attack concepts and the defence of Central Europe' and Emerging technologies and European security': Rik Coolsat, 'NATO strategy: under different influences', *ADIU Report* 6 (6), Nov.–Dec. 1984, pp. 4–8; General Bernard W. Rogers, 'Follow-on Forces Attack (FOFA): myths and realities', *NATO Review* 32 (6), Dec. 1984, pp. 1–9; Dan Plesch, AirLand Battle and NATO's military posture', *ADIU Report* (2), March–April 1985, pp. 7–11; General Sir Hugh Beach, Emerging tecnology and the Soviet dilemma', *Defense Analysis* 1 (2), June 1985, pp. 131–3; Richard Ned Lebow, 'The Soviet offensive in Europe: the Schlieffen Plan revisited?', *International Security* 9 (4), spring 1985, pp. 44–78; North Atlantic Assembly Military Committee, *Final Report of the Sub-Committee on Conventional Defence: New Strategies and Operational Concepts* (Karsten Voigt, rapporteur, September 1987); Sally Stoecker, 'Soviets plan counter-measures to FOFA', *IDR* 19 (11), 1986, pp. 1607–8; Michael J. Sterling, *Soviet Reactions to NATO's Emerging Technologies for Deep Attack* (RAND Note N-2294-AF, August 1985); Bjorn Moller, 'The need for an alternative NATO strategy', *Journal of Peace Research* 24 (1), March 1987, pp. 61–74; *Power and Policy: Doctrine, the Alliance and Arms Control* (Adelphi Paper 206, spring 1986), especially the papers by James F. Brown and Dennis M. Gormley on 'The impact of NATO doctrinal choices on the policies and strategic choices of Warsaw Pact states,; Frank Barnaby and Marlies ter Borg (eds), *Emerging Technologies and Military Doctrine: A Political Assesment* (Macmillan, 1986; Jacob W. Kipp, 'Conventional force modernization and the asymmetries of military doctrine: historical reflections on Air/Land Battle and the Operational Manoeuvre Group', in Carl G. Jacobsen (ed.), *The Uncertain Course: New Weapons, Strategies, and Mind-Sets* (OUP/SIPRI, 1987); *Discriminate Deterrence: report of the Commission on Integral Long-Term Strategy* (co-chairmen Fred C Ikle and Albert Wohlstetter, Jan. 1988); Dale R. Herspring, 'Nikolay Ogarkov and the scientific-technical revolution in Soviet military affairs', *Comparative Strategy* 6 (1), 1987, pp. 29–59.

78 Gareev, *M. V. Frunze*, p. 203.
79 *The Military Balance 1986–1987*, p. 225.
80 See Mark Urban, 'Red flag over Germany, part I', *Armed Forces* 4 (2), Feb. 1985, pp. 69–74. Also Andrew Kelly, *The Myth of Soviet Superiority*; Lutz Unterseher, *Conventional Land Forces for Central Europe: A Military Threat Assessment*; Malcolm Chalmers and Lutz Unterseher, *Is There A Tank Gap? A Comparative Assessment of the Tank Fleets of NATO and the Warsaw Pact* (Peace Research Reports 14, 15 and 19, Bradford University School of Peace Studies, 1987).
81 *The Military Balance 1987–1988*, pp. 226–31.
82 MccGwire 1986, pp. 682–3.

Chapter 5 Arms Control and Disarmament Policy

1 Allen Lynch, *The Soviet Study of International Relations* (Cambridge University Press, 1987). For an analysis which places more emphasis on continuities, see Margot Light, *The Soviet Theory of International Relations* (Wheatsheaf, 1988). See also Julian Lider, *Correlation of Forces: An Analysis of Marxist-Leninist Concepts* (Gower, 1986).
2 See P. H. Vigor, *The Soviet View of War, Peace and Neutrality* (Routledge and Kegan Paul, 1975), and *The Soviet View of Disarmament* (Macmillan, 1986).
3 For example David Holloway, *The Soviet Union and the Arms Race* (Yale University Press, 1983); Raymond L. Garthoff, *Detente and Confrontation: American–Soviet Relations From Nixon to Reagan* (The Brookings Institution, 1985), and 'The Soviet military and SALT', in Jiri Valenta and William C. Potter (eds), *Soviet Decision-making for National Security* (Allen and Unwin, 1984); Peter M. E. Volten, *Brezhnev's Peace Program: A Study of Soviet Domestic Political Process and Power* (Westview, 1982).
4 See Jane Sharp, 'Troop reductions in Europe: a status report', *ADIU Report* vol. 5, no. 5, Sept.–Oct. 1983, pp. 4–7, and 'Security through detente and arms control', in David Holloway and Jane M. O. Sharp (eds), *The Warsaw Pact: Alliance in Transition?* (Macmillan, 1984); Jonathan Dean, *Watershed in Europe: Dismantling the East–West Military Confrontation* (Lexington Books, 1987), chapter 6.
5 For example: Georgi Arbatov, *Cold War or Detente? The Soviet Viewpoint* (Zed Books, 1983); D. Proektor, *The Foundations of Peace in Europe: Political and Military Aspects* (Nauka, 1984); Garthoff, *Detente and Confrontation*, chapter 22; Horst Ehmke, 'A second phase of detente', *World Policy Journal* IV (3), summer 1987, pp. 363–82.
6 Richard F. Kaufman, 'Causes of the slowdown in Soviet defense', *Survival* XXVII (4), July/August 1985, pp. 179–92.
7 The fullest account is in John Borawski, *From the Atlantic to the Urals: Negotiating Arms Control at the Stockholm Conference* (Pergamon-Brassey's, 1988), with the full document at appendix B. For additional discussions, see: Martin A. Cichock, 'Soviet goal articulations and involvement at the European disarmament conference', *Coexistence* 23 (3), 1986, pp. 189–207; 'Breakthrough in arms control?',

Non-Offensive Defence 5, 1986, pp. 1–2; James E. Goodby, 'Reducing the risks of war: the Stockholm Agreement', *Disarmament* IX (3), autumn 1986, pp. 53–61; John Borawski, Stan Weeks and Charlotte E. Thompson, 'The Stockholm Agreement of September 1986', *Orbis* 30 (4), winter 1987, pp. 643–62; Jane Sharp, 'The future of European arms control', *ADIU Report* 9 (5), Sept.–Oct. 1987, pp. 1–5; John Borawski, 'Toward conventional stability in Europe?', *The Washington Quarterly* 10 (4), autumn 1987, pp. 13–29.

8 Borawski, *From the Atlantic to the Urals*, p. 222.

9 *Soviet News* 18 June 1986, p. 284; *Address of Warsaw Treaty member states to NATO member states, to all European countries with a programme of reducing armed forces and conventional armaments in Europe*. Russian original in *Pravda* 12 June 1986.

10 For text, see Conference on Disarmament document CD/780, 11 August 1987: 'Letter dated 4 August 1987 addressed to the President of the Conference on Disarmament by the Permanent Representative of the Polish People's Republic transmitting the text of the 'Memorandum of the Government of the Polish People's Republic on Arms Reduction and Confidence-Building in Central Europe'.' See also reports in *Pravda* 9 and 10 May 1987, *International Herald Tribune* 9 May 1987.

11 Yazov's article was in *Pravda* 8 February 1988. For commentaries on the background issues, see: CRS Report for Congress, *Conventional Arms Control and Military Stability in Europe*, by Stanley R. Sloan, Steven R. Bowman, Paul E. Gallis, Stuart D. Goldman (Congressional Research Service, 16 October 1987); David S. Yost, 'Beyond MBFR: the Atlantic to the Urals gambit', *Orbis* 31 (1), spring 1987, pp. 99–134; Jonathan Dean, 'Military security in Europe', *Foreign Affairs* 66 (1), fall 1987, pp. 22–40; Karl Kaiser, 'Conventional arms control: the future agenda', *The World Today*, February 1988, pp. 22–7; Gen.-Maj. V. Tatarnikov, 'Do urovnei razumnoi dostatochnosti: na ocheredi – sokrashchenie arsenalov obychnykh vooruzhenii', *Krasnaya Zvezda* 5 January 1988; V. Nazarenko, 'Na puti k mandatu', *Krasnaya Zvezda* 2 March 1988; *The Guardian* 13 and 16 June 1988; *Soviet News* 8 and 15 June 1988 (15 June, Shevardnadze speech to UN incorporating a three-stage plan for European cuts); *Soviet News* 13 July 1988 (Gorbachev speech) and 20 July 1988 (PCC statement).

12 Anatolii Gromyko, Vladimir Lomeiko, *Novoe myshlenie v yadernyi vek* (Mezhdunarodnye Otnosheniya, 1984).

13 Margot Light, '"New thinking" in Soviet foreign policy?', *Coexistence* 24 (3), 1987, pp. 233–43.

14 Anatolii Gromyko and Vladimir Lomeiko, 'New way of thinking and "new globalism"', *International Affairs* [Moscow] 5, 1986, pp. 15–27.

15 A selection of items over the 1984–8 period would include: G. Kh. Shakhnazarov, 'Logika politicheskogo myshleniya v yadernuyu eru', *Voprosy Filosofii* 5, 1984, pp. 63–74 (and a useful commentary by Jeff Gleisner in *Detente* 1, Oct. 1984, pp. 12–14); O. Bykov, 'Vseobshchaya bezopasnost' – vlastnoe trebovanie vremeni', *MEMO* 3, 1986, pp. 28–39; E. Primakov, 'XXVII s'ezd KPSS i issledovanie problem mirovoi ekonomiki i mezhdunarodnykh otnoshenii', *MEMO* 5, 1986, pp. 3–14; A. Dobrynin, 'Za bez'yadernyi mir, navstrechu XXI veku', *Kommunist* 9, 1986; I. Frolov, 'Nauchit'sya myslit' i deistvovat' po-novomu', *MEMO* 8, 1986, pp. 3–7; A. Bovin 'Novoe myshlenie – trebovanie yadernogo veka', *Kommunist* 10, 1986, pp. 113–24; G. A. Trofimenko, 'Novye real'nosti i novoe myshlenie', *SSHA* 2, 1987, pp. 3–15; Nikolai Kapchenko, 'The political philosophy of peace in the nuclear-missile age', *Inter-*

national Affairs [Moscow] 3, 1987, pp. 12–29; Yuri Slepukhin, 'Do we believe in the reality of the threat?', *XX Century and Peace* 4, 1987, pp. 20–5; Professor Tair Tairov, 'Moment of truth', *New Times* no. 19, 18 May 1987, pp. 12–13; Editorial – 'Dialektika novogo myshleniya', *Kommunist* 18, 1987, pp. 3–12; V. Petrovskii, 'Doverie i vyzhivanie chelovechestva', *MEMO* 11, 1987, pp. 15–26; E. Primakov, 'Sovetskaya politika v regional'nykh konfliktakh', *Mezhdunarodnaya Zhizn'* 5, 1988, pp. 3–9; A. Bovin, 'Novoe myshlenie – novaya politika', *Kommunist* 9, 1988, pp. 115–25; E. A. Shevardnadze, 'Na puti k bezopasnomu miru', *Mezhdunarodnaya Zhizn'* 7, 1988, pp. 3–16.

16 Important statements since Gorbachev's appointment as General Secretary in March 1985 are: Statement by M. S. Gorbachev, General Secretary of the CPSU Central Committee, *Pravda* 16 January 1986, and English version in *Soviet News* 22 January 1986; Report by Mikhail Gorbachev to 27th Congress of the CPSU, *Pravda* and *Soviet News* 26 February 1986; Programme of the Communist Party of the Soviet Union, *Pravda* 7 March 1986, and *Soviet News* 19 March 1986; Mikhail Gorbachev's address to Moscow forum, *Pravda* 17 February 1987 and *Soviet News* 18 February 1987; Mikhail Gorbachev, 'The reality and guarantees of a secure world', *Pravda* 17 September 1987 and *Soviet News* 23 September 1987; Mikhail Gorbachev, *Perestroika: New Thinking for Our Country and the World* (Collins, 1987); Mikhail Gorbachev, 'October and perestroika: the revolution continues', *Pravda* 3 November 1987 and *Soviet News* 4 November 1987; Mikhail Gorbachev's speech at CPSU CC plenum, *Pravda* 19 February 1988 and *Soviet News* 24 February 1988. Mikhail Gorbachev, 'On progress in implementing the decisions of the 27th Party Congress and the tasks for promoting perestroika', Report at 19th All-Union Conference of the CPSU, 28 June 1988 *Pravda* 29 June 1988 and *Soviet News* 6 July 1988.

17 For details of the organization and personnel changes, see: Margot Light, *Coexistence* 24 (3), 1987; Gary Thatcher, 'Moscow shifts arms control team', *Christian Science Monitor* 30 July 1986; Philip Taubman, 'Gorbachev overhauls foreign policy system', *International Herald Tribune*, 11 August 1986; 'Perestroika in Soviet diplomacy: from Soviet Minister of Foreign Affairs Edvard Shevardnadze's report at a conference of diplomatic staff', supplement to *Moscow News*, no. 48, 1987; Archie Brown, 'Soviet political developments and prospects', *World Policy Journal* IV (1), winter 1986–7, pp. 55–87.

18 See Jerry F. Hough, *The Struggle for the Third World: Soviet Debates and American Options* (The Brookings Institution, 1986); and Elizabeth Kridl Valkenier, 'East–West economic competition in the Third World', in Marshall D. Shulman (ed.), *East–West Tensions in the Third World* (W.W. Norton, 1986).

19 *Soviet News* 19 March 1986, p. 146.

20 Gorbachev's remarks are in his report to the 27th Congress, *Soviet News* 26 February 1986, p. 78.

21 Patrick Litherland, 'Nuclear arms: a one-horse race?', *Detente* 6, spring 1986, pp. 7–9, and *Gorbachev and Arms Control: Civilian Experts and Soviet Policy* (Peace Research Report number 12, University of Bradford School of Peace Studies, November 1986; Stephen Shenfield, *The Nuclear Predicament: Explorations in Soviet Ideology* (Chatham House Papers no. 37, Routledge and Kegan Paul/ RIIA, 1987).

22 Bogomolov's letter, *Literaturnaya Gazeta* 16 March 1988 and *Detente* 12, 1988, p. 11; Vyacheslav Dashichev, 'Vostok-Zapad: poisk novykh otnoshenii – O prioritetakh vneshnei politiki Sovestkogo gosudarstva', *Literaturnaya Gazeta* 18 May 1988.

23 *Theses of the CPSU Central Committee for the 19th All-Union Party Conference* (Novosti, 1988), pp. 26–7.
24 V. Zagladin, 'Kursom razuma i gumanizma', *Pravda* 13 June 1988; 'Vneshnyaya politika i perestroika', *Pravda* 26 June 1988; 'Ot balansa sil – k balansu interesov', *Literaturnaya Gazeta* 29 June 1988; Igor Malashenko 'Freedom of choice', *New Times* 29, July 1988, pp. 11–12; A. Bovin, 'Mirnoe sosushchestvovanie i mirovaya sistema sotsializma', *MEMO* 7, 1988, pp. 5–15; A. Bovin, 'Let's break the ice on foreign policy', *Moscow News* 24, 12 June 1988, p. 6; Editorial – 'Partkonferentsiya: vneshnepoliticheskoe izmerenie', *Mezhdunarodnaya Zhizn'* 7, 1988, pp. 74–80.
25 *Soviet News* 6 July 1988, p. 243, and *Pravda* 29 June 1988.
26 Coverage in *Pravda* 30 June 1988 to 3 July 1988; resolutions published in *Soviet News* 13 July 1988 and *Pravda* 4 July 1988.
27 Shevardnadze addresses conference on foreign policy and diplomacy, BBC SWB SU/0214, 27 July 1988, pp. A1/2–A1/5; Ligachev's speech to Gorkiy oblast party activists, BBC SWB SU/0224, 8 August 1988, pp. B/1–B/5. A fuller version of Shevardnadze's speech is in *Vestnik MID SSSR* 15, 15 August 1988, pp. 27–46.
28 See V. V. Zhurkin, S. A. Karaganov, A. V. Kortunov, 'O razumnoi dostatochnosti', *SSHA* 12, 1987, pp. 11–21, p. 11.
29 See Stephen Shenfield, 'The USSR: Viktor Girshfeld and the concept of "sufficient defence"', *ADIU Report* 6 (1), Jan.–Feb. 1984, p. 10; M. A. Gareev, *M. V. Frunze: Voennyi Teoretik* (Voenizdat, 1985), p. 399.
30 *Soviet News* 26 February 1986, p. 91.
31 *Soviet News* 19 March 1986, p. 136.
32 *Constitution (Fundamental Law) of the Union of Soviet Socialist Republics* (Novosti, 1980), Article 32, p. 34.
33 *Soviet News* 19 March 1986, p. 145.
34 For example: Lev Semeiko, 'Concerning parity', *New Times* no. 20, 25 May 1987, pp. 16–17; V. Petrovskii, 'Sovetskaya kontseptsiya vseobshchei bezopasnosti' *MEMO* 6, 1986, pp. 3–13.
35 Committee of Soviet Scientists For Peace, Against the Nuclear Threat, *Strategic Stability Under the Conditions of Radical Nuclear Arms Reductions: Report On A Study (Abridged)* (Moscow, 1987); V. V. Zhurkin, S. A. Karaganov, A. V. Kortunov, 'O razumnoi dostatochnosti' *SSHA* 12, 1987, pp. 11–21; A. A. Kokoshin, 'Sokrashchenie yadernykh vooruzhenii i strategicheskaya stabil'nost'', *SSHA* 2, 1988, pp. 3–12; A. Arbatov, 'Glubokoe sokrashchenie strategicheskikh vooruzhenii', 2 parts, *MEMO* 4, 1988, pp. 10–22, and *MEMO* 5, 1988, pp. 18–30. See also Stephen Shenfield, *Rival Soviet Schemes for Minimum Nuclear Deterrence*, paper prepared for the Center for Foreign Policy Development at Brown University, Providence, RI, USA, July 1988.
36 Stephen Shenfield, 'The militarisation of space through Soviet eyes', in S. Kirby and G. Robson (eds). *The Militarisation of Space* (Wheatsheaf, 1987); Rip Bulkeley, 'Soviet military responses to the Strategic Defense Initiative', *Current Research on Peace and Violence* 4, 1987, pp. 129–42.
37 *Soviet News* 10 April 1985 and *Pravda* 8 April 1985; *Pravda* 2 August 1985.
38 *Soviet News* 9 October 1985 and *Pravda* 4 October 1985.
39 *Soviet News* 22 January 1986 and *Pravda* 16 January 1986.
40 *Soviet News* 26 February 1986, p. 89, and *Pravda* 26 February 1986.
41 Gorbachev statement in *Soviet News* 4 March 1987 and *Pravda* 1 March 1987.
42 Bovin in *Moscow News* 8 March 1987; Bessmertnykh in *New Times* no. 46, 23 November 1987, p. 7.

43 For the treaty text, see *USSR–US Summit: Documents and Materials* (Novosti, 1987). On re-targeting, see Leon V. Sigal, 'INF deal faces conservative opposition', *Bulletin of the Atomic Scientists*, May 1987, pp. 14–16.

44 For a useful overview of Nato debates, written before the signature of the treaty, see John Baylis, 'NATO strategy: the case for a new strategic concept', *International Affairs* [London] 64 (1), winter 1987/8, pp. 43–59.

45 The best source for following developments in the various proposals for chemical- and nuclear-free zones is the monthly digest *Arms Control Reporter*. The SED–SPD initiative on chemical weapons can be found in: 'For a zone free of chemical weapons in Europe: joint political initiative by the Socialist Unity Party of Germany and the Social Democratic Party of Germany, Intertext, Dresden 1985. See also Ralf Trapp (ed.), *Chemical Weapon Free Zones?* (SIPRI, 1987), which has contributions from the FRG, GDR and Czechoslovakia.

46 Mary C. Fitzgerald, 'The strategic revolution behind Soviet arms control', *Arms Control Today* June 1987, pp. 16–19; George C. Weickhardt, 'The military consensus behind Soviet arms control proposals', *Arms Control Today* September 1987, pp. 20–4.

47 See Matthew Evangelista, 'The new Soviet approach to security', *World Policy Journal* III (4), fall 1986, pp. 561–99; also Jonathan Dean, 'Gorbachev's arms control moves', *Bulletin of the Atomic Scientists* June 1987, pp. 34–40.

48 Stephen F. Cohen, 'Gorbachev's detente: dangerous illusions?', *International Herald Tribune* 3 June 1986; Franklyn Griffiths, '"New thinking" in the Kremlin', *Bulletin of the Atomic Scientists* April 1987, pp. 20–4.

49 Dennis M. Gormley, '"Triple zero" and Soviet military strategy', *Arms Control Today* January/February 1988, pp. 17–20.

50 Dennis M. Gormley, 'A new dimension to Soviet theater strategy', *Orbis* 29 (3), fall 1985, pp. 537–69; for a different view see Matthew Evangelista, 'Exploiting the Soviet "threat" to Europe', *Bulletin of the Atomic Scientists* Jan/Feb 1987, pp. 14–18.

51 See an opinion poll in *Pravda* 17 December 1987, reported in *The Times* 18 December 1987, and expressions of concern or mention of them in *Krasnaya Zvezda* 3 February 1988, *Moscow News* no. 6, 7 February 1988, *New Times* no. 6, February 1988, and *Izvestiya* 16 March 1988.

52 V. Ivanov 'Bez'yadernyi mir i obshchestvennoe mnenie', *Kommunist* 5, 1987, pp. 117–19; see also a commentary in *Detente* 9/10, winter 1987/8, pp. 46–8, pointing out the discrepancies between responses to various questions in this survey.

53 Marshal S. F. Akhromeev, 'Na puti k yadernomu razoruzheniyu', *Pravda* 16 December 1987; General D. T. Yazov, 'O voennom balanse sil i raketno-yadernom paritete', *Pravda* 8 February 1988; *Pravda* and *Krasnaya Zvezda* 10 February 1988 (Supreme Soviet session, including Shevardnadze speech); *Krasnaya Zvezda* 20 February 1988 (report of Akhromeev's evidence to the Supreme Soviet's preparatory commission); *MEMO* 2, 1988, pp. 3–34 (assessments of the treaty by E. Primakov, O. Bykov and V. Baranovskii); *Krasnaya Zvezda* 29 May 1988 (report of ratification).

54 See the very first page of Gorbachev's book, where he says: 'Any delay in beginning perestroika could have led to an exacerbated internal situation in the near future, which, to put it bluntly, would have been fraught with serious social, economic and political crises' (*Perestroika*, p. 17); and Peter Frank, 'Gorbachev's dilemma: social justice or political instability', *The World Today* 42 (6), June 1986, pp. 93–5.

55 See 'Mikhail Gorbachev's speech at international meeting', *Soviet News* 11 November 1987, and in *Pravda* 5 November 1987; E. Primakov, 'Novaya filosofiya vneshnei politiki', *Pravda* 10 July 1987. It is interesting to compare this piece by Primakov with one from a year earlier, in *MEMO* 5, 1986, in which he was much harsher about capitalism's problems, and more restrained about Soviet economic difficulties (see note 15 above).

56 See Primakov in *Pravda* 10 July 1987, and A. Lizichev, 'Oktyabr' i leninskoe uchenie o zashchite revolyutsii', *Kommunist* 3, 1987, pp. 85–96. Also Gorbachev's own comments about unspecified confusion in some people's minds about the essence of New Thinking, in his CC plenum speech in February 1988, *Pravda* 19 February 1988 and *Soviet News* 24 February 1988.

57 See V. V. Zhurkin, S. A. Karaganov, A. V. Kortunov, 'Razumnaya dostatochnost' ili kak razorvat' porochnyi krug', *Novoe Vremya* no. 40, 2 October 1987, pp. 13–15; 'O razumnoi dostatochnosti', *SSHA* 12, 1987, pp. 11–21; 'Vyzovy bezopasnosti – starye i novye', *Kommunist* 1, 1988, pp. 42–50. Also A. Izyumov, A. Kortunov, 'Sovetskii Soyuz v menyayushchem mire', *Mezhdunarodnaya Zhizn'* 7, 1988, pp. 53–64.

58 See Gorbachev's statement on Afghanistan in *Pravda* 8 February 1988 and *Soviet News* 10 February 1988; and some comments by Shevardnadze in the Supreme Soviet's discussion of the INF Treaty, *Pravda* 10 February 1988: 'The signature of this treaty has no less significance in the context of creating conditions beneficial to the resolution of regional problems.'

59 The phrase 'incomplete superpower' is Paul Dibb's, in *The Soviet Union: The Incomplete Superpower* (Macmillan/IISS, 1986). For general discussions of late–1980s geopolitics, see the essays in Mary Kaldor, Gerard Holden and Richard Falk (eds), *The New Detente: Rethinking East–West Relations* (Verso/United Nations University, 1989).

Chapter 6   Alternatives

1 McGeorge Bundy, George Kennan, Robert McNamara and Gerard Smith, 'Nuclear weapons and the Atlantic alliance', *Foreign Affairs* 60 (4), spring 1982, pp. 753–68. This was followed in 1986 by: McGeorge Bundy, Morton M. Halperin, William W. Kaufman, George F. Kennan, Robert S. McNamara, Madalene O'Donnell, Leon V. Sigal, Gerard C. Smith, Richard H. Ullman, and Paul C. Warnke, 'Back from the brink', *The Atlantic* 258 (2), August 1986, pp. 35–41.

2 *Common Security: A Programme for Disarmament: The Report of the Independent Commission on Disarmament and Security Issues under the Chairmanship of Olof Palme* (Pan Books, 1982).

3 See *Policies for Common Security* (Taylor and Francis for SIPRI, 1985), in particular the chapters by Mary Kaldor and Emma Rothschild.

4 See Lord Philip Noel-Baker, 'Historical developments on disarmament', in *Disarm or Die: A Disarmament Reader for the Leaders and the Peoples of the World* (Taylor and Francis, 1978), and Lutz Unterseher, 'Emphasizing defence: an ongoing non-debate in the Federal Republic of Germany', in Frank Barnaby and Marlies ter Borg (eds), *Emerging Technologies and Military Doctrine: A Political Assessment* (Macmillan, 1986).

5 From Egbert Boeker and Lutz Unterseher, 'Emphasizing defence', in Barnaby and ter Borg, ibid.

6 Anders Boserup, 'Non-offensive defence in Europe', in Derek Paul (ed.), *Defending Europe: Options for Security* (Taylor and Francis, 1985).

7 Material in English on the range of West German proposals includes: Boeker and Unterseher in Barnaby and ter Borg, *Emerging Technologies and Military Doctrine*; Andreas von Bülow, 'Defensive entanglement: an alternative strategy for Nato', in Andrew J. Pierre (ed.), *The Conventional Defense of Europe: New Technologies and New Strategies* (Council on Foreign Relations, 1986) (an SPD discussion document); several contributions to Hylke Tromp (ed.), *Non-Nuclear War in Europe* (Groningen University Press, 1986); David Gates, 'Area defence concepts: the West German debate', *Survival* XXIX (4), July–August 1987, pp. 301–17; Jonathan Dean, 'Alternative defence: answer to NATO's Central Front problems?', *International Affairs* [London] 64 (1), winter 1987/8, pp. 61–82.

8 The Labour Party, 'Defence and Security for Britain', statement to 1984 annual conference by the National Executive Committee.

9 For example Bjorn Moller, *Disengagement and Non-Offensive Defence in Europe* (CPCRUC working paper 1987/2), and *Common Security and Military Posture* (CPCRUC working paper 1987/5).

10 Gene Sharp, *Making Europe Unconquerable: The Potential of Civilian-based Deterrence and Defence* (Taylor and Francis, 1985); Appeal for European Nuclear Disarmament, launched on 28 April 1980, in E. P. Thompson and Dan Smith (eds), *Protest and Survive* (Penguin, 1980).

11 For example, Michael Clarke, *The Alternative Defence Debate: Non-Nuclear Defence Policies for Europe* (ADIU Occasional Paper no. 3, 1985); Barry Buzan, 'Common security, non-provocative defence and the future of Western Europe', *Review of International Studies* 13 (4), October 1987, pp. 265–79.

12 *Defence Without the Bomb: The Report of the Alternative Defence Commission* (Taylor and Francis, 1983); shortened version published as *Without the Bomb: Non-nuclear Defence Policies for Britain* (Paladin, 1985).

13 *The Politics of Alternative Defence: A Policy for a Non-nuclear Britain* (Paladin, 1987).

14 Notably E. P. Thompson in 'Notes on exterminism, the last stage of civilization', in Edward Thompson et al. *Exterminism and Cold War* (Verso, 1982), and *Beyond the Cold War* (Merlin Press/END, 1982).

14 See David Holloway, 'War, militarism and the Soviet state', in Thompson and Smith, *Protest and Survive*, and Roy and Zhores Medvedev's contribution, 'The USSR and the arms race', in *Exterminism and Cold War*.

16 Charles J. Dick, 'Soviet responses to emerging technology weapons and new defensive concepts', in Barnaby and ter Borg, *Emerging Technologies and Military Doctrine*, and dialogue (with Lutz Unterseher) on the military effectiveness of non-provocative defence, ibid.; David Gates, *Non-Offensive Defence: A Strategic Contradiction?* (IEDSS Occasional Paper no. 29, 1987).

17 Stephan Tiedtke, 'Alternative military defence strategies as a component of detente and Ostpolitik', *Bulletin of Peace Proposals* 15 (1), 1984, pp. 13–23.

18 I am aware that before his death in 1986, Stephan Tiedtke published a book which dealt with these questions in more detail. The book is *Abschreckung und ihre Alternativen. Die sowjetische Sicht einer westlichen Debatte* (Texte und Materialen der Forschungsstätte der Evangelischen Studiengemeinschaft, Reihe A/20, Heidelberg 1986). Not being a German reader, I have been unable to use this material. A short paper based on the book appeared in the same year: Hans-Joachim Spanger and Stephan Tiedtke, 'Alternative approaches to

security and Soviet attitudes: basic problems and tentative answers', *Bulletin of Peace Proposals* 17 (2) 1986, pp. 141–9.

19 E. P. Thompson's own account of the period makes fascinating reading: *Double Exposure* (Merlin Press, 1985). The best source of regular coverage ever since its first issue in December 1982 has been the London-based *END: Journal of European Nuclear Disarmament*.

20 For example: D. M. Proektor, 'European security: the problems of the 1980s', in V. S. Shaposhnikov (ed.), *Problems of Common Security* (Progress, 1984), p. 193.

21 See *Policies for Common Security*, and Paul, *Defending Europe: Options for Security*. Paul's editorial comment is at page 238.

22 Stephen Shenfield, 'The USSR: Viktor Girshfeld and the concept of "sufficient defence"', *ADIU Report* 6 (1), Jan.–Feb. 1984, p. 10.

23 'Colonel X's warning: our mistakes plus your hysteria', *Detente* 1, October 1984, pp. 2–3; and Viktor Olenev 'The Threat from above: the USSR and the militarization of space', *Detente* 5, winter 1986, pp. 22–7.

24 László Valki, 'The concept of defensive defence', in Pál Dunay (ed.), *Studies in Peace Research* (Centre for Peace Research Coordination of the Hungarian Academy of Sciences, 1986); 'Arguments and counter-arguments concerning defensive defence', in Barnaby and ter Borg, *Emerging Technologies and Military Doctrine*; 'Certainties and uncertainties about military doctrines', in *Proceedings of the Thirty-Sixth Pugwash Conference on Science and World Affairs, Budapest 1–6 September 1986*.

25 Valki, The Concept of Defensive Defence, ibid., p. 153.

26 Bjorn Moller, 'The need for an alternative Nato strategy', *Journal of Peace Research* 24 (1), 1987, pp. 61–74.

27 See Stephen Tunnicliffe (ed.), Department of Theological Studies of the Federation of Protestant Churches in the GDR, *Security Partnership and Peace in Europe* (END Churches Register pamphlet no. 1, 1985).

28 See the synopsis of Romberg's (German-language only) book on *Crisis-Stable Military Security in Central Europe – Criteria, Models and Ethical Aspects* in *Non-Offensive Defence* 5, November 1986, pp. 16–17.

29 Alfred Bönisch, 'East–West co-operation and European security', *ADIU Report* 8 (2), March–April 1986, pp. 7–9. See also a later paper by Bönisch, 'Theoretical and practical problems of security policy in Europe: the case of the chemical weapon free zone', *Disarmament and Peace* 8 (2), autumn 1987, pp. 60–9.

30 *International Affairs* [Moscow] 9, 1985, p. 94 (part of an exchange of views on 'For peace and security in Europe').

31 Denis Healey, *Beyond Nuclear Deterrence* (Fabian tract no. 510, March 1986), p. 9.

32 E. Silin, 'Ways of safeguarding European security', *International Affairs* [Moscow] 3, 1986, pp. 89–97, and A. A. Kokoshin, '"Plan Rodgersa", al'ternativnye kontseptsii oborony i bezopasnost' v Evrope', *SShA* 9, 1985, pp. 3–14.

33 *XX Century and Peace* 6, 1986, pp. 30–8.

34 Pages 7 and 12 of Kokoshin's article in *SShA* 9, 1985.

35 *Disarmament and Security 1986*, yearbook of the IMEMO, USSR Academy of Sciences, 2 vols (Novosti, 1987), vol. I, chapter 10.

36 *Krasnaya Zvezda* 9 May 1984, partially translated in *Survival* XXVI (4), July/August 1984, pp. 187–8, and fully in *Soviet Press Selected Translations* no. 5, 1984, pp. 148–53. For a fuller examination see Dale R. Herspring, 'Nikolay Ogarkov

and the scientific-technical revolution in Soviet military affairs', *Comparative Strategy* 6 (1), 1987, pp. 29–59.

37 See the abridged paper by Colonel Peter Deak and Dr László Valki, 'Certainties and uncertainties about the military doctrine of WTO', in *Pugwash Newsletter* 24 (3), January 1987, pp. 63–6.

38 *Pugwash Newsletter* 23 (4), April 1986, pp. 113–15.

39 *Soviet News* 26 February 1986, p. 89.

40 *Soviet News* 23 April 1986, p. 203. Russian original in *Pravda* 19 April 1986.

41 'Address of Warsaw Treaty member states to NATO member states, to all European countries with a programme of reducing armed forces and conventional armaments in Europe.' *Soviet News* 18 June 1986, p. 284, Russian original in *Pravda* 12 June 1986.

42 *Soviet News* 30 July 1986, p. 342.

43 *Soviet News* 18 February 1987, p. 60, original in *Pravda* 17 February 1987.

44 *XX Century and Peace* 8, 1987, pp. 16–23.

45 V. Abakov, V. Baranovskii, 'V interesakh sokhraneniya tsivilizatsii', *MEMO* 4, 1987, pp. 19–33.

46 *Soviet News* 4 March 1987, original in *Pravda* 26 February 1987.

47 *Soviet News* 15 April 1987, p. 128; original in *Pravda* 11 April 1987.

48 *Soviet News* 29 April 1987, and *Pravda* 31 March 1987.

49 V. Petrovskii, 'Bezopasnost' cherez razoruzhenie', *MEMO* 1, 1987, pp. 3–13.

50 Professor Genrikh Trofimenko, 'Stop the drift to nuclear catastrophe', *Soviet News* 2 July 1987, p.311.

51 G. A. Trofimenko, 'Novye real'nosti i novoe myshlenie', *SSHA* 2, 1987, pp. 3–15, p. 12.

52 A. F. Dobrynin, 'Za bez'yadernyi mir, navstrechu XXI veku', *Kommunist* 9, 1986, pp. 18–31. English translation available as 'For a nuclear-free world at the approaches to the 21st century', in P. N. Fedoseev (ed.), *Peace and Disarmament: Academic Studies 1987* (Progress, 1987).

53 For example: Patrick Cockburn in *Financial Times* 13 March 1987; John Keegan in the *Daily Telegraph* 2 March 1987; Martin Walker in the *Guardian* 15 April 1987.

54 WTO CFM communiqué in *Pravda* 26 March 1987; Dobrynin speech in *Pravda* 5 May 1987 and *Soviet News* 6 May 1987.

55 *Pravda* 30 May 1987 and *Soviet News* 3 June 1987.

56 See Raymond L. Garthoff, 'New thinking in Soviet military doctrine', *The Washington Quarterly* 11 (3), summer 1988, pp. 131–158.

57 Reports of the meetings of this group include that in *Arms Control Reporter* 3/1987, p. 402 B 144.

58 *Krasnaya Zvezda* 23 June 1987.

59 Yazov in *Pravda* 27 July 1987, published in English in *International Affairs* [Moscow] 10, 1987, pp. 3–8; Sergei Akhromeyev, 'The doctrine of averting war and defending peace and socialism', *World Marxist Review* 30 (12), December 1987, pp. 37–47.

60 *Krasnaya Zvezda* 23 February 1988.

61 M. A. Gareev, *M. V. Frunze: voennyi teoretik* (Voennoe Izdatel'stvo, 1985), p. 422.

62 As well as Dobrynin's speech in May 1986, see Alexander Yakovlev, *Modern Socialism Must First and Foremost Know Itself* (Novosti, 1987), p. 26.

63 I have taken this account from two of MccGwire's articles: 'Update: Soviet military objectives', *World Policy Journal* IV (4), fall 1987, pp. 723–31, and

'Rethinking war: the Soviets and European security', *The Brookings Review* 6 (2), spring 1988, pp. 3–12. For a fuller account, see his new book *Perestroika and Soviet National Security*.

64 For example: A. Utkin, 'O rasshirenii sfery deistviya NATO', *MEMO* 5, 1987, pp. 32–42.

65 See William P. Baxter, *Soviet Airland Battle Tactics* (Presidio, 1986), chapter 4. For more general discussions of operational questions in Afghanistan, see *Janes's Defence Weekly* 5 March 1988 (Ian Kemp, 'Abdul Haq: Soviet mistakes in Afghanistan, and Mark Urban, *War in Afghanistan* (Macmillan, 1988).

66 V. V. Zhurkin, S. A. Karaganov, A. V. Kortunov, 'razumnoi dostatochnosti', *SSHA* 12, 1987, pp. 11–21; Rowland T. Maddock, 'The Soviet defence burden and arms control', *Journal of Peace Research* 24 (4), 1987, pp. 381–91.

67 Jeffrey Smith, 'Soviet army chief reveals budget cut', *Guardian* 28 July 1988.

68 Martin Walker, 'New Moscow institute puts Soviet stress on Europe', *Guardian* 18 November 1987. See also Jonathan Haslam, 'Soviets take fresh look at Europe', *Bulletin of the Atomic Scientists* May 1988, pp. 38–42; Michael Lucas, 'The United States and post-INF Europe', *World Policy Journal* V (2), spring 1988, pp. 183–233; Jerry F. Hough, 'Gorbachev's strategy' *Foreign Affairs* 64 (1), fall 1985, pp. 33–55; Robert A. Manning, 'Moscow's Pacific future: Gorbachev rediscovers Asia', *World Policy Journal* V (1), winter 1987–88, pp. 55–78; Bonnie S. Glaser, *Soviet, Chinese and American Perspectives on Arms Control in Northeast Asia* (Australian National University Peace Research Centre, working paper no. 28, February 1988); Dan L. Strode, 'Soviet China policy in flux', *Survival* XXX (4), July/August 1988, pp. 332–50.

69 On air forces see James T. Westwood, 'Developments in Soviet air defence', *Armed Forces* 7 (2), February 1988, and *Arms Control Reporter* 5/1987 p. 401 B 141, report of a 1985 CIA/DIA study which has not been published but was referred to by the US Secretary of the Air Force in April 1987. On naval operations, see report of Admiral William Studeman, Director of US Naval Intelligence, presenting an intelligence assessment to the House Armed Services Committee, *Jane's Defence Weekly* 26 March 1988, p. 600. A different view is given in Carl G. Jacobsen, 'Soviet strategy: the naval dimension', in Carl G. Jacobsen (ed.), *The Uncertain Course: New Weapons, Strategies and Mind-sets* (SIPRI/Oxford University Press, 1987). On problems arising from the pre-1941 overemphasis on the offensive, see: S. Akhromeev, 'Prevoskhodstvo sovetskoi voennoi nauki i sovetskogo voennogo iskusstva – odin iz vaz-hneishikh faktorov pobedy v velikoi otechestvennoi voine', *Kommunist* 3, 1985, pp. 44–63, and Yu. G. Perechnev, 'O nekotorykh problemakh podgotovki strany i Vooruzhennykh Sil k otrazheniyu fashistskoi agressii', *Voenno-Istoricheskii Zhurnal* 4, 1988, pp. 42–50. See also Gareev, *M. V. Frunze*, pp. 230–31. On the distinction between operational-tactical and strategic defence, see Stephen R. Covington, *The Role of the Defence in Soviet Military Thinking: Operational-Tactical Defence, Strategic Defence* (Soviet Studies Research Centre, RMA Sandhurst, September 1987). See also *Soviet Military Power: An Assessment of the Threat 1988* (US DoD, 1988), pp. 12, 69, 73–4, 113.

70 Andreas von Bülow and Lev Semeiko in *Moskovskie Novosti* 23, 7 June 1987; James Eberle and A. A. Kokoshin in *Pravda* 21 August 1987 (and a shortened version in *Soviet Military Review* 1, 1988, pp. 26–7); Dan Smith in *Novoe Vremya* 42, 16 October 1987, pp. 12–13; Jonathan Steele and I. Zelin in *Pravda* 2 September 1987 (translation in *END Journal* 31, December–January 1987/8); Stephen Shenfield and Anatoly Utkin in *Moscow News* 6, 7 February 1988; John

Keegan and Lev Semeiko in *Moscow News* 12, 20 March 1988 (translation in the *Daily Telegraph* 16 March 1988).

71 *Pravda* 21 August 1987.

72 For the Gorbachev correspondence, see *FAS Public Interest Report* 41 (2), February 1988, pp. 14–15; the slightly misleading account was in the *Independent* 14 December 1987.

73 For a useful commentary see Stephen Shenfield, 'In quest of sufficient defence', *Detente* 11, 1988, pp. 26–9.

74 I. Malashenko, 'O razumnoi dostatochnosti i illyuziyakh prevoskhodstva', *Novoe Vremya* 24, 12 June 1987, pp. 18–20; Vitalii Zhurkin, Sergei Karaganov, Andrei Kortunov, 'Razumnaya dostatochnost', ili kak razorvat' porochnyi krug', *Novoe Vremya* 40, 2 October 1987, pp. 13–15, and 'O razumnoi dostatochnosti' *SSHA* 12, 1987, pp. 11–21.

75 'O razumnoi dostatochnosti, neprochnom paritete i mezhdunarodnoi bezopasnosti' *Novoe Vremya* 27, 3 July 1987, pp. 18–21 (participants M. A. Mil'shtein, A. R. Astaf'ev, V. I. Makarevskii, E. A. Nozhin); 'Reasonable means sufficient', *XX Century and Peace* 12, 1987, pp. 2–9 (L. Semeiko, S. Fedorenko, A. Yefremov, A. Astafyev, A. Nikonov, Yu. Streltsov, A. Kireyev, G. Sturua, V. Zhurkin); 'From realistic positions', *Soviet Military Review* 1, 1988, pp. 51–4 (L. Semeiko, R. Simonyan, V. Makarevsky).

76 A. Kokoshin, V. Larionov, 'Kurskaya bitva v svete sovremennoi oboronitel'noi doktriny', *MEMO* 8, 1987, pp. 32–40.

77 A. Kokoshin, 'Razvitie voennogo dela i sokrashchenie vooruzhennykh sil i obychnykh vooruzhenii', *MEMO* 1, 1988, pp. 20–32; A. Kokoshin, V. Larionov, 'Protivostoyanie sil obshchego naznacheniya v kontekste strategicheskoi stabil'nosti', *MEMO* 6, 1988, pp. 23–31. See also A. A. Kalinin, A. Yu. Koshmarov, 'Al'ternativnaya oborona: sushchnost' i varianty', *SSHA* 7, 1988, pp. 109–15.

78 Dmitrii Volkogonov, 'Doktrina antivoiny', *Novoe Vremya* 25, 19 June 1987, pp. 14–15

79 Editorial, 'Strategiya bez'yadernogo mira', *Mezhdunarodnaya Zhizn* 7, 1987, pp. 3–9; A. Slobodenko, 'Voenaya doktrina SSHA – stavka na silu', *Mezhdunarodnaya Zhizn'* 8, 1987, pp. 42–51; I. Lyutov, 'Leninskie idei zashchity sotsializma i formirovanie voennoi doktriny', *Mezhdunarodnaya Zhizn'* 12, 1987, pp. 13–20.

80 'Doktrina sokhraneniya mira', *Krasnaya Zvezda* 25 September 1987, and *FBIS* 30 September 1987.

81 'Reliable defence first and foremost', *Moscow News* 8, 21 February 1988.

82 V. I. Varennikov, 'Klassicheskii primer nastupleniya gruppy frontov', *Voenno-Istoricheskii Zhurnal* 8, 1987, pp. 12–19; and three pieces in *Voenno-Istoricheskii Zhurnal* 3, 1988, pp. 26–48: V. I. Ul'yanov, 'Razvitie teorii glubokogo nastupatel'nogo boya v predvoennye gody'; A. P. Maryshev, 'Proryv oborony protivnika'; S. N. Mikhalev, 'Nastuplenie 2-go Belorusskogo fronta v Poles'e'.

83 *Voennyi Vestnik* 1, 1988, p. 93, 'K nashim chitatelyam'; 3, 1988, pp. 18–21 (G. Ionin, 'Osnovy sovremennogo oboronitel'nogo boya'); and 4, 1988, pp. 18–29 (Yu. Morenko, V. Lebedev, V. Sadovnokiv, 'Na rubezhakh oborony').

84 *Washington Times*, 10 March 1988 and 12 November 1988.

85 P. Lushev, 'Na strazhe zavoevanii revolyutsii', *Mezhdunarodnaya Zhizn'* 8, 1987, pp. 60–70; Colonel-General Makhmut Gareyev, 'For lasting peace', *Soviet Military Review* 12, 1987, pp. 3–5; N. Chervov, 'Moguchii faktor mira', *Mezhdunarodnaya Zhizn'* 2, 1988, pp. 10–18.

86 D. T. Yazov, *Na strazhe sotsializma i mira* (Voennoe Izdatel'stvo, 1987).
87 Ibid., pp. 32–3.
88 D. T. Yazov, 'O voennom balanse sil i raketno-yadernom paritete' *Pravda* 8 February 1988.
89 *Washington Post* 17 March 1988; *Christian Science Monitor, Financial Times, Krasnaya Zvezda*, all 18 March 1988; see also *Krasnaya Zvezda* 30 April 1988 and, for Carlucci's account, *International Herald Tribune*, 7–8 May 1988, and *Soviet Military Power 1988*, Preface.
90 'Defence sufficiency' was in Gorbachev's speech, *Soviet News* 6 July 1988, p. 244; Primakov in *Pravda* 2 July 1988, p. 8; WTO CDM communique in *Soviet News* 13 July 1988 and *Krasnaya Zvezda* 9 July 1988, p. 1.
91 Alexei Arbatov, 'Military doctrines', in *Disarmament and Security 1987*, Yearbook of the Institute of World Economy and International Relations, USSR Academy of Sciences (Novosti, 1988).
92 The competing models here are those of: Roman Kolkowicz, *The Soviet Military and the Communist Party* (Princeton University Press, 1967); Timothy J. Colton, *Commissars, Commanders and Civilian Authority* (Harvard University Press, 1979); Edward L. Warner III, *The Military in Contemporary Soviet Politics: An Institutional Analysis* (Praeger, 1977).
93 Useful commentaries include: Dale R. Herspring, 'The Soviet military in the aftermath of the 27th Party Congress', *Orbis* 30 (2), summer 1986, pp. 297–315, and 'Marshal Akhromeyev and the future of the Soviet armed forces', *Survival* XXXVIII (6), Nov.–Dec. 1986, pp. 524–35; Condoleezza Rice, 'The party, the military and decision authority in the Soviet Union', *World Politics* XL (1), October 1987, pp. 55–81. On civilian involvement in security discussions, see chapter 5 note 17, and also interview with Andrei Kokoshin in *Defense News* 21 March 1988. On the high command personnel, see Malcolm Mackintosh, 'Changes in the Soviet high command under Gorbachev', *RUSI Journal* 133 (1), spring 1988, pp. 49–56.
94 See Joergen Dragsdahl, 'Are the Soviets really serious?', *Nuclear Times* May/June 1988, pp. 22–5.
95 Jack Snyder, 'The Gorbachev revolution: a waning of Soviet expansionism?', *International Security* 12 (3), winter 1987/88, pp. 93–131.
96 See Yazov, *Na strazhe sotsializma i mira*, chapters 2 and 3, and a number of his other public interventions: *Krasnaya Zvezda* 18 July 1987 (report of a speech at the Ministry of Defence's party *aktiv*); 'Perestroika v rabote voennykh kadrov', *Voenno-Istoricheskii Zhurnal* 7, 1987, pp. 3–12. See also Dale R. Herspring, 'On *Perestroyka*: Gorbachev, Yazov, and the military', *Problems of Communism* XXXVI (4), July–August 1987, pp. 99–107; and other publications including M. Popkov, 'Uspekh perestroiki reshayut kadry', *Voennyi Vestnik* 5, 1987, pp. 3–6; V. T. Tkachev (ed.), 'Na putyakh perestroiki', Voennoe Izdatel'stvo, 1987; Editorial in *Krasnaya Zvezda* 15 January 1988; *International Herald Tribune* 22 January 1988 (Bill Keller, 'Soviet defense chief criticizes the press'); Marshal V. G. Kulikov, 'Strazh mira i sotsializma', *Krasnaya Zvezda* 21 February 1988; *Krasnaya Zvezda* 25 May 1988 (Yazov criticisms of shortcomings in GSFG).
97 See Andrew Wilson in the *Observer* 21 June 1987 on 'Young Turk' circles in the Soviet military who might be pleased to see Gorbachev's disarmament diplomacy fail.
98 *Soviet News* 6 July 1988, p. 244. See also the contribution to the conference by Lieut.-Gen. B. V. Gromov, Commander of Soviet forces in Afghanistan, *Krasnaya Zvezda* 2 July 1988, and Yazov's speech to military academy graduates, *Krasnaya Zvezda* 13 July 1988.

99 To take two examples from the time of writing of this chapter. *Defense News* 21 March 1988 ('Soviets fashion tougher battle tank'), and *Jane's Defence Weekly* 26 March 1988 (report on new Soviet bridging systems in the GDR).
100 For example, G. Shevchenko, 'Obostrenie ideologicheskogo protivoborstva mezhdu sotsializmom i kapitalizmom', *Kommunist Vooruzhennykh Sil* 6, 1988, pp. 84–9.
101 See reports in the *Guardian* 9 March 1987 and 4 April 1987, and also note 55 above; also *Daily Telegraph* 19 May 1988, *Guardian* and *Independent* 11 July 1988. On the GDR, see Dale R. Herspring, 'The military factor in East German Soviet policy', *Slavic Review* 47 (1), spring 1988, pp. 89–107.
102 Margaret Thatcher was reported in early 1988 as saying to a meeting of NATO ambassadors that 'the Russian bear was easier to deal with when it looked more like a bear than it does now' (*Independent* 22 February 1988.)
103 See *Non-Offensive Defence* 8, February 1988, pp. 28–31; Pál Dunay, *Hungary's Security Policy* (Institut für Friedensforschung und Sicherheitspolitik an der Universität Hamburg, 1987), p. 51; report from the GDR in *Arms Control Reporter* 9/1987, p. 401 B 168; Manfred Müller, 'European security and non-offensive defence', *Scientific World* 32 (1), 1988, pp. 11–13. For some general discussions of Eastern European threat perceptions, see Tamás Lovassy, 'The case of Hungary', and Adam Daniel Rotfeld, 'The case of Poland', in Sverre Lodgaard and Karl Birnbaum (eds), *Overcoming Threats to Europe: A New Deal for Confidence and Security* (SIPRI/OUP, 1987).
104 For example in his article, 'the reality and guarantees of a secure world', in *Pravda* 17 September 1987 and *Soviet News* 23 September 1987.
105 *Pravda* 19 March 1988 and *Soviet News* 23 March 1988. See also reports in the *Guardian* 19 March 1988 and *International Herald Tribune* 19–20 March 1988.
106 *Soviet News* 16 March 1988, p. 94; *Soviet News* 25 May 1988, p. 185.
107 SED–SPD document *Conflicting Ideologies and Common Security*, issued 27 August 1987 (text in *Strategic Digest*, October 1987, pp. 1942–8).

Conclusion

1 For background discussions, see: Karen Dawisha, 'Gorbachev and Eastern Europe: a new challenge for the West?', *World Policy Journal* III (2), spring 1986, pp. 277–99, and *Eastern Europe, Gorbachev and Reform: The Great Challenge* (Cambridge University Press, 1988); Ivan Volgyes, 'Troubled friendship or mutual dependence? Eastern Europe and the USSR in the Gorbachev era', *Orbis* 30 (2), summer 1986, pp. 343–53; Karen Dawisha and Jonathan Valdez, 'Socialist internationalism in Eastern Europe'. *Problems of Communism* XXXVI (2), March–April 1987, pp. 1–14; Charles Gati, 'Gorbachev and Eastern Europe', *Foreign Affairs* 65 (5), summer 1987, pp. 958–75; Zdenek Kavan, 'Gorbachev and the world: the political side', in David Dyker (ed.), *The USSR Under Gorbachev: Prospects For Reform* (Croom Helm, 1987); Michael Shafir, 'Eastern Europe', in Martin McCauley (ed.), *The Soviet Union Under Gorbachev* (Macmillan/SSEES, 1987), Neal Ascherson, Misha Glenny, Michael Simmons, George Kolankewicz, 'A spectre haunts the East', *Marxism Today* February 1988, pp. 22–9.
2 See Margot Light, *The Soviet Theory of International Relations* (Wheatsheaf, 1988), chapter 10, and Dawisha and Valdez, ibid.
3 See *Pravda* and *Soviet News*, 22 April 1987; *Guardian* 9 November 1987 and 25 March 1988; Jiri Dienstbier, 'Gorbachev's reforms and a European perspective' (paper for November 1987 seminar in Budapest); 'Katyń: an open letter to Soviet

intellectuals', *East European Reporter* 3 (2), 1988, p. 23. For Soviet material on the historians' commission, see *Literaturnaya Gazeta* 11 May 1988; *Mezhdunarodnaya Zhizn'* 5, 1988; *Guardian* 30 May 1988 (report of a Moscow Radio broadcast).

4 For example Neal Ascherson in *Marxism Today* February 1988; Kate Soper in *END Journal* 28/29, summer 1987.

5 Mikhail Gorbachev's speech at international meeting, *Soviet News* 11 November 1987 and *Pravda* 5 November 1987; 'Restructuring in the USSR and the Socialist world', in *Perestroika* (Collins, 1987), p. 165.

6 A. Bovin, 'Mirnoe sosushchestvovanie i mirovaya sistema sotsializma', *MEMO* 7, 1988, pp. 5–15. Gorbachev's comment in *Soviet Weekly* supplement, 7 November 1987, p. xvi.

7 See coverage in *East European Reporter* 2 (4), 1987, pp. 56–8 ('Freedom and peace international seminar, Warsaw, 7–10 May 1987'); *END Journal* 28/29, summer 1987 ('Provoking peace in Poland'); *East European Reporter* 3 (2), 1988 ('German Democratic Republic' and 'Conscientious objection appeal').

8 Interview with Adam Michnik, *The Times Literary Supplement* 19–25 February 1988, pp. 188–9.

9 *Guardian* 10 April 1987, *Observer* 12 April 1987; *Guardian* 2 May 1987.

10 Kevin Ball, 'Only rock'n'roll?', *Labour Focus on Eastern Europe* 9 (2), July–October 1987, p. 48.

11 See Mark Frankland in the *Observer* 17 July 1988.

12 See Zdenek Mlynar, *Relative Stabilization of the Soviet Systems in the 1970s* (study no. 2, Research Project on Crises in Soviet-Type Systems, Munich 1983), and Günter Minnerup, 'New life at 70?', *Labour Focus on Eastern Europe* 9 (3), Nov. 1987–Feb. 1988, pp. 3–4.

13 For some interesting discussions, see Michael Checinski, 'Warsaw Pact/CEMA military-economic trends', *Problems of Communism* XXXVI (2), March–April 1987, pp. 15–28; Andras Köves, 'Problems and prospects of East–West economic cooperation: an East European view', in Mary Kaldor, Gerard Holden and Richard Falk (eds), *The New Detente: Rethinking East–West Relations* (Verso/United Nations University, 1989); Anders Aslund, 'The new Soviet policy towards international economic organizations', *The World Today*, February 1988, pp. 27–30; Timothy Garton Ash, 'The empire in decay', *New York Review of Books* September 29, 1988.

14 Paul Kennedy, *The Rise and Fall of the Great Powers* (Unwin Hyman, 1988).

15 William G. Hyland, 'Reagan–Gorbachev III', *Foreign Affairs* 66 (1), fall 1987, pp. 7–21.

16 Zbigniew Brzezinski, 'Cracks in the Soviet empire', *Independent* 4 February 1988.

17 For example James Chace, 'A new grand strategy', *Foreign Policy* no. 70, spring 1988, pp. 3–25.

18 *Moscow News* 2, 10 January 1988, p. 5.

19 See Immanuel, Wallerstein, 'The Reagan non-revolution or the limited choices of the US', offprint to *Millenium: Journal of International Studies* 16 (3), winter 1987, pp. 467–72A. For the centre-to-left debates in British publications, see: Martin Walker, *The Waking Giant: The Soviet Union Under Gorbachev* (Michael Joseph, 1986); Hillel Ticktin, 'The political economy of the Gorbachev era', *Critique* 17, 1986, pp. 113–35; Anthony Barnett, *Soviet Freedom* (Picador, 1988); Boris Kagarlitsky, 'Perestroika: the dialectic of change', *New Left Review*, 169, May/June 1988, pp. 63–83; John Keane, 'The democracy facing Gorbachev',

New Statesman 20 May 1988; Paul Hirst, 'Soviet freedom', *New Statesman* 10 June 1988; Alec Nove, 'The Muscovite marketeers', *New Socialist*, May/June 1988, pp. 11–12; Mike Haynes, 'Understanding the Soviet crisis', *International Socialism* 2:34, 1987, pp. 3–41; Ralph Miliband, Leo Panitch, John Savile (eds), *Socialist Register 1988 – Problems of Socialist Renewal: East and West* (Merlin Press, 1988).

20 See *Sovetskaya Rossiya* 13 March 1988 (BBC SWB 14 April 1988, SU/0126 B1-6) and *Pravda* 5 April 1988 (*Soviet News* 13 April 1988, extracts). For commentary, see Martin Walker, 'What Is To Be Done?', *Marxism Today* June 1988, pp. 12–15. On Yeltsin's interview, see the *Guardian* 31 May 1988.

21 Mikhail Gorbachev, 'On progress in implementing the decisions of the 27th Party Congress and the tasks for promoting perestroika', report at the 19th All-Union Conference of the CPSU, 28 June 1988, *Pravda* 29 June 1988 and *Soviet News* 6 July 1988. For commentary, see 'Moscow in motion', interview with Roy Medvedev, *Marxism Today* August 1988, pp. 14–17.

22 Richard Falk, 'The superpowers and a sustainable detente for Europe', in Kaldor, Holden and Falk, *The New Detente*. On the 'Reagan doctrine', see Fred Halliday, *Beyond Irangate: The Reagan Doctrine and the Third World* (Transnational Institute issue papers no. 1, 1987).

23 For a more extensive discussion, see Mammo Muchie and Hans van Zon, 'Soviet foreign policy under Gorbachev and revolution in the Third World: an ideological retreat or refinement?', in Kaldor, Holden and Falk, *The New Detente*.

Bibliography

Soviet and Eastern European books and monographs
Alexandrov, Valentin, *The Warsaw Treaty and Peace in Europe*, Novosti, 1980.
Arbatov, Georgi, *Cold War or Detente? The Soviet Viewpoint*, Zed Press, 1983.
Babakov, A. A., *Vooruzhennye sily SSSR posle voiny: (1945–1986gg) istoriya stroitel'stva*, Voennoe Izdatel'stvo, 1987.
Batov, P. I., *Forsirovanie rek 1942–1945gg (iz opyta 65–i armii)*, Voennoe Izdatel'stvo, 1986.
Bykov, O., *Creating a Climate of Confidence*, Nauka, 1986.
Committee of Soviet Scientists For Peace, Against the Nuclear Threat, *Strategic Stability Under the Conditions of Radical Arms Reductions: Report On A Study (Abridged)*, Moscow, 1987.
Disarmament and Security 1986, Yearbook of the IMEMO, USSR Academy of Sciences, Novosti, 1987, 2 vols.
Disarmament and Security 1987, Yearbook of the Institute of World Economy and International Relations, USSR Academy of Sciences, Novosti, 1988.
Dunay, Pál, *Hungary's Security Policy*, Hamburg Institut für Friedensforschung und Sicherheitspolitik, 1987.
——(ed.), *Studies in Peace Research*, Centre for Peace Research Coordination of the Hungarian Academy of Sciences, 1986.
Fedoseev, P. N., (ed.), *Peace and Disarmament 1987: Academic Studies*, Progress, 1987.
Gareev, M. A., *M. V. Frunze – voennyi teoretik*, Voennoe Izdatel'stvo, 1985.
Gorbachev, Mikhail, *Perestroika: New Thinking for Our Country and the World*, Collins, 1987.
Gromyko, Anatolii, and Vladimir Lomeiko, *Novoe myshlenie v yadernyi vek*, Mezhdunarodnye Otnosheniya, 1984.
Gromyko, A. A. and B. N. Ponomarev *Soviet Foreign Policy Volume II, 1945–1980, Progress, 1981.*
Khrushchev, N. S., Khrushchev Remembers Volume 1, tr. Strobe Talbott, Sphere, 1971.
——*Khrushchev Remembers, Volume 2 – The Last Testament*, Tr. and ed. Strobe Talbott, Penguin, 1977.
Mal'tsev, V. F. (ed.), *Organizatsiya Varshavskogo Dogovora 1955–1985, dokumenty i materialy*, Izdatel'stvo Politicheskoi Literatury, 1986.
Matsulenko, V. A., *Operatsii i boi na okruzhenie*, Voennoe Izdatel'stvo, 1983.
Medvedev, Roy, *Khrushchev*, Basil Blackwell, 1982
Milovidov, A. S.,*Voenno-teoreticheskoe nasledie V. I. Lenina i problemy sovremennoi voiny*, Voennoe Izdatel'stvo, 1987.
Nekrasov, Vadim, *The Roots of European Security*, Novosti, 1984.
Ogarkov, N. V., *Istoriya uchit bditel'nosti*, Voennoe Izdatel'stvo, 1985.
Olteanu, Constantin, *The Romanian Armed Power Concept: A historical approach*, Military Publishing House, Bucharest 1982.
Petrovsky, V., *Soviet Security Concept*, Nauka, 1986.
Proektor, D. *The Foundations of Peace in Europe: Political and Military Aspects*, Nauka, 1984.
Savinov, K. I., *Varshavskii Dogovor: faktor mira, shchit sotsializma*, Mezhdunarodnye Otnosheniya, 1986.

Savkin, V., *The Basic Principles of Operational Art and Tactics* (A Soviet View), Moscow 1972, tr. and publ. under the auspices of the United States Air Force, Soviet Military Thought Series, Washington, DC, no date.

Shaposhnikov, V. S., (ed.), *Problems of Common Security*, Progress, 1984.

Sidorenko, A. A., *The Offensive*, Moscow 1970, tr. and publ. under the auspices of the United States Air Force, Soviet Military Thought Series, Washington, DC, no date.

Sokolovsky, V., (Soviet) *Military Strategy*, 3rd edn, ed. with analysis and commentary by H. F. Scott, Crane Russak, 1975.

Sovetskaya Voennaya Entsiklopediya (SVE), several volumes, Voennoe Izdatel'stvo.

Ten Years After Helsinki: The Results and Prospects of the Process of European Security and Co-operation, report of the Soviet Committee for European Security and Co-operation, Progress, 1985.

Tiuskevich, S. A. *Voina i sovremmenost'*, Nauka, 1986.

——*Kritika burzhuaznykh kontseptsii po voprosam sovetskogo voennogo stroitel,'stva*, Voennoe Izdatel'stvo, 1987.

Tkachev, V. T., (ed.), *Na putyakh perestroiki*, Voennoe Izdatel'stvo, 1987.

Valki, László, *A Flexible Response to Defensive Defence*, Annales Universitatis Scientiarum Budapestinensis de Rolando Eötvös Nominatae, Separatum Sectio Iuridica, tomus XXVII, Budapest 1986.

Voennyi Entsiklopedicheskii Slovar' (VES), Voennoe Izdatel'stvo, 1983.

Volkogonov, D. A., (ed.), *Armii stran Varshavskogo Dogovora – spravochnik*, Voennoe Izdatel'stvo, 1985.

Volkogonov, D. A., A. S. Milovidov and S. A. Tiushkevich (eds), *Voina i armiya – filosofsko-sotsiologicheskii ocherk*, Voennoe Izdatel'stvo, 1977.

The Warsaw Treaty Organization: Alliance for Peace, Novosti, 1984.

Yakovlev, Alexander, *Modern Socialism Must First and Foremost Know Itself*, Novosti, 1987.

Yazov, D. T., *Na strazhe sotsializma i mira*, Voennoe Izdatel'stvo, 1987.

Zhilin, P. A., (ed.), *Stroitel'stvo armii evropeiskikh stran sotsialisticheskogo sodruzhestva 1949–1980*, Izdatel'stvo Nauka, 1984.

——*Istoriya voennogo iskusstva*, Voennoe Izdatel'stvo, 1986.

Soviet and Eastern European articles

Abakov, V., and V. Baranovskii, 'V interesakh sokhraneniya tsivilizatsii', *MEMO* 4, 1987, pp. 19–33.

Akhromeev, S., 'Prevoskhodstvo sovetskoi voennoi nauki i sovetskogo voennogo iskusstva – odin iz vazhneishikh faktorov povedy v velikoi otechestvennoi voine', *Kommunist* 3, 1985, pp. 49–63.

——'The Doctrine of averting war and defending peace and socialism', *World Marxist Review* 30 (12), December 1987, pp. 37–47.

Belov, M., and V. Schukin, 'Razvedyvatel'no-porazhayushchie kompleksy armii SSHA', *Voennyi Vestnik* 1, 1985, pp. 86–9.

Bönisch, Alfred, 'East–West co-operation and European security', *ADIU Report* 8 (2), March–April 1986, pp. 7–9.

Bovin, A., 'Novoe myshlenie – trebovanie yadernogo veka', *Kommunist* 10, 1986, pp. 113–24.

——'Novoe myshlenie – novaya politika', *Kommunist* 9, 1988, pp. 115–25.

——'Mirnoe sosushchestvovanie i mirovaya sistema sotsializma', *MEMO* 7, 1988, pp. 5–15.

Bykov, O., 'Vseobshchaya bezopasnost' – vlastnoe trebovanie vremeni', *MEMO* 3, 1986, pp. 28–39.
Chervov, N., 'Moguchii faktor mira', *Mezhduranodnaya Zhizn'* 2, 1988, pp. 10–18.
Deak, Peter, and László Valki, 'Certainties and uncertainties about the military doctrine of WTO', *Pugwash Newsletter* 24 (3), January 1987, pp. 63–6.
Dobrynin, A., 'Za bez'yadernyi mir, navstrechu XXI veku', *Kommunist* 9, 1986, pp. 18–31.
Frolov, I., 'Nauchit'sya myslit' i deistvovat' po-novomu', *MEMO* 8, 1986, pp. 3–7.
Gareev, M. A., 'Tvorcheskii kharakter sovetskoi voennoi nauki v Velikoi Otechestvennoi Voine', *Voenno-Istoricheskii Zhurnal* 7, 1985, pp. 22–30.
——'For lasting peace', *Soviet Military Review* 12, 1987, pp. 3–5.
Gorbachev, M. S., statement by M. S. Gorbachev, General Secretary of the CPSU Central Committee, *Pravda* 16 January 1986 and *Soviet News* 22 January 1986.
——report by Mikhail Gorbachev to 27th Congress of the CPSU, *Pravda* 26 February 1986 and *Soviet News* 26 February 1986.
——'Mikhail Gorbachev's address to Moscow forum', *Pravda* 17 February 1987 and *Soviet News* 18 February 1987.
——'The reality and guarantees of a secure world', *Pravda* 17 September 1987 and *Soviet News* September 1987.
——'October and perestroika: the revolutions continues', *Pravda* 3 November 1987 and *Soviet News* 4 November 1987.
——'Mikhail Gorbachev's speech at CPSU CC plenum', *Pravda* 19 February 1988 and *Soviet News* 24 February 1988.
——'On progress in implementing the decisions of the 27th Party Congress and the tasks for promoting perestroika', report at the 19th All-Union Conference of the CPSU, 28 June 1988, *Pravda* 29 June 1988 and *Soviet News* 6 July 1988.
Gromyko, A. and V. Lomeiko, 'New way of thinking and "new globalism"', *International Affairs* [Moscow] 5, 1986, pp. 15–27.
Gribkov, A. I., 'Brat'ya po klassu, brat'ya po oruzhiyu', *Voennyi Vestnik* 5, 1985, pp. 11–14.
——'30 let na strazhe mira i sotsializma', *Voenno-Istoricheskii Zhurnal* 5, 1985, pp. 82–91.
Ionin, G., 'Osnovy sovremmenogo oboronitel'nogo boya', *Voennyi Vestnik* 1, 1988, pp. 18–21.
Ivanov, V., 'Bez'yadernyi mir i obshchestvennoe mnenie', *Kommunist* 5, 1987, pp. 117–19.
Kagarlitsky, Boris, 'Perestroika: the dialectic of change', *New Left Review* 169, May/June 1988, pp. 63–83.
Kapchenko, Nikolai, 'The political philosophy of peace in the nuclear-missile age', *International Affairs* [Moscow] 3, 1987, pp. 12–29.
Kokoshin, A. A., 'Plan Rodgersa', al'ternativnye kontseptsii oborony i bezopasnost' v Evrope', *SSHA* 9, 1985, pp. 3–14.
——'Razvitie voennogo dela i sokrashchenie vooruzhennykh sil i obychnykh vooruzhenii', *MEMO* 1, 1988, pp. 20–32.
——'Sokrashchenie yadernykh vooruzhenii i strategicheskaya stabil'nost'', *SSHA* 2, 1988, pp. 3–12.
Kokoshin, A. A. and A. Larionov, 'Kurskaya bitva v svete sovremennoi oboronitel'noi doktriny', *MEMO* 8, 1987, pp. 32–40.
——'Protivostoyanie sil obshchego naznacheniya v kontekste strategicheskoi stabil'nosti', *MEMO* 6, 1988, pp. 23–31.
Kulikov, V. G., 'Nadezhnyi shchit mira', *Kommunist* 8, 1985, pp. 67–76.

Lizichev, A., 'Oktyabr' i leninskoe uchenie o zashchite revolyutsii' *Kommunist* 3, 1987, pp. 85–96.

Lushev, P., 'Na strazhe zavoevanii revolyutsii', *Mezhdunarodnaya Zhizn'* 8, 1987, pp. 60–70.

Lyutov, I., 'Leninskie idei zashchity sotsializma i, formirovanie voennoi doktriny', *Mezhdunarodnaya Zhizn'* 12, 1987, pp. 13–20.

Malashenko, I. 'O razumnoi dostatochnosti i illyuziyakh prevoskhodstva', *Novoe Vremya* 24, 1987, pp. 18–20.

Maryshev, A. P., 'Proryv oborony protivnika', *Voenno-Istoricheskii Zhurnal* 3, 1988, pp. 34–40.

Mikhalev, S. N., 'Nastuplenie 2-go Belorusskogo fronta v Poles'e', *Voenno-istoricheskii Zhurnal* 3, 1988, pp. 41–8.

Molostov, Yu., 'Zashchita ot vysokotochnogo oruzhiya', *Voennyi Vestnik* 2, 1987, pp. 83–5.

Molostov, Yu., and A. Novikov, 'High-precision weapons against tanks', *Soviet Military Review* 1, 1988, pp. 12–13.

Morenko, Yu., V. Lebedev, and V. Sadovnikov, 'Na rubezhakh oborony', *Voennyi Vestnik* 4, 1988, pp. 18–29.

Müller, Manfred, 'European security and non-offensive defence', *Scientific World* 32 (1), 1988, pp. 11–13.

Mututshika, Sigeo, 'Fundamental directions of Romanian foreign policy for the strengthening of its national sovereignty', *Revue Roumaine d'Études Internationales* XX (5), Sept.–Oct. 1986, pp. 427–43.

Nezhinsky, L., 'An alliance for world peace and security', *International Affairs* [Moscow] 6, 1985, pp. 60–99.

Nikitin, N., 'Nastavlenie dlya voisk NATO', *Voennyi Vestnik* 8, 1987, pp. 86–9.

Ogarkov, N.V., 'Na strazhe mirnogo truda', *Kommunist* 10, 1981, pp. 80–91.

Perechnev, Yu., 'O nekotorykh problemakh podgotovki strany i Vooruzhennykh Sil k otrazheniyu fashistskoi agressii', *Voenno-Istoricheskii Zhurnal* 4, 1988, pp. 42–50.

Petrovskii, V., 'Sovetskaya kontseptsiya vseobshchei bezopasnosti', *MEMO* 6, 1988, pp. 3–13.

——'Bezopasnost' cherez razoruzhenie', *MEMO* 1, 1987, pp. 3–13.

——'Doverie i vyzhivanie chelovechestva', *MEMO* 11, 1987, pp. 15–26.

Popkov, M., 'Uspekh perestroiki reshayut kadry', *Voennyi Vestnik* 5, 1987, pp. 3–6.

Primakov, E., 'XXVII s'ezd KPSS i issledovanie problem mirovoi ekonomiki i mezhdunarodnykh otnoshenii', *MEMO* 5, 1986, pp. 3–14.

——'Novaya filosofiya vneshnei politiki', *Pravda* 10 July 1987.

——'Sovetskaya politika v regional'nykh konfliktakh', *Mezhdunarodnaya Zhizn'* 5, 1988, pp. 3–9.

Semeiko, Lev 'Concerning parity', *New Times* 20, 1987, pp. 16–17.

Shakhnazarov, G. Kh., 'Logika politicheskogo myshleniya v yadernuyu eru', *Voprosy Filosofii* 5, 1984, pp. 63–74.

Shevardnadze, E. A., 'Na puti k bezopasnomu miru', *Mezhdunarodnaya Zhizn'* 7, 1988, pp. 3–16.

Shevchenko, Aleksandr, 'What lies behind the "Rogers Plan"', *Soviet Military Review* 3, 1986, pp. 46–7.

Shevchenko, G., 'Obostrenie ideologicheskogo protivoborstva mezhdu sotsializmom i kapitalizmom', *Kommunist Vooruzhennykh Sil* 6, 1988, pp. 84–9.

Silin, E., 'Ways of safeguarding European security', *International Affairs* [Moscow] 3, 1986, pp. 89–97.

Slepukhin, Yuri, 'Do we believe in the reality of the threat?', *XX Century and Peace* 4, 1987, pp. 20–5.
Slobodenko, A., 'Voennaya doktrina SSHA – stavka na silu', *Mezhdunarodnaya Zhizn'* 8, 1987, pp. 42–51.
Smorigo, N., 'Varshavskii Dogovor – nadezhnyi instrument ukrepleniya mezhdunarodnoi bezopasnosti', *Partiinaya Zhizn'* 10, 1985, pp. 27–33.
Svetlov, A., 'Varshavskii Dogovor na sluzhbe mira i bezopasnosti', *MEMO* 5, 1985, pp. 24–36.
Tairov, Tair, 'Moment of truth', *New Times* 19, 1987, pp. 12–13.
Trofimenko, G. A., 'Novye real'nosti i novoe myshlenie', *SSHA* 2, 1987, pp. 3–15.
Ul'yanov, V. I., 'Razvitie teorii glubokogo nastupatel'nogo boya v predvoennye gody', *Voenno-Istoricheskii Zhurnal* 3, 1988, pp. 26–33.
Utkin, A., 'O rasshirenii sfery deistviya NATO', *MEMO* 5, 1987, pp. 32–42.
Varennikov, V. I., 'Klassicheskii primer nastupleniya gruppy frontov', *Voenno-Istoricheskii Zhurnal* 8, 1987, pp. 12–19.
Voitenko, S. P., and K. F. Pavlikov, 'Velikaya sila Varshavskogo Dogovora i bessilie ego kritikov', *Voenno-Istoricheskii Zhurnal* 4, 1987, pp. 71–8.
Volkogonov, Dmitrii, 'Doktrina antivoiny', *Novoe Vremya* 25, 1987, pp. 14–15.
Vorobyov, I., 'Tactics today', *Soviet Military Review* 3, 1985, pp. 10–12.
——'New weapons require sound tactics', *Soviet Military Review* 1 and 2, 1987, pp. 16–18, 16–18.
Vorontsov, G., 'SSHA, NATO i gonka obychnykh vooruzhenii', *MEMO* 5, 1985, pp. 49–60.
Yakovlev, A., 'Mezhdunarodnoe znachenie Varshavskogo Dogovora', *MEMO* 7, 1985, pp. 14–25.
Yazov, D. T., 'Perestroika v rabote voennykh kadrov', *Voenno-Istoricheskii Zhurnal* 7, 1987, pp. 3–12.
Zhurkin, V. V., S. A. Karaganov and A. V. Kortunov, 'Razumnaya dostatochnost' ili kak razorvat' porochnyi krug', *Novoe Vremya* 40, 1987, pp. 13–15.
——'O razumnoi dostatochnosti', *SSHA* 12, 1987, pp. 11–21.
——'Vyzovy bezopasnosti – starye i novye', *Kommunist* 1, 1988, pp. 42–50.

Western books and monographs

Alperowitz, Gar, *Atomic Diplomacy: Hiroshima and Potsdam – The Use of the Atomic bomb and the American Confrontation with Soviet Power*, Penguin, 1985.
Alternative Defence Commission, *Defence Without the Bomb: The Report of the Alternative Defence Commission*, Taylor and Francis, 1983.
——*Without the Bomb: Non-Nuclear Policies for Britain*, Paladin, 1985.
——*The Politics of Alternative Defence: A Role for a Non-nuclear Britain*, Paladin, 1987.
Arkin, William M., and Richard W. Fieldhouse, *Nuclear Battlefields: Global Links in the Arms Race*, Institute of Policy Studies, Ballinger, 1985.
Ascherson, Neal, *The Polish August*, Penguin, 1981.
Bahro, Rudolf, *The Alternative in Eastern Europe*, Verso, 1981.
Ball, Desmond, *Can Nuclear War Be Controlled?* Adelphi Paper, 169, autumn 1981.
Barnaby, Frank, and Marlies ter Borg (eds), *Emerging Technologies and Military Doctrine: A Political Assessment*, Macmillan, 1986.
Barnett, Anthony, *Soviet Freedom*, Picador, 1988.
Baxter, William P., *Soviet Airland Battle Tactics*, Presidio, 1986.
Baylis, John, and Gerald Segal, (eds), *Soviet Strategy*, Croom Helm, 1981.
Berman, Robert P. and John C. Baker, *Soviet Strategic Forces: Requirements and*

Responses, The Brookings Institution, 1982.

Bialer, Seweryn (ed.), *The Domestic Context of Soviet Foreign Policy*, Croom Helm, 1981.

Bloomfield, Lincoln P., Walter C. Clemens Jr and Franklyn Griffiths, *Krushchev and the Arms Race: Soviet Interests in Arms Control and Disarmament. 1954–1964*, MIT Press, 1966.

Borawski, John, *From the Atlantic to the Urals: Negotiating Arms Control at the Stockholm Conference*, Pergamon-Brassey's, 1988.

Boutwell, Jeffrey D, Paul Doty and Gregory Treverton (eds), *The Nuclear Confrontation in Europe*, Croom Helm for the Center for Science and International Affairs, Harvard University, 1986.

Bracken, Paul, *The Command and Control of Nuclear Forces*, Yale University Press, 1983.

Brandt, Willy, *A Peace Policy for Europe*, Holt, Rinehart and Winston, 1969.

Braun, Aurel, *Romanian Foreign Policy Since 1965: The Political and Military Limits of Autonomy*, Praeger, 1978.

Brzezinski, Zbigniew K., *The Soviet Bloc: Unity and Conflict*, Praeger, 1962.

Buzan, Barry, *People, States and Fear: The National Security Problem in International Relations*, Wheatsheaf, 1983.

Campbell, Duncan, *The Unsinkable Aircraft Carrier: American Military Power in Britain*, Paladin, 1986.

Chalmers, Malcolm, and Lutz Unterseher, *Is There A Tank Gap? A Comparative Assessment of the Tank Fleets of NATO and the Warsaw Pact*, Peace Research Report 19, Bradford University School of Peace Studies, 1987.

Childs, David, *The GDR: Moscow's German Ally*, Allen and Unwin, 1983.

Clarke, Michael, *The Alternative Defence Debate: Non-Nuclear Defence Policies for Europe*, ADIU Occasional Paper 3, 1985.

Clawson, Robert W., and Lawrence S. Kaplan, *The Warsaw Pact: Political Purpose and Military Means*, Scholarly Resources, 1982.

Cockburn, Andrew, *The Threat: Inside the Soviet Military Machine*, Hutchinson, 1983.

Colton, Timothy J., *Commissars, Commanders and Civilian Authority*, Harvard University Press, 1979.

Common Security: A Programme for Disarmament: The Report of the Independent Commission on Disarmament and Security Issues under the Chairmanship of Olof Palme, Pan, 1982.

Covington, Stephen R., *The Role of the Defence in Soviet Military Thinking: Operational-Tactical Defence, Strategic Defence*, Soviet Studies Research Centre, RMA Sandhurst, September 1987.

Dawisha, Karen, *The Kremlin and the Prague Spring*, University of California Press, 1984.

——*Eastern Europe, Gorbachev and Reform: The Great Challenge*, Cambridge University Press, 1988.

Dawisha, Karen, and Philip Hanson (eds), *Soviet-East European Dilemmas*, Heinemann, 1981.

Dean, Jonathan, *Watershed in Europe: Dismantling the East–West Military Confrontation*, Lexington Books, 1987.

Deutscher, Isaac, *The Great Contest: Russia and the West*, Oxford University Press, 1960.

Dibb, Paul, *The Soviet Union: The Incomplete Superpower*, Macmillan/IISS, 1986.

Dinter, E., and P. Griffith, *Not over by Christmas: NATO's Central Front in World War III*, Anthony Brett, 1983.

Donnelly, Christopher, *Heirs of Clausewitz: Change and Continuity in the Soviet War Machine*, Institute for European Defence and Strategic Studies Occasional Paper 16, 1985.

Drachkovitch, Milorad M. (ed.), *East Central Europe: Yesterday, Today, Tomorrow*, Hoover Institution Press, 1982.

Dyker, David (ed.), *The USSR Under Gorbachev: Prospects for Reform*, Croom Helm, 1987.

Dyson, Kenneth (ed.), *European detente: Case studies of the politics of East–West relations*, Frances Pinter, 1986.

Edmonds, Robin, *Soviet Foreign Policy: The Brezhnev Years*, Oxford University Press, 1982.

Erickson, John, Lynn Hansen and William Schneider, *Soviet Ground Forces: An Operational Assessment*, Westview/Croom Helm, 1986.

Ermarth, Fritz, *Internationalism, Security and Legitimacy: The Challenge to Soviet Interests in East Europe, 1964–1968*, RAND Memorandum RM–5909 PR, March 1969.

'ESECS Report'/Report of the European Security Study, *Strengthening Conventional Deterrence in Europe: Proposals for the 1980s*, Macmillan, 1983.

Evangelista, Matthew A., *Innovation and the Arms Race: How the United States and the Soviet Union Develop New Military Technologies*, Cornell University Press, 1988.

Fejtö, Francois, *A History of the People's Democracies: Eastern Europe Since Stalin*, Penguin, 1977.

Fischer, Dietrich, *Preventing War in the Nuclear Age*, Rowland and Allanheld, 1984.

Ford, Daniel, *The Button: The Nuclear Trigger – Does it Work?*, Unwin, 1986.

Forster, Thomas M., *The East German Army: The Second Power in the Warsaw Pact*, Allen and Unwin, 1980.

Freedman, Lawrence, *The Evolution of Nuclear Strategy*, Macmillan, 1981.

Gaddis, John Lewis, *The United States and the Origins of the Cold War 1941–1947*, Columbia University Press, 1972.

Galtung, Johan, *There Are Alternatives! Four Roads to Peace and Security*, Spokesman, 1984.

Garner, William V., *Soviet Threat Perceptions of NATO's Eurostrategic Missiles*, Atlantic Papers 52–3, The Atlantic Institute for International Affairs, 1983.

Garthoff, Raymond L., *Detente and Confrontation: American–Soviet Relations from Nixon to Reagan*, The Brookings Institution, 1985.

Garton, Ash, Timothy, *The Polish Revolution: Solidarity*, Coronet, 1985.

Gates, David, *Non-Offensive Defence: A Strategic Contradiction?*, IEDSS Occasional Paper 29, 1987.

Goldblat, J., S. Lodgaard and F. Blackaby, *No First Use*, SIPRI/Taylor and Francis, 1984.

Hahn, Werner G., *Postwar Soviet Politics: The Fall of Zhdanov and the Defeat of Moderation, 1946–53*, Cornell University Press, 1982.

Hale, Julian, *Ceausescu's Romania*, Harrap, 1971.

Halliday, Fred, *The Making of the Second Cold War*, Verso, 2nd edn 1986.

Harbutt, Fraser J., *The Iron Curtain: Churchill, America and the Origins of the Cold War*, Oxford University Press, 1986.

Harman, Chris, *Class Struggles in Eastern Europe, 1945–83*, Pluto, 1983.

Healey, Denis, *Beyond Nuclear Deterrence*, Fabian Tract 510, 1986.

Holloway, David, *The Soviet Union and the Arms Race*, Yale University Press, 1983.

Holloway, David, and Jane M. O. Sharp (eds), *The Warsaw Pact: Alliance in Transition?*, Macmillan, 1984.

Hough, Jerry F., *The Struggle for the Third World: Soviet Debates and American Options*,

Bibliography

The Brookings Institution, 1986.

Howard, Michael, *Disengagement in Europe*, Penguin, 1958.

Hutchings, Robert L., *Soviet–East European Relations: Consolidation and Conflict 1968–1980*, University of Wisconsin Press, 1983.

Iklé, Fred C. and Albert Wohlstetter (co-chairmen), *Discriminate Deterrence: report of the Commission on Integrated Long-Term Strategy*, 1988.

International Institute for Strategic Studies, *The Military Balance*, annual publication.

Isby, David, *Weapons and Tactics of the Soviet Army*, Jane's, 1981.

Jacobsen, Carl G. (ed), *The Uncertain Course: New Weapons, Strategies, and Mind-Sets*, Oxford University Press/SIPRI, 1987.

Jahn, Egbert (ed.), *Soviet Foreign Policy: Its Social and Economic Conditions*, Allison and Busby, 1978.

Jahn, Egbert, Pierre Lemaitre and Ole Waever, *European Security: Problems of Research on Non-military Aspects*, Copenhagen Papers 1, August 1987.

Jones, Christopher D., *Soviet Influence in Eastern Europe: Political Autonomy and the Warsaw Pact*, Praeger, 1981.

Kaldor, Mary, *The Disintegrating West*, Pelican, 1979.

——*The Baroque Arsenal*, Andre Deutsch, 1982.

——*The Imaginary War*, Basil Blackwell, forthcoming.

Kaldor, Mary, and Richard Falk (eds), *Dealignment: A New Foreign Policy Perspective*, Basil Blackwell, 1987.

Kaldor, Mary, and Dan Smith (eds), *Disarming Europe*, Merlin, 1982.

Kaldor, Mary, Gerard Holden and Richard Falk (eds), *The New Detente: Rethinking East–West Relations*, Verso/United Nations University, 1989.

Kaplan, Stephen S., *Diplomacy of Power: Soviet Armed Forces as a Political Instrument*, The Brookings Institution, 1981.

Kaser, Michael, *COMECON: Integration Problems of the Planned Economies*, Oxford University Press, 1967.

Kelly, Andrew, *The Myth of Soviet Superiority: A Critical Analysis of the Current Balance of Conventional Forces on the Central Front in Europe and of Possible Defence Alternatives for NATO*, University of Bradford Peace Research Report 14, 1987.

Kennedy, Paul, *The Rise and Fall of the Great Powers*, Unwin Hyman, 1988.

Kirby, S., and G. Robson (eds), *The Militarisation of Space*, Wheatsheaf, 1987.

Kissinger, Henry, *The White House Years*, Weidenfeld and Nicolson and Michael Joseph, 1979.

Kolkowicz, Roman, *The Soviet Military and the Communist Party*, Princeton University Press, 1967.

Krause, Joachim, *Prospects for Conventional Arms Control in Europe*, Institute for East–West Security Studies Occasional Paper 8, 1988.

Kusin, V. V. (ed.), *The Czechoslovak Reform Movement 1968*, International Research Documents, 1969.

Labour Party, The, *Defence and Security for Britain*, statement to 1984 annual conference by the National Executive Committee.

Lafeber, Walter, *America, Russia and the Cold War 1945–1984*, 5th edn, Alfred A. Knopf, 1985.

Leebaert, Derek (ed.), *Soviet Military Thinking*, Allen and Unwin, 1981.

Lewis, William J., *The Warsaw Pact: Arms, Doctrine, and Strategy*, McGraw-Hill, 1982.

Lider, Julian, *Correlation of Forces: An Analysis of Marxist-Leninist Concepts*, Gower, 1986.

Light, Margot, *The Soviet Theory of International Relations*, Wheatsheaf, 1988.

Litherland, Patrick, *Current Soviet Thinking on the Use of Intermediate-Range Nuclear Forces*, Peace Studies Briefing, University of Bradford, 1984.
——*Gorbachev and Arms Control: Civilian Experts and Soviet Policy*, Peace Research Report 12, University of Bradford, 1986.
Lodgaard, Sverre, and Karl Birnbaum (eds), *Overcoming Threats to Europe: A New Deal for Confidence and Security*, SIPRI/OUP, 1987.
Lodgaard, Sverre, and Marek Thee (eds), *Nuclear Disengagement in Europe*, SIPRI/Pugwash, Taylor and Francis, 1983.
Lomax, Bill, *Hungary 1956*, St Martin's Press, 1976.
Lynch, Allen, *The Soviet Study of International Relations*, Cambridge University Press, 1987.
Mackintosh, Malcolm, *The Evolution of the Warsaw Pact*, Adelphi Paper 58, 1969.
Mako, William P., *US Ground Forces and the Defense of Central Europe*, The Brookings Institution, 1983.
Malcher, George C., *Poland's Politicized Army: Communists in Uniform*, Praeger, 1984.
Mastny, Vojtech, *Russia's Road to the Cold War: Diplomacy, Warfare, and the Problems of Communism, 1941–1945*, Columbia University Press, 1979.
McAdams, A. James, *East Germany and Detente: Building Authority After the Wall*, Cambridge University Press, 1985.
McCagg, William O. Jr, *Stalin Embattled 1943–1948*, Wayne State University Press, 1978.
McCauley, Martin (ed.), *Khrushchev and Khrushchevism*, Macmillan/SSEES, 1987.
——*The Soviet Union Under Gorbachev*, Macmillan/SSEES, 1987.
MccGwire, Michael (ed.), *Soviet Naval Developments: Capability and Context*, Praeger, 1973.
——*Military Objectives in Soviet Foreign Policy*, The Brookings Institutions, 1987.
McGwire, Michael, Ken Booth and John McDonnell (eds), *Soviet Naval Policy: Objectives and Constraints*, Praeger, 1975.
MccGwire, Michael, and John McDonnell (eds), *Soviet Naval Influence: Domestic and Foreign Dimensions*, Praeger, 1975.
McLean, Scilla (ed.), *How Nuclear Weapons Decisions Are Made*, Macmillan/Oxford Research Group, 1986.
Mearsheimer, John J., *Conventional Deterrence*, Cornell University Press, 1983.
Meyer, Stephen M., *Soviet Theatre Nuclear Forces, Part I: Development of Doctrine and Objectives; Part II: Capabilities and Implications*, Adelphi Papers 187 and 188, 1983/4.
Mylnar, Zdenek, *Night Frost in Prague: The End of Humane Socialism*, Hurst, 1980.
——*Relative Stabilization of the Soviet Systems in the 1970s*, study no. 2, Research Project on Crises in Soviet-Type Systems, Munich 1983.
Moller, Bjorn, *Disengagement and Non-Offensive Defence in Europe*, CPCRUC Working Paper 1987/2.
——*Common Security and Military Posture*, CPCRUC Working Paper 1987/5.
Moreton, Edwina, *East Germany and the Warsaw Alliance: The Politics of Detente*, Westview, 1978.
Moreton, Edwina, and Gerald Segal (eds), *Soviet Strategy Towards Western Europe*, Allen and Unwin, 1984.
Möttölä, Kari (ed.), *Ten Years After Helsinki: The Making of the European Security Regime*, Westview, 1986.
Nato Handbook, NATO Information Service, 1986.
Nelson, Daniel N. (ed.), *Soviet Allies: The Warsaw Pact and the Issue of Reliability*, Westview, 1984.

——*Alliance Behavior in the Warsaw Pact*, Westview, 1986.

Noel-Baker, Philip, *The Arms Race: A Programme for World Disarmament*, Atlantic Books, 1958.

——*Disarm or Die: A Disarmament Reader for the Leaders and the Peoples of the World*, Taylor and Francis, 1978.

North Atlantic Assembly Military Committee, *Final Report of the Sub-Committee on Conventional Defence: New Strategies and Operational Concepts*, Karsten Voigt, rapporteur, September 1987.

Oldberg, Ingmar (ed.), *Unity and Conflict in the Warsaw Pact*, Swedish National Defence Research Establishment, 1984.

ORAE Extra-Mural Papers, *Warsaw Pact: The Question of Cohesion*. No. 29, February 1984: *The Greater Socialist Army: Integration and Reliability*; no. 33, November 1984: *Poland, German Democratic Republic and Romania*; no. 39, March 1986: *Union of Soviet Socialist Republics, Bulgaria, Czechoslovakia, and Hungary*. All Operational Research and Analysis Establishment, Department of National Defence, Canada.

Paul, Derek (ed.), *Defending Europe: Options for Security*, Taylor and Francis, 1985.

Phillips, Ann L., *Soviet Policy Towards East Germany Reconsidered: The Postwar Decade*, Greenwood, 1986.

Pierre, Andrew J. (ed.), *The Conventional Defence of Europe: New Technologies and New Strategies*, Council on Foreign Relations, 1986.

Ploss, Sidney I., *Moscow and the Polish Crisis: an interpretation of Soviet policies and intentions*, Westview, 1986.

Policies for Common Security, Taylor and Francis for SIPRI, 1985.

Remington, Robin Alison (ed.), *Winter in Prague: Documents on Czechoslovak Communism in Crisis*, MIT Press, 1969.

——*The Warsaw Pact: Case Studies in Communist Conflict Resolution*, MIT Press, 1971.

Rice, Condoleezza, *The Soviet Union and the Czechoslovak Army, 1948–1983: Uncertain Allegiance*, Princeton University Press, 1984.

Rigby, T. H., and Ferenc Feher (eds), *Political Legitimacy in Communist States*, Macmillan/St Antony's College, 1982.

Rogers, Paul, *Guide to Nuclear Weapons*, Berg, 1988.

Ross Johnson, A., Robert W. Dean and Alexander Alexiev, *East European Military Establishments: The Warsaw Pact Northern Tier*, Crane Russak, 1982.

Ryan, H. Butterfield, *The Vision of Anglo-America,: The US–UK Alliance and the Emerging Cold War, 1943–1946*, Cambridge University Press, 1987.

Sanford, George, *Military Rule in Poland: The Rebuilding of Communist Power, 1981–1983*, Croom Helm, 1986.

Scott, Harriet Fast, and William F. Scott, *The Armed Forces of the USSR*, Westview, 1979.

Sharp, Gene, *Making Europe Unconquerable: The Potential of Civilian-based Deterrence and Defence*, Taylor and Francis, 1985.

Shenfield, Stephen, *The Nuclear Predicament: Explorations in Soviet Ideology*, Routledge and Kegan Paul, 1987.

Simon, Jeffrey, *Warsaw Pact Forces: Problems of Command and Control*, Westview, 1985.

Simon, Jeffrey, and Trond Gilberg (eds), *Security Implications of Nationalism in Eastern Europe*, Westview, 1986.

Simpkin, Richard, in association with John Erickson, *Deep Battle: The Brainchild of Marshal Tukhachevskii*, Brassey's, 1987.

Sloan, Stanley R., Steven R. Bowman, Paul E. Gallis and Stuart D. Goldman, *Conventional Arms Control and Military Stability in Europe*, Congressional Research Service, 1987.

Smith, Dan, and E. P. Thompson (eds), *Prospectus for a Habitable Planet*, Penguin, 1987.

Soviet Armed Forces Review Annual, successive years.

Soviet Military Power, successive years.

Steele, Jonathan, *Socialism With a German Face: The state that came in from the cold*, Cape, 1977.

——*The Limits of Soviet Power: The Kremlin's Foreign Policy – Brezhnev to Chernenko*, Penguin, 1985.

Steinke, Rudolf, and Michael Vale (eds), *Germany Debates Defence: The NATO Alliance at the Crossroads*, M. E. Sharpe, 1983.

Sterling, Michael J., *Soviet Reactions to NATO's Emerging Technologies for Deep Attack*, RAND Note N-2294-AF, August 1985.

Suvorov, Viktor, *The Liberators*, Hamish Hamilton, 1981.

——*Inside the Soviet Army*, Hamish Hamilton, 1982.

Tatu, Michel, *Power in the Kremlin: From Khrushchev's Decline to Collective Leadership*, Collins, 1969.

Terry, Sarah Meiklejohn (ed.), *Soviet Policy in Eastern Europe*, Yale University Press, 1984.

Thomas, Andy, and Ben Lowe, *How Britain Was Sold – Why the US bases came to Britain*, Peace News/Housmans, 1984.

Thomas, Hugh, *Armed Truce: The Beginnings of the Cold War*, Hamish Hamilton, 1986.

Thompson, Edward, *Beyond the Cold War*, Merlin/END, 1982.

——*Double Exposure*, Merlin, 1985.

Thompson, Edward, and Dan Smith (eds), *Protest and Survive*, Penguin 1980.

Thompson, Edward, et al., *Exterminism and Cold War*, Verso, 1982.

Trapp, Ralf (ed.), *Chemical Weapon Free Zones?* SIPRI, 1987.

Tromp, Hylke (ed.), *Non-Nuclear War in Europe*, Groningen University Press, 1986.

Ulam, Adam B., *Expansion and Coexistence: Soviet Foreign Policy, 1917–73*, Holt, Rinehart and Winston, 1974.

Unterseher, Lutz, *Conventional Land Forces for Central Europe: A Military Threat Assessment*, Peace Research Report 19, Bradford University 1987.

Urban, Mark, *War in Afghanistan*, Macmillan, 1988.

Valenta, Jiri, *Soviet Intervention in Czechoslovakia, 1968: Anatomy of a Decision*, Johns Hopkins University Press, 1979.

Valenta, Jiri, and William C. Potter (eds), *Soviet Decisionmaking for National Security*, Allen and Unwin, 1984.

Vigor, P. H., *The Soviet View of War, Peace and Neutrality*, Routledge and Kegan Paul, 1975.

——*Soviet Blitzkrieg Theory*, Macmillan, 1983.

——*The Soviet View of Disarmament*, Macmillan, 1986.

Vine, Richard D. (ed.), *Soviet–East European Relations As A Problem for the West*, Croom Helm, 1987.

Volgyes, Ivan, *The Political Reliability of the Warsaw Pact Armies: The Southern Tier*, Duke University Press, 1982.

Volten, Peter M. E., *Brezhnev's Peace Program: A Study of Soviet Domestic Political Process and Power*, Westview, 1982.

von Beyme, Klaus, *The Soviet Union in World Politics*, Gower, 1987.

Walker, Martin, *The Waking Giant: The Soviet Union Under Gorbachev*, Michael Joseph, 1986.

Warner, Edward L. III, *The Military in Contemporary Soviet Politics: An Institutional*

Analysis, Praeger, 1977.
Werth, Alexander, *Russia: The Post-War Years*, Robert Hale, 1971.
Wiener, Friedrich, *The Armies of the Warsaw Pact Nations*, Carl Ueberreuter, 1981.
Windass, Stan (ed.), *Avoiding Nuclear War*, Brassey's, 1985.
Windsor, Philip and Adam Roberts, *Czechoslovakia 1968: Reform, Repression, and Resistance*, Chatto and Windus, 1969.
Wolfe, Alan, *The Rise and Fall of the 'Soviet Threat': Domestic Source of the Cold War Consensus*, Institute for Policy Studies, 1979.
Wolfe, Thomas W., *Soviet Power and Europe, 1945–70*. Johns Hopkins Press, 1970.
Yergin, Daniel, *Shattered Peace: The Origins of the Cold War and the National Security State*, Deutsch, 1978.

Western articles

Alexiev, Alex, 'Romania and the Warsaw Pact: the defence policy of a reluctant ally', *Journal of Strategic Studies* 4 (1), March 1981, pp. 5–15.
Anderson, Richard D. Jr, 'Soviet decision-making and Poland', *Problems of Communism* XXXI (2), March–April 1982, pp. 22–36.
Asmus, Ronald D., 'The dialectics of detente and discord: the Moscow–East Berlin–Bonn triangle', *Orbis* 28 (4) winter 1985, pp. 743–74.
Atkeson, Edward B., 'The "fault line" in the Warsaw Pact: implications for NATO strategy', *Orbis* 30 (1), spring 1986, pp. 111–31.
Baylis, John, 'NATO strategy: the case for a new strategic concept', *International Affairs* [London] 64 (1), winter 1987/8, pp. 43–59.
Beach, Hugh, 'Emerging technology and the Soviet dilemma', *Defense Analysis* 1 (2), June 1985, pp. 131–3.
Beatty, Jack, 'In harm's way', *The Atlantic* May 1987, pp. 37–53.
Bellamy, Chris, 'Antecedents of the modern OMG', *RUSI Journal* 27 (3), Sept. 1984, pp. 50–8.
Bodansky, Yossef, 'Reorganizing the Soviet high command for war', *Defense and Foreign Affairs* August 1985, pp. 27–32.
Borawski, John, 'Toward conventional stability in Europe?', *Washington Quarterly* 10 (4), autumn 1987, pp. 13–29.
Borawski, John, Stan Weeks and Charlotte E. Thompson, 'The Stockholm Agreement of September 1986', *Orbis* 30 (4), winter 1987, pp. 643–62.
Bowker, Mike, and Phil Williams, 'Helsinki and West European security', *International Affairs* [London] 61 (4), autumn 1985, pp. 607–18.
Brown, Archie, 'Soviet political developments and prospects', *World Policy Journal* IV (1), winter 1986–7, pp. 55–87.
Bulkeley, Rip, 'Soviet military responses to the Strategic Defense Initiative', *Current Research on Peace and Violence* 4, 1987, pp. 129–42.
Bundy, McGeorge, et al. 'Nuclear weapons and the Atlantic alliance', *Foreign Affairs* 60 (4), spring 1982, pp. 753–68.
——'Back from the brink', *The Atlantic* 258 (2), August 1986, pp. 35–41.
Burke, David P., 'Defense and mass mobilization in Romania', *Armed Forces and Society* 7 (1), fall 1980, pp. 31–49.
Buzan, Barry, 'Common security, non-provocative defence and the future of Western Europe', *Review of International Studies* 13 (4), October 1987, pp. 265–79.
Chace, James, 'A new grand strategy', *Foreign Policy* no. 70, Spring 1988, pp. 3–25.

Checinski, Michael, 'Warsaw Pact/CEMA military-economic trends', *Problems of Communism* XXXVI (2), March–April 1987, p. 15–28.

Cichock, Martin A., 'Soviet goal articulations and involvement at the European disarmament conference', *Coexistence* 23 (3), 1986, pp. 189–207.

Coolsaet, Rik, 'NATO strategy: under different influences', *ADIU Report* 6 (6), Nov.–Dec. 1984, pp. 4–8.

Cox, Mick, 'The Cold War as a system', *Critique* 17, 1986, pp. 17–82.

Currie, Kenneth, 'Soviet General Staff's new role', *Problems of Communism* XXXIII (2), March–April 1984, pp. 32–40.

Cutshaw, Charles Q., 'Who's in charge', *Proceedings of the US Naval Institute*, April 1986, pp. 79–83.

Dawisha, Karen, 'Gorbachev and Eastern Europe: a new challenge for the West?' *World Policy Journal* III (2), spring 1986, pp. 277–99.

Dawisha, Karen, and Jonathan Valdez, 'Socialist internationalism in Eastern Europe', *Problems of Communism* XXXVI (2), March–April 1987, pp. 1–14.

Dean, Jonathan, 'Directions in inner-German relations', *Orbis* 29 (3), fall 1985, pp. 609–32.

——'Military security in Europe', *Foreign Affairs* 66 (1), fall 1987, pp. 22–40.

——'Alternative defence: answer to NATO's Central Front problems?', *International Affairs* [London] 64 (1), winter 1987/8, pp. 61–82.

Deane, Michael J, Ilana Kass and Andrew G. Porth, 'The Soviet command structure in transformation', *Strategic Review* XII (2), 1984, pp. 55–70.

Dick, C. J., 'Soviet Operational Manoeuvre Groups – a closer look', *International Defense Review* 16 (6), 1983, pp. 769–76.

——'Soviet operational concepts, parts I and II', *Military Review* LXV (9 and 10), Sept. and Oct. 1985.

——'Catching NATO unawares – Soviet Army surprise and deception techniques', *International Defense Review* 19 (1), 1986, pp. 21–6.

Donnelly, Christopher, 'Tactical problems facing the Soviet army – recent debates in the Soviet military press', *International Defense Review* 11 (9), 1978, pp. 1405–12.

——'The development of Soviet military doctrine', *International Defense Review* 14 (12), 1981, pp. 1589–96.

——'The Soviet Operational Manoeuvre Group – a new challenge for NATO', *International Defense Review* 15 (9), 1982, pp. 1177–86.

——'The development of the Soviet concept of echeloning', *NATO Review* 32 (6), Dec. 1984, pp. 9–17.

Dragsdahl, Joergen, 'Are the Soviets really serious?' *Nuclear Times* May/June 1988, pp. 22–5.

Ehmke, Horst, 'A second phase of detente', *World Policy Journal* IV (3), summer 1987, pp. 363–82.

English, Robert, 'Eastern Europe's doves', *Foreign Policy* 56, fall 1984, pp. 44–60.

Erickson, John, 'The ground forces in Soviet military policy', *Strategic Review* winter 1978, pp. 64–79.

——'The Soviet view of deterrence: a general survey', *Survival* XXIV, (26), Nov.–Dec. 1982, pp. 242–50.

——'The implications of Soviet military power', *Catalyst* 1 (2), Summer 1985, pp. 11–18.

Evangelista, Matthew A., 'Stalin's postwar army reappraised', *International Security* 7 (3), winter 1982/1983, pp. 110–38.

——'The new Soviet approach to security', *World Policy Journal* III (4), fall 1986, pp. 561–99.

Fitzgerald, Mary C., 'Marshal Ogarkov on the modern theater operation', *Naval War College Review* XXXIX (4), autumn 1986, pp. 6–25.

——'Marshal Ogarkov and the new revolution in Soviet military affairs', *Defense Analysis* 3 (1), March 1987, pp. 3–19.

——'The strategic revolution behind Soviet arms control', *Arms Control Today* June 1987, pp. 16–19.

Gaddis, John Lewis, 'The emerging post-revisionist synthesis on the origins of the Cold War', *Diplomatic History* summer 1983, pp. 171–204.

Garthoff, Raymond L., 'The Soviet SS-20 decision', *Survival* XXV (3), May/June 1983, pp. 110–19.

——'New thinking in Soviet military doctrine', *The Washington Quarterly* 11 (3), summer 1988, pp. 131–158.

Gates, David, 'Area defence concepts: the West German debate', *Survival* XXIX (4), July–August 1987, pp. 301–17.

Gati, Charles, 'Gorbachev and Eastern Europe', *Foreign Affairs* 65 (5), summer 1987, pp. 958–75.

Gerrits, André, 'Limits of influence: the Kremlin and the Polish crisis 1980–1981', *Bulletin of Peace Proposals* 19 (2), 1988, pp. 231–9.

Goodby, James E., 'Reducing the risks of war: the Stockholm Agreement', *Disarmament* IX (3), autumn 1986, pp. 53–6.

Gormley, Dennis M., 'A new dimension to Soviet theater strategy', *Orbis* 29 (3), fall 1985, pp. 537–69.

——'"Triple zero" and Soviet theater strategy', *Arms Control Today* January/February 1988, pp. 17–20.

Gray, Colin S., 'Maritime strategy and the Pacific: the implications for NATO', *Naval War College Review* XXXX (1), winter 1987, pp. 8–19.

Hagelin, Bjorn, 'Swords into daggers: a study of Soviet missile R&D with special reference to the SS-20', *Bulletin of Peace Proposals* 15 (4), 1984, pp. 341–53.

Hasegawa, Tsuyoshi, 'Soviets on nuclear-war-fighting', *Problems of Communism* XXXV (4), July–August 1986, pp. 68–79.

Herspring, Dale R., 'The Soviet military in the aftermath of the 27th Party Congress', *Orbis* 30 (2), summer 1986, pp. 297–315.

——'Marshal Akhromeyev and the future of the Soviet armed forces', *Survival* XXXVIII (6), Nov.–Dec. 1986, pp. 524–35.

——'Nikolay Ogarkov and the scientific-technical revolution in Soviet military affairs', *Comparative Strategy* 6 (1), 1987, pp. 29–59.

——'On *perestroyka*: Gorbachev, Yazov and the military', *Problems of Communism* XXXVI (4), July–August 1987, pp. 99–107.

——'The military factor in East German Soviet policy', *Slavic Review* 47 (1), spring 1988, pp. 89–197.

Hines, J. G. and P. A. Petersen, 'The conventional offensive in Soviet theater strategy', *Orbis* 27 (3), fall 1983, pp. 695–739.

——'Changing the Soviet system of control: focus on theater warfare', *International Defense Review* 19 (3), 1986, pp. 281–9.

——'Is NATO thinking too small? a comparison of command structures', *International Defense Review* 19 (5), 1986, pp. 563–72.

Hough, Jerry F., 'Gorbachev's strategy', *Foreign Affairs* 64 (1), fall 1985, pp. 33–55.

Howard, Michael, 'Reassurance and deterrence', *Foreign Affairs* 61 (2), winter 1982–3, pp. 309–24.

——'The future of deterrence', *RUSI Journal* 131 (2), June 1986, pp. 3–10.

Hyland, William G., 'Reagan–Gorbachev III', *Foreign Affairs* 66 (1), fall 1987, pp. 7–21.

Kaiser, Karl, 'Conventional arms control: the future agenda', *The World Today* February 1988, pp. 22–7.

Kass, Ilana, and Michael J. Deane, 'The role of nuclear weapons in the modern theater battlefield: the current Soviet view', *Comparative Strategy* 4 (3), 1984.

Kaufman, Richard F., 'Causes of the slowdown in Soviet defense', *Survival* XXVII (4), July/August 1985, pp. 179–92.

Kramer, Mark N., 'Civil–military relations in the Warsaw Pact: the East European component', *International Affairs* [London] 61 (1), winter 1984/5, pp. 45–66.

Kuklinski, Ryszard, 'The crushing of Solidarity', *Orbis* 32 (1), winter 1988, pp. 7–31.

Lebow, Richard Ned, 'The Soviet offensive in Europe: the Schlieffen Plan revisited?' *International Security* 9 (4), spring 1985, pp. 44–78.

Light, Margot, 'New thinking" in Soviet foreign policy?', *Coexistence* 24 (3), 1987, pp. 233–43.

Lippert, Günter, 'GSFG: spearhead of the Red Army', *International Defense Review* 20 (5), 1987, pp. 553–63.

Löwenthal, Richard, 'The limits of intra-bloc pluralism: the changing threshold of Soviet intervention', *International Journal* XXXVII (2), spring 1982, pp. 263–84.

Lucas, Michael, 'The United States and post-INF Europe', *World Policy Journal* V (2), spring 1988, pp. 183–233.

Mackay, S. V., 'The maritime strategy: an Allied reaction', *Proceedings of the US Naval Institute* April 1987, pp. 82–9.

Mackintosh, Malcolm, 'Changes in the Soviet high command under Gorbachev', *RUSI Journal* 133 (1), spring 1988, pp. 49–56.

Maddock, Rowland T., 'The Soviet defence burden and arms control', *Journal of Peace Research* 24 (4), 1987, pp. 381–91.

Mastny, Vojtech, 'Kremlin politics and the Austrian settlement', *Problems of Communism* XXXI (4), July–August 1982, pp. 37–51.

McAdams, A. James, 'Inter-German detente: a new balance', *Foreign Affairs* 65 (1), fall 1986, pp. 136–53.

McCausland, Jeff, 'The East German army – spear point or weakness?', *Defense Analysis* 2 (2), 1986, pp. 137–53.

McConnell, James M. 'Shifts in Sovet views on the proper focus of military development', *World Politics* XXXVII (3), April 1985, pp. 317–43.

——'The irrelevance today of Sokolovskiy's book *Military Strategy*', *Defense Analysis* 1 (4), December 1985, pp. 243–54.

——'SDI, the Soviet investment debate and Soviet military policy', *Strategic Review* XVI (1), winter 1988, pp. 47–62.

MccGwire, Michael, 'Dilemmas and delusions of deterrence', *World Policy Journal* 1 (4), summer 1984, p. 745–67.

——'Deterrence: the problem – not the solution', *International Affairs* [London] 62 (1), winter 1985–6, pp. 55–70.

——'Soviet military objectives', *World Policy Journal* III (4), fall 1986, pp. 667–95.

——'Update: Soviet military objectives', *World Policy Journal* IV (4), fall 1987, pp. 723–31.

——'Rethinking war: the Soviets and European security', *The Brookings Review* 6, (2), spring 1988, pp. 3–12.

Mearsheimer, John J., 'Why the Soviets can't win quickly in Central Europe', *International Security* 7 (1), summer 1982, pp. 3–39.

——'A strategic misstep: the maritime strategy and deterrence in Europe', *Inter-*

national Security 11 (2), fall 1987.

Menning, Bruce W. 'The deep strike in Russian and Soviet military history', *The Journal of Soviet Military Studies* 1 (1), April 1988, pp. 9–28.

Moller, Bjorn, 'The need for an alternative NATO strategy', *Journal of Peace Research* 24 (1), March 1987, pp. 61–74.

Paul, David W., 'Soviet foreign policy and the invasion of Czechoslovakia: a theory and a case study', *International Studies Quarterly* 15 (2), June 1971, pp. 159–202.

Petersen, Phillip A., 'Soviet offensive operations in Central Europe', *NATO's Sixteen Nations* 32 (5), August 1987, pp. 26–32.

Plesch, Dan, 'AirLand Battle and NATO's military posture', *ADIU Report* 7 (2), March–April 1985, pp. 4–8.

Posen, B. R., 'Measuring the European conventional balance: coping with complexity in threat assessment', *International Security* 9 (3), winter 1984–5, pp. 47–88.

Remington, Robin Alison, 'Western images of the Warsaw Pact', *Problems of Communism* XXXVI (2), March–April 1987, pp. 69–80.

Rice, Condoleezza, 'The party, the military and decision authority in the Soviet Union', *World Politics* XL (1), October 1987, pp. 55–81.

Rogers, Bernard W., 'Follow-on Forces Attack (FOFA): myths and realities', *NATO Review* December 1984, pp. 1–9.

Schulz-Torge, Ulrich-Joachim, 'The Soviet military high command, parts I and II', *Military Technology* IX (8 and 9), 1985, pp. 111–21, 102–11.

Sharp, Jane, 'Troop reductions in Europe: a status report', *ADIU Report* 5 (5), Sept.–Oct. 1983, pp. 4–7.

——'Understanding the INF debacle: arms control and alliance cohesion', *Arms Control* 5 (2), September 1984, pp. 95–127.

——'The future of European arms control', *ADIU Report* 9 (5), Sept.–Oct. 1987, 1–5.

Shenfield, Stephen, 'The USSR: Viktor Girshfeld and the concept of "sufficient defence"', *ADIU Report* 6 (1), Jan.–Feb. 1984, p. 10.

——'Nuclear winter and the USSR', *Millenium, Journal of International Studies* 15 (2), summer 1986, pp. 197–208.

——'In quest of sufficient defence', *Detente* 11, 1988, pp. 26–9.

Smith, D. L. and A. L. Meier, 'Ogarkov's revolution: Soviet military doctrine for the 1990s', *International Defense Review* 20 (7), 1987, pp. 869–73.

Snyder, Jack, 'The Gorbachev revolution: a waning of Soviet expansionism?', *International Security* 12 (3), winter 1987/8, pp. 93–131.

——'Limiting offensive conventional forces: Soviet proposals and Western options', *International Security* 12 (4), spring 1988, pp. 48–77.

Spanger, Hans-Joachim, and Stephen Tiedtke, 'Alternative approaches to security and Soviet attitudes: basic problems and tentative answers', *Bulletin of Peace Proposals* 17 (2), 1986, pp. 141–9.

Suvorov, Viktor, 'Strategic command and control: the Soviet approach', *International Defense Review* 17 (12), 1984, pp. 1813–20.

Ticktin, Hillel, 'The political economy of the Gorbachev era', *Critique* 17, 1986, pp. 113–35.

Tiedtke, Stephan, 'Alternative military defence strategies as a component of detente and Ostpolitik', *Bulletin of Peace Proposals* 15 (1) 1984, pp. 13–23.

Urban, Mark L., 'Romanian land forces today', *Jane's Defence Review* 4 (5), 1983, pp. 475–8.

——'Major re-organization of Soviet air forces', *International Defense Review* 16 (6), 1983, p. 756.

——'Red flag over Germany, part I', *Armed Forces* 4 (2), February 1985, pp. 69–74.

Vego, Milan, 'Command and control of the Warsaw Pact navies', *Proceedings of the US Naval Institute*, September 1987, pp. 115–18.

Volgyes, Ivan, 'Troubled friendship or mutual dependence?: Eastern Europe and the USSR in the Gorbachev era', *Orbis* 30 (2), summer 1986, pp. 343–53.

Wallerstein, Immanuel, 'The Reagan non-revolution or the limited choices of the US', offprint to *Millenium, Journal of International Studies*, 16 (3), winter 1987, pp. 467–72A.

Watkins, James D., 'The maritime strategy', supplement to *Proceedings of the US Naval Institute*, January 1986.

Weickhardt, George C., 'Ustinov versus Ogarkov', *Problems of Communism* XXXIV (1), Jan.–Feb. 1985, pp. 77–82.

——'The military consensus behind Soviet arms control proposals', *Arms Control Today*, September 1987, pp. 20–4.

Westwood, James T., 'Developments in Soviet air defence', *Armed Forces* 7 (2), Feb. 1988, pp. 64–7.

Yost, David S., 'Beyond MBFR: the Atlantic to the Urals gambit', *Orbis* 31 (1), spring 1987, pp. 99–134.

Index

Abakov, V., 125
ABM Treaty, 98, 107, 108
ADC *see* Alternative Defence
  Commission
Adenauer, Konrad, 7
Afghanistan, 35, 112, 113, 131
Afheldt, Horst, 121, 122
Akhromeev, Marshal S., 61, 64, 76,
  129, 137
ALB (Airland Battle), 94, 120, 128,
  133
Albania, 6, 8–9, 12, 24, 46
Albrecht, Ulrich, 40
Alexiev, Alexander, 86
alternative defence, 115–46
Alternative Defence Commission
  (ADC), 82, 117, 118, 119, 142
America *see* USA
Andropov, Yuri, 36, 37, 108
Anzus alliance, 7
Arbatov, Alexei, 137
Arbatov, Georgii, 116
arms control, 98–101, 157
Ash, Timothy Garton, 26, 153
Atlanticist reformers, 116
Austrian State Treaty, 8

Baghdad Pact, 7
Baranovskii, V., 125
Berlin, 30, 32, 47, 55
Bessmertnykh, Aleksandr, 108
bloc: consolidation, 145; dissolution,
  118, 142–3, 156
Boeker, Egbert, 116
Bogomolov, Oleg, 104
Bönisch, Alfred, 122, 123
Boserup, Anders, 117, 125, 134, 135
Bovin, Aleksandr, 105, 108, 151
Brandt, Willy, 31, 32
Bratislava declaration, 23
Brezhnev, Leonid, 44, 58, 92, 108
Brezhnev doctrine, 19, 22, 23, 27–8,
  39, 143

Britain *see* UK
Brzezinski, Zbigniew, 153–4
Budapest appeal, 100, 110, 124
Bulganin, Nikolai, 8, 73
Bulgaria, 6, 46, 47, 52, 164, 166
Bülow, Andreas von, 133
Bush, George, 155

Carlucci, Frank, 137
CDM *see* Committee of Defence
  Ministers
Ceausescu, Nicolae, 24, 37, 59
CFM *see* Committee of Foreign
  Ministers
Chernenko, Konstantin, 38, 39
Chervov, N., 37
China, 12, 24–5, 55
coalition warfare, 20, 85
Cold War, 69–73, 153
Comecon, 6, 12, 152–3
Committee of Defence Ministers (of
  WTO), 15, 42–4, 148
Committee of Foreign Ministers (of
  WTO), 15, 16–17, 25, 34, 37, 148
common security, 116, 120, 122
Conference on Confidence and
  Security-Building Measures and
  Disarmament in Europe, 99
Conference on Security and
  Co-operation in Europe (CSCE),
  12, 33, 98, 99
counterdeployments, 35–8, 87, 92,
  110
CSCE *see* Conference on Security and
  Co-operation in Europe
Czechoslovakia, 6, 152;
  counterdeployments, 37, 38, 55;
  Gottwald Memorandum/press
  conference, 43, 86; military forces,
  46, 47–8, 52, 164, 166; 1968
  intervention, 11–12, 22–3, 56, 86,
  141, 148; public opinion, 39–40;
  USSR forces, 46

Index by G. M. Riordan